SERIAL KILLER

RAPISTS

Serial Killer Quick Reference Guides #2

SERIAL KILLER
RAPISTS

Serial Killer Quick Reference Guides #2

Kevin Smith

Killer.Cloud - the Serial Killer Database
a Mindlock Innovation - Pigeon Forge, Tennessee

Serial Killer Rapists

Serial Killer Quick Reference Guides #2

by Kevin Smith

Published by Mindlock Innovations, Pigeon Forge, Tennessee

ISBN: 978-1-7336306-1-0

First Printing April 2019

Print Revision July 2019 (revised)

Killer.Cloud the Serial Killer Database, an ongoing research project which aims to sort and classify serial killers based on documented references from books written about serial killers as well as other online resources. This book is a portion of the Killer.Cloud website. While every precaution has been taken in the preparation of this book, the publisher and the author collectively, assumes no responsibility for errors or omissions, or for damages resulting from the use of the information contained herein.

https://www.killer.cloud

20190707205855

Table of Contents

Introduction

Serial Killer Rapists *Serial Killer Quick Reference Guides #2* contains 266 serial killers who have been known to rape at least one victim during their acts as a serial killer. Each serial killer profile contains 30 points of data backed by our publicly accessible serial killer database. QR codes included in each profile leads the reader to the killers online profile on Killer.Cloud the serial killer database. Killer.Cloud's data is crossed linked to other online datasets, easily referenced by short codes for readers as well as at the bottom of each serial killers online profile page.

Killer.Cloud the Serial Killer Database, an ongoing research project which aims to sort and classify serial killers based on documented references from books written about serial killers as well as other online resources.

The database currently contains 642 serial killers that are classified into serial killer types. Serial killer types are based on acts committed during a killers serial spree such as: torture, sexual assault *rape*, stalking, strangulation, consumption of human flesh or organs *cannibalism*, consumption of human blood *vampirism*, and/or sexual assault after death *necrophilia*. Killer's can belong to more than one serial killer type.

Serial Killer The unlawful killing of two or more victims by the same offender(s), in separate events. Serial Killer as defined by the FBI at the 2005 symposium. While this definition has been altered and changed over the years, our database contains killers that are currently labeled as a serial killer either by the authorities or local media in the area where the crimes took place.

Rape usually defined as having sexual intercourse with a person who does not want to, or cannot consent.

Serial Killer Rapists killers known to rape their victims during their acts as a serial killer.

Confirmed Victims the number of confirmred victims killed in association with a killers serial spree. Some serial killers may have other possible victims that were either unproven or the motives and/or methods were unrelated to the spree the killer is being documented as.

Years Active the amount of time between the first and last kills associated with the killers serial killing spree. Some serial killers may have killed victims prior to their killing spree where the motives and/or methods were unrelated to the spree the killer is being documented as.

Thank You, by purchasing this book you have helped fund future versions of Killer.Cloud the Serial Killer Database. The money will be used to update servers, write new code, create new entries and update exsisting entires in the database. Our general interest will drive us to continue following news stories and updating the database, but with your help we get coffee while we work.

How To

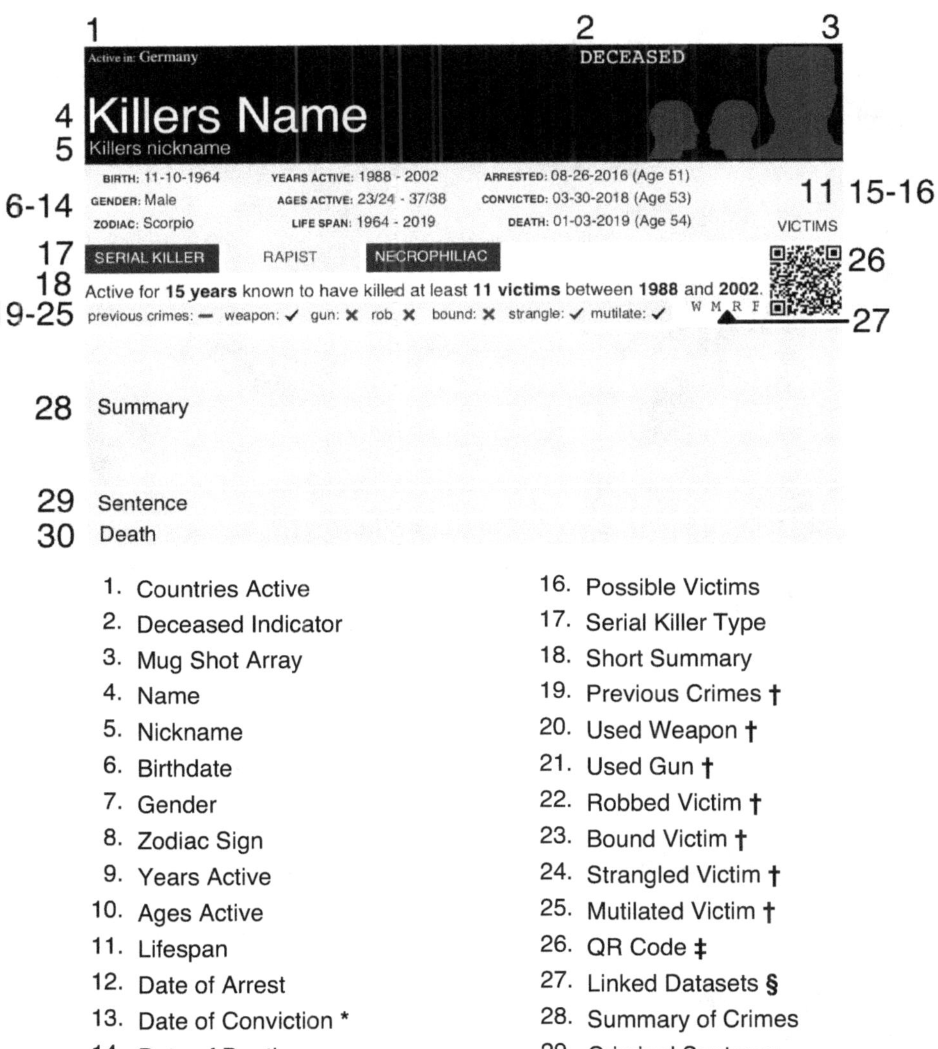

1. Countries Active
2. Deceased Indicator
3. Mug Shot Array
4. Name
5. Nickname
6. Birthdate
7. Gender
8. Zodiac Sign
9. Years Active
10. Ages Active
11. Lifespan
12. Date of Arrest
13. Date of Conviction *
14. Date of Death
15. Confirmed Victims
16. Possible Victims
17. Serial Killer Type
18. Short Summary
19. Previous Crimes †
20. Used Weapon †
21. Used Gun †
22. Robbed Victim †
23. Bound Victim †
24. Strangled Victim †
25. Mutilated Victim †
26. QR Code ‡
27. Linked Datasets §
28. Summary of Crimes
29. Criminal Sentence
30. Location and Cause of Death

* Where conviction dates were unavailable, sentenced dates were used.

† Boolean Values: (✓ True) (✗ False) (— No Answer)

‡ each QR Code leads readers to the killers online profile on Killer.Cloud
Scan the QR code with your smartphone's camera or a standalone QR reader.

§ The below linked datasets are available through the QR code above.
(W) en.wikipedia.org (M) murderpedia.org
(R) maamodt.asp.radford.edu (F) skdb.fgcu.edu

SERIAL KILLER RAPISTS A-Z

Some serial killers on this list may be unidentified or using an alias as their main name, alphabetical order is a very loose term. Also consider that in many parts of Asia, as well as some parts of Europe and Africa, the family name is placed before a person's given name. In these cases, for simplicity, we have used the last section of the name.

SERIAL KILLER
RAPISTS

Active in: United States

Rodney Alcala

Dating Game Killer

BIRTH: 08-23-1943 YEARS ACTIVE: 1971 - 1979 ARRESTED: 08-24-1979 (Age 36)
GENDER: Male AGES ACTIVE: 27/28 - 35/36 CONVICTED: 06-20-1986 (Age 42)
ZODIAC: Leo LIFE SPAN: 1943 - DEATH:

8-100 VICTIMS

SERIAL KILLER | RAPIST | TORTURER | STRANGLER

Active for **9 years** known to have killed at least **8 victims** between **1971** and **1979**.
previous crimes: ✓ weapon: ✗ gun: ✓ rob: ✗ bound: ✓ strangle: ✓ mutilate: ✓ W M R F

Rodney Alcala an American serial killer known as the Dating Game Killer for appearing on the game show The Dating Game in the middle of his killing spree. Alcala was convicted of five murders, though his actual total is estimated to be much higher. Alcala had a locker filled with thousands of photographs of women and children, most in sexually explicit poses, and it is suspected that some of the women photographed may be among Alcala's additional victims. Rodney Alcala remains in California State Prison in Corcoran pending further appeals of his death sentences.

Sentence: death at California State Prison in Corcoran, California.

BIRTH: 01-02-1967 YEARS ACTIVE: 1991 - 1991 ARRESTED: 12-18-1991 (Age 24)
GENDER: Male AGES ACTIVE: 23/24 - 23/24 CONVICTED: 04-26-1993 (Age 26)
ZODIAC: Capricorn LIFE SPAN: 1967 - DEATH:

14 VICTIMS

SERIAL KILLER | RAPIST | NECROPHILIAC | VAMPIRE | STRANGLER

Active for **1 year** known to have killed at least **14 victims** in **1991**.
previous crimes: ✓ weapon: ✗ gun: ✗ rob: ✓ bound: ✗ strangle: ✓ mutilate: ✓ W M

Marcelo Costa de Andrade a Brazilian serial killer known as The Vampire of Niterói. Andrade raped and killed fourteen children in Niterói and Rio de Janeiro during 1991. He was known to rape, strangle, beat and drink the blood of his victims. He confessed to committing acts of necrophilia with at least one of his victims body. Marcelo was caught after one of the victims escaped and alerted the authorities. He confessed to killing the fourteen boys and was preventively detained at the Heitor Carrilho Psychiatric Hospital in Rio de Janeiro, Brazil.

Sentence: preventively detained at the Heitor Carrilho Psychiatric Hospital in Niterói, State of Rio de Janeiro, Brazil.

Active in: United States

John Eric Armstrong

BABYDOLL, Opie

BIRTH: 11-23-1973 YEARS ACTIVE: 1992 - 1999 ARRESTED: 04-12-2000 (Age 26)

GENDER: Male AGES ACTIVE: 18/19 - 25/26 CONVICTED: 06-18-2001 (Age 27)

ZODIAC: Sagittarius LIFE SPAN: 1973 - DEATH:

5-18 VICTIMS

SERIAL KILLER RAPIST STRANGLER

Active for **8 years** known to have killed at least **5 victims** between **1992** and **1999**.

previous crimes: ✗ weapon: ✗ gun: ✗ rob: ✓ bound: ✗ strangle: ✓ mutilate: ✗ M R

John Eric Armstrong an American serial killer and rapist nicknamed Babydoll and Opie. On April 10th 2000, police found the bodies of three strangled prostitutes in a railroad yard in southwest Detroit. Armstrong pleaded guilty to the deaths of Robbin Brown, 20; Rose Marie Felt, 32; and Monica Johnson, 31. Armstrong also pleaded guilty to one assault charge and no contest to another assault charge. A third assault and unarmed robbery case was dismissed as part of a plea bargain. Ultimately, he was sentenced to life in prison for the death of Kelly Jean Hood, 34. All of the victims bodies were found in Detroit, Michigan.

Sentence: life imprisonment at Earnest C. Brooks Correctional Facility, West Shoreline Correctional Facility in Muskegon Heights, Michigan, US.

Active in: Russia

Valery Asratyan

The Director

BIRTH: YEARS ACTIVE: 1988 - 1990 ARRESTED:

GENDER: Male AGES ACTIVE: - CONVICTED: 06-18-1992

ZODIAC: LIFE SPAN: - DEATH:

3 VICTIMS

SERIAL KILLER RAPIST

Active for **3 years** known to have killed at least **3 victims** between **1988** and **1990**.

previous crimes: ✓ weapon: ✓ gun: ✗ rob: ✓ bound: ✓ strangle: ✗ mutilate: ✗ W M

Valery Asratyan (Valery Georgievich Asratyan) a Soviet serial killer, rapist and child molester known as The Director. He was known to drug, rape and murder his victims between 1988 and 1990 in Moscow, Russia. Asratyan received his nickname because he posed as film director Svetoslav Chaplygin in order to gain the trust of the young women. He was previously convicted of over twenty rapes of girls and young women during the 1980s. In 1990, he confessed to two murders and admitted to seventeen rapes. Asratyan was convicted of killing two women and was sentenced to death. Valery Asratyan was executed by firing squad in 1992.

Sentence: death by firing squad in 1992 at a prison location in Moscow, Russia.

Active in: United States DECEASED

Benjamin Atkins

The Woodward Corridor Killer

BIRTH: 08-26-1968 YEARS ACTIVE: 1991 - 1992 ARRESTED:
GENDER: Male AGES ACTIVE: 22/23 - 23/24 CONVICTED: 05-11-1994 (Age 25)
ZODIAC: Virgo LIFE SPAN: 1968 - 1997 DEATH: 09-17-1997 (Age 29)

11 VICTIMS

SERIAL KILLER RAPIST TORTURER STRANGLER

Active for **2 years** known to have killed at least **11 victims** between **1991** and **1992**.
previous crimes: — weapon: ✗ gun: ✗ rob: ✗ bound: ✗ strangle: ✓ mutilate: ✗ W M F

Benjamin Atkins an American serial killer and rapist known as The Woodward Corridor Killer. Atkins murdered, tortured, and raped eleven women in Highland Park and Detroit, Michigan, during a period of nine months between December 1991 and August 1992. He raped and strangled his victims before abandoning their bodies in vacant buildings in Highland Park and Detroit, Michigan. He was sentenced to eleven life terms in 1994. In 1997, Benjamin Atkins died from an infection caused by HIV while serving his life sentence at the Charles Egeler Reception and Guidance Center in Jackson, Michigan.

Sentence: life imprisonment, eleven life terms at Charles Egeler Reception and Guidance Center in Jackson, Michigan, US. **Death:** cause of death: natural causes, AIDS at Charles Egeler Reception and Guidance Center in Jackson, Michigan, US.

Active in: United States

Johnny Avalos

San Antonio serial killer

BIRTH: 12-01-1986 YEARS ACTIVE: 2012 - 2015 ARRESTED: 04-22-2015 (Age 28)
GENDER: Male AGES ACTIVE: 25/26 - 28/29 CONVICTED: 02-19-2019 (Age 32)
ZODIAC: Sagittarius LIFE SPAN: 1986 - DEATH:

5 VICTIMS

SERIAL KILLER RAPIST NECROPHILIAC STRANGLER

Active for **4 years** known to have killed at least **5 victims** between **2012** and **2015**.
previous crimes: ✓ weapon: ✗ gun: ✗ rob: ✓ bound: ✗ strangle: ✓ mutilate: ✗

Johnny Avalos (Johnny Joe Avalos) an American serial killer and rapist known as the San Antonio serial killer. Avalos murdered five women in San Antonio, Texas between 2012 and 2015. He would strangle his victims, raping some after death. His previous charges range from making terroristic threats, criminal mischief and possession of a controlled substance. Avalos confessed to killing Vanessa Lopez in 2012, Natalie Chavez in 2014, Rosemary Perez and Celia Lopez in 2015. He also admitted to attacking Genevieve Ramirez who later died of her injuries in 2015. He was arrested in 2015. On February 19th 2019, Johnny Avalos was sentenced to two terms of life without the possibility of parole.

Sentence: life imprisonment, two terms at the James H. Byrd Jr. Unit in Huntsville, Texas, US.

Active in: United States

DECEASED

Cesar Barone

Adolph James Rode

BIRTH: 12-04-1960 YEARS ACTIVE: 1991 - 1993 ARRESTED: 02-27-1993 (Age 32)
GENDER: Male AGES ACTIVE: 30/31 - 32/33 CONVICTED: 12-06-1995 (Age 35)
ZODIAC: Sagittarius LIFE SPAN: 1960 - 2009 DEATH: 12-24-2009 (Age 49)

4 VICTIMS

SERIAL KILLER RAPIST STRANGLER

Active for **3 years** known to have killed at least **4 victims** between **1991** and **1993**.
previous crimes: ✓ weapon: ✓ gun: ✓ rob: ✓ bound: ✗ strangle: ✓ mutilate: ✗ W M R

Cesar Barone (Cesar Francesco Barone) (born Adolph James Rode) an American serial killer who assaulted, raped and murdered four women in the Portland area between 1991 and 1993. In 1990, Barone was kicked out of the army after he exposed himself to a female officer, his superiors also learned that he had changed his identity and had spent several years in prison prior to joining the army. Barone was arrested in 1993 and sentenced to death in 1995. He met serial killer Ted Bundy while they were both inmates at Florida State Prison. In 2009, Cesar Barone died of natural causes at the Oregon State Penitentiary in Salem, Oregon.

Sentence: death at Oregon State Penitentiary in Salem, Oregon, US. **Death:** cause of death: natural causes at Oregon State Penitentiary in Salem, Oregon, US.

Active in: Mexico

Juana Barraza

La Mataviejitas, The Old Lady Killer

BIRTH: 12-27-1957 YEARS ACTIVE: 1998 - 2006 ARRESTED: 01-24-2006 (Age 48)
GENDER: Female AGES ACTIVE: 40/41 - 48/49 CONVICTED: 03-31-2008 (Age 50)
ZODIAC: Capricorn LIFE SPAN: 1957 - DEATH:

11-49 VICTIMS

SERIAL KILLER RAPIST STRANGLER

Active for **9 years** known to have killed at least **11 victims** between **1998** and **2006**.
previous crimes: — weapon: ✓ gun: ✗ rob: ✓ bound: ✗ strangle: ✓ mutilate: ✗ W M

Juana Barraza a Mexican professional wrestler and female serial killer known as La Mataviejitas (The Old Lady Killer) and La Dama del Silencio (The Lady of Silence). Barraza killed by bludgeoning or strangling elderly women to rob them, forty-two to forty-nine total victims. She was found guilty on sixteen charges of murder and aggravated burglary, including eleven separate counts of murder. Barraza's mother, Justa Samperio, was an alcoholic who reportedly exchanged her for three beers to a man who repeatedly raped her in his care. Juana Barraza was sentenced to 759 years in 2008.

Sentence: life imprisonment, 759 years at a prison in Mexico City, Mexico.

Active in: United States DECEASED

Robert Berdella

The Kansas City Butcher, The Collector

BIRTH: 01-31-1949 YEARS ACTIVE: 1984 - 1987 ARRESTED: 04-02-1988 (Age 39)
GENDER: Male AGES ACTIVE: 34/35 - 37/38 CONVICTED: 12-19-1988 (Age 39)
ZODIAC: Aquarius LIFE SPAN: 1949 - 1992 DEATH: 10-08-1992 (Age 43)

6 VICTIMS

SERIAL KILLER RAPIST TORTURER

Active for **4 years** known to have killed at least **6 victims** between **1984** and **1987**.
previous crimes: — weapon: — gun: — rob: — bound: — strangle: — mutilate: — W M R F

Robert Berdella (Robert Andrew Berdella Jr.) an American serial killer, known as The Kansas City Butcher and The Collector. Berdella abducted, raped, tortured, and murdered at least six men between 1984 and 1987. He would hold victims captive for periods of up to six weeks. Berdella dissected his victims' bodies and dispose of the body parts in garbage bags. His last victims escaped and alerted the police. Berdella was found guilty of six murders in 1988 and was sentenced to life imprisonment. He died of a heart attack while incarcerated at the Missouri State Penitentiary in 1992.

Sentence: life imprisonment without the possibility of parole at the Missouri State Penitentiary in Jefferson City, Missouri, US. **Death:** cause of death: natural causes, heart attack, myocardial infarction at the Missouri State Penitentiary in Jefferson City, Missouri, US.

Active in: Colombia

Manuel Octavio Bermudez

El Monstruo de los Cañaduzales, The Monster of the Cane Fields

BIRTH: 10-15-1961 YEARS ACTIVE: 1999 - 2003 ARRESTED: 07-18-2003 (Age 41)
GENDER: Male AGES ACTIVE: 37/38 - 41/42 CONVICTED: 03-20-2004 (Age 42)
ZODIAC: Libra LIFE SPAN: 1961 - DEATH:

21-50 VICTIMS

SERIAL KILLER RAPIST STRANGLER

Active for **5 years** known to have killed at least **21 victims** between **1999** and **2003**.
previous crimes: — weapon: ✗ gun: ✗ rob: ✗ bound: ✗ strangle: ✓ mutilate: ✗ W M

Manuel Octavio Bermudez (Manuel Octavio Bermúdez Estrada) a Colombian rapist, pedophile and serial killer known as El Monstruo de los Cañaduzales (The Monster of the Cane Fields). Bermudez confessed to murdering twenty-one children in remote areas of Colombia, only seventeen of bodies were officially found. Police searched a room he rented in El Cairo and found newspaper clippings of the murders, syringes, Lidocaine, and the wristwatch of one of his victims. Bermúdez is suspected of killing over fifty children in several towns of Valle del Cauc between 1999 and 2003. Manuel Octavio Bermudez was sentenced to forty years imprisonment at a unknown prison in Colombia.

Sentence: forty years imprisonment at a prison in Colombia.

Active in: Canada

Paul Kenneth Bernardo

Scarborough Rapist, Schoolgirl Killer

BIRTH: 08-27-1964 YEARS ACTIVE: 1990 - 1992 ARRESTED: 02-17-1993 (Age 28)
GENDER: Male AGES ACTIVE: 25/26 - 27/28 CONVICTED: 09-01-1995 (Age 31)
ZODIAC: Virgo LIFE SPAN: 1964 - DEATH:

3-5
VICTIMS

SERIAL KILLER | RAPIST | TORTURER | STALKER | STRANGLER

Active for **3 years** known to have killed at least **3 victims** between **1990** and **1992**.

previous crimes: ✓ weapon: ✗ gun: ✗ rob: ✗ bound: ✓ strangle: ✓ mutilate: ✓ W M R

Paul Kenneth Bernardo a Canadian serial killer and rapist known as the Schoolgirl Killer, the Scarborough Rapist and Paul Jason Teale. Bernardo raped and murdered at least three minors between 1990 and 1992. Bernardo attacked most of his victims after stalking them as they got off of public transportation buses in Scarborough, Canada. Bernardo gained worldwide media attention when he raped, tortured and murdered two Ontario teenage girls with the assistance of his wife, Karla Homolka. Homolka and Bernardo were arrested in 1993. In 1995, Paul Kenneth Bernardo was convicted of a number of offenses, including the two first-degree murders, and was sentenced to life in prison without parole for at least twenty-five years.

Sentence: life imprisonment without the possibility of parole for twenty-five years at Kingston Penitentiary in Kingston, Ontario, Canada.

Active in: United States

Kenneth Alessio Bianchi

Hillside Stranglers

BIRTH: 05-22-1951 YEARS ACTIVE: 1977 - 1978 ARRESTED: 01-12-1979 (Age 27)
GENDER: Male AGES ACTIVE: 25/26 - 26/27 CONVICTED: 10-21-1983 (Age 32)
ZODIAC: Gemini LIFE SPAN: 1951 - DEATH:

12-15
VICTIMS

SERIAL KILLER | RAPIST | TORTURER | STALKER | STRANGLER

Active for **2 years** known to have killed at least **12 victims** between **1977** and **1978**.

previous crimes: ✓ weapon: ✗ gun: ✗ rob: ✗ bound: ✓ strangle: ✓ mutilate: ✗ W M R F

Kenneth Alessio Bianchi an American serial killer, kidnapper and rapist known as the Hillside Stranglers. Bianchi was convicted of strangling twelve females between the ages of 12 and 28, he is also suspected in another three cases. Kenneth Alessio Bianchi is one of the Hillside Stranglers the other is his cousin, Angelo Buono. Bianchi is also a suspect in the alphabet murders, three unsolved murders in his home city of Rochester, New York. He was known to kidnap, rape and torture victims prior to murdering them. Kenneth Alessio Bianchi was convicted and sentenced to life imprisonment on October 21st 1983. Bianchi is serving his sentence at Washington State Penitentiary in Walla Walla, Washington.

Sentence: life imprisonment with possibility of parole at Washington State Penitentiary in Walla Walla, Washington, US.

Active in: United States

DECEASED

Richard Biegenwald

The Thrill Killer

BIRTH: 08-24-1940 **YEARS ACTIVE:** 1958 - 1983 **ARRESTED:** 01-22-1983 (Age 42)
GENDER: Male **AGES ACTIVE:** 17/18 - 42/43 **CONVICTED:** 11-08-1983 (Age 43)
ZODIAC: Virgo **LIFE SPAN:** 1940 - 2008 **DEATH:** 03-10-2008 (Age 67)

9-11 VICTIMS

SERIAL KILLER RAPIST

Active for **26 years** known to have killed at least **9 victims** between **1958** and **1983**.
previous crimes: ✓ weapon: ✓ gun: ✓ rob: ✓ bound: ✗ strangle: ✗ mutilate: ✓ W M F

Richard Biegenwald an American serial killer known as The Thrill Killer. Biegenwald killed at least nine people in Monmouth County, New Jersey between 1958 and 1983. He is suspected in at least two other murders. Biegenwald was sentenced to death, his sentence was commuted to four terms of life at the New Jersey State Prison in Trenton, New Jersey. In 2008, Richard Biegenwald died of natural causes at the St. Francis Medical Center in Trenton, New Jersey.

Sentence: death commuted to four terms of life at New Jersey State Prison, Trenton, New Jersey, US.
Death: cause of death: natural causes, kidney failure at St. Francis Medical Center in Trenton, New Jersey, US.

Active in: Iran

DECEASED

Mohammed Bijeh

Tehran Desert Vampire, the hyenas

BIRTH: 02-07-1975 **YEARS ACTIVE:** 2004 - 2004 **ARRESTED:** 09-01-2004 (Age 29)
GENDER: Male **AGES ACTIVE:** 28/29 - 28/29 **CONVICTED:** 10-14-2004 (Age 29)
ZODIAC: Aquarius **LIFE SPAN:** 1975 - 2005 **DEATH:** 03-16-2005 (Age 30)

16-20 VICTIMS

SERIAL KILLER RAPIST NECROPHILIAC VAMPIRE

Active for **1 year** known to have killed at least **16 victims** in **2004**.
previous crimes: — weapon: ✓ gun: ✗ rob: ✗ bound: ✗ strangle: ✗ mutilate: ✗ W M

Mohammed Bijeh an Iranian serial killer and rapist known as the Tehran Desert Vampire and the hyenas. Bijeh raped and killed at least sixteen boys and teenagers with an accomplice named Ali Baghi (Ali Gholampour). The pair would stun their victims with blows from a stone to the head, they raped and buried the bodies in a shallow grave. They allegedly placed dead animals near the graves to cover up the smell of the rotting corpses. In 2005, Bijeh was executed after being lashed a hundred times in front of a crowd. In 2004 early in the case police officers were arrested on charges of derailing the investigations by refusing to identify the murderers earlier at Tehran Police's Bureau of Investigation.

Sentence: death by hanging at a prison in Pakdasht, Iran. **Death:** cause of death: capital punishment, executed by hanging after being publicly flogged a hundred times at a prison in Pakdasht, Iran.

Active in: United States

DECEASED

Jake Bird

The Tacoma Ax-Killer

BIRTH: 12-14-1901 YEARS ACTIVE: 1930 - 1947 ARRESTED: 10-30-1947 (Age 45)
GENDER: Male AGES ACTIVE: 28/29 - 45/46 CONVICTED: 11-26-1947 (Age 45)
ZODIAC: Sagittarius LIFE SPAN: 1901 - 1949 DEATH: 07-15-1949 (Age 47)

12-46 VICTIMS

SERIAL KILLER RAPIST STALKER

Active for **18 years** known to have killed at least **12 victims** between **1930** and **1947**.
previous crimes: ✓ weapon: ✓ gun: ✗ rob: ✓ bound: ✗ strangle: ✗ mutilate: ✓ W M

Jake Bird an American serial killer and rapist known as The Tacoma Ax-Killer. Bird had an extensive criminal record including burglary and attempted murder. Bird was arrested in 1947 and was sentenced to death for the murders of two victims. In 1948, Bird was scheduled for execution but it was postponed when he confessed to a total of forty-six murders. Eleven of the forty-six victims were substantiated and he was considered a prime suspect in the remaining crimes. In 1949, Jake Bird was executed by public hanging at Washington State Penitentiary in Walla Walla, Washington.

Sentence: death by hanging at the Washington State Penitentiary in Walla Walla, Washington, US.
Death: cause of death: capital punishment, executed by hanging at Washington State Penitentiary in Walla Walla, Washington, US.

Active in: Russia

DECEASED

Anatoly Biryukov

The Baby Hunter

BIRTH: 02-18-1944 YEARS ACTIVE: 1977 - 1977 ARRESTED: 10-24-1977 (Age 33)
GENDER: Male AGES ACTIVE: 32/33 - 32/33 CONVICTED:
ZODIAC: Aquarius LIFE SPAN: 1944 - 1979 DEATH: 02-24-1979 (Age 35)

5 VICTIMS

SERIAL KILLER RAPIST NECROPHILIAC

Active for **1 year** known to have killed at least **5 victims** in **1977**.
previous crimes: ✓ weapon: ✓ gun: ✗ rob: ✗ bound: ✗ strangle: ✗ mutilate: ✗ W M

Anatoly Biryukov (Anatoliy Nikolaevich Biryukov) a Soviet serial killer and child rapist known as The Baby Hunter. Biryukov was convicted for kidnapping, raping and subsequent murder of five infants from Moscow in the fall of 1977. Biryukov abducted his victims and committed violent sexual intercourse with the infants before murdering and discarding the body. He committed acts of necrophilia on at least one of his victims. In 1977, Biryukov attempted a kidnapping when he was chased by Chekhov citizens which later led to his arrest. He was sentenced to death for the five murders in 1978. Biryukov attempted multiple failed suicides while awaiting execution. In 1979, Anatoly Biryukov was executed by firing squad.

Sentence: death by firing squad at a prison in the Soviet Union. **Death:** cause of death: executed by firing squad at a prison in the Soviet Union.

Active in: United States

Lawrence Bittaker

Tool Box Killers

BIRTH: 09-27-1940 **YEARS ACTIVE:** 1979 - 1979 **ARRESTED:** 11-20-1979 (Age 39)
GENDER: Male **AGES ACTIVE:** 38/39 - 38/39 **CONVICTED:** 03-24-1981 (Age 40)
ZODIAC: Libra **LIFE SPAN:** 1940 - **DEATH:**

5 VICTIMS

SERIAL KILLER | RAPIST | TORTURER | STALKER | STRANGLER

Active for **1 year** known to have killed at least **5 victims** in **1979**.
previous crimes: ✓ weapon: ✓ gun ✗ rob: ✗ bound: ✓ strangle: ✓ mutilate: ✗ W M R F

Lawrence Bittaker (Lawrence Sigmund Bittaker) an American serial killer and rapists who along with his accomplice, Roy Lewis Norris are known as the Tool Box Killers. In 1979, Bittaker and Norris kidnapped, raped, tortured, and murdered five teenage girls over a period of five months in southern California. Bittaker and Norris used standard tools such as pliers, ice picks and sledgehammers to torture and murder their victims. Bittaker was sentenced to death for five of the murders in 1981. Lawrence Bittaker is currently incarcerated on death row at San Quentin State Prison in San Quentin, California.
Sentence: death at San Quentin State Prison in San Quentin, California, US.

BIRTH: 04-21-1947 **YEARS ACTIVE:** 1981 - 1986 **ARRESTED:** 07-14-1990 (Age 43)
GENDER: Male **AGES ACTIVE:** 33/34 - 38/39 **CONVICTED:** 05-19-1994 (Age 47)
ZODIAC: Aries **LIFE SPAN:** 1947 - 2016 **DEATH:** 01-12-2016 (Age 68)

4-18 VICTIMS

SERIAL KILLER | RAPIST | TORTURER | STRANGLER

Active for **6 years** known to have killed at least **4 victims** between **1981** and **1986**.
previous crimes: ✓ weapon: ✗ gun ✗ rob: ✗ bound: ✓ strangle: ✓ mutilate: ✗ W M R F

Robert Black a Scottish serial killer and pedophile known as the M1 Maniac and Smelly Bob. Black was convicted of kidnapping, raping and murdering four girls in the United Kingdom from 1981 to 1986. He was a possible suspect in several other earlier unsolved child murder cases in the UK and other European countries. He was found guilty on all counts and sentenced to a life term for each murder. Black died of a myocardial infarction weeks before he was to be charged with a fifth child murder.
Sentence: life imprisonment with out the possibility of parole for thirty-five years at HM Prison Maghaberry in Lisburn, Northern Ireland. **Death:** cause of death: heart attack at HM Prison Maghaberry in Lisburn, Northern Ireland.

Active in: United States

Terry Blair

BIRTH: 09-16-1961 **YEARS ACTIVE:** 1982 - 2004 **ARRESTED:** 09-14-2004 (Age 42)
GENDER: Male **AGES ACTIVE:** 20/21 - 42/43 **CONVICTED:** 03-27-2008 (Age 46)
ZODIAC: Virgo **LIFE SPAN:** 1961 - **DEATH:**

7-9 VICTIMS

SERIAL KILLER RAPIST STRANGLER

Active for **23 years** known to have killed at least **7 victims** between **1982** and **2004**.
previous crimes: ✓ weapon: ✗ gun: ✗ rob: ✗ bound: ✗ strangle: ✓ mutilate: ✗ W M F

Terry Blair (Terry A. Blair) an American serial killer who raped and killed at least seven women in Kansas City, Missouri between 1982 and 2004. In 1982, Blair murdered the mother of his two children, she was pregnant at the time of her death. He was sentenced to twenty-five years imprisonment and was released on parole after serving twenty-one years. In 2004, Blair was charged with eight counts of murder, two counts were later dropped due to lack of evidence. A 911 call claimed responsibility for the murders. The caller stated that they were all prostitutes and scum which is why they were killed. Blair's semen was found on at least one of his victims. In 2008, Terry Blair was sentenced to six life sentences for the six murders in 2004.

Sentence: life imprisonment, six life terms at the Potosi Correctional Center in Potosi, Missouri, US.

Active in: Canada DECEASED

Wayne Boden

the Vampire Rapist

BIRTH: 01-01-1948 **YEARS ACTIVE:** 1968 - 1971 **ARRESTED:** 05-19-1971 (Age 23)
GENDER: Male **AGES ACTIVE:** 20/20 - 23/23 **CONVICTED:** 02-16-1972 (Age 24)
ZODIAC: Capricorn **LIFE SPAN:** 1948 - 2006 **DEATH:** 03-27-2006 (Age 58)

4 VICTIMS

SERIAL KILLER RAPIST VAMPIRE STRANGLER

Active for **4 years** known to have killed at least **4 victims** between **1968** and **1971**.
previous crimes: — weapon: ✗ gun: ✗ rob: ✗ bound: ✗ strangle: ✓ mutilate: ✗ W M

Wayne Boden (Wayne Clifford Boden) a Canadian serial killer and rapist known as the Vampire Rapist. Boden killed four women between 1968 and 1971 in Montreal and Calgary, Canada. He would rape and strangle his victims. He was known to bite the breasts of at least three of his victims. Boden was the first murderer to be convicted in North America based on odontological evidence. Boden received four life sentences in 1972. In 2006, Wayne Boden died from skin cancer at Kingston General Hospital after being confined in the hospital for six weeks.

Sentence: life imprisonment, four terms at the Kingston Penitentiary in Kingston, Ontario, Canada.

Death: cause of death: natural causes, cancer, skin cancer at Kingston General Hospital in Kingston, Ontario, Canada.

Active in: Israel

Nicolai Bonner

Haifa serial killer, The Homeless Murderer

BIRTH: | **YEARS ACTIVE:** 2005 - 2005 | **ARRESTED:** 05-29-2005
GENDER: Male | **AGES ACTIVE:** - | **CONVICTED:** 05-06-2007
ZODIAC: | **LIFE SPAN:** - | **DEATH:**

4 VICTIMS

SERIAL KILLER RAPIST

Active for **1 year** known to have killed at least **4 victims** in **2005**.

previous crimes: — weapon: ✓ gun: ✗ rob: ✗ bound: ✗ strangle: ✗ mutilate: ✓ W M

Nicolai Bonner a Moldovan-born Israeli serial killer and rapist known as the Haifa serial killer and The Homeless Murderer. In 2005, Bonner beat or stabbed to death four fellow immigrants from the former Soviet Union. Three of his victims were homeless vagrants in the industrial area of Haifa, Israel. He drank alcohol with the three victims prior to murdering them in an abandoned building by the Haifa market. Two of his victims were male and two were female. Bonner set three of his victims bodies on fire and attempted to set fire to the fourth victims body. Nicolai Bonner was sentenced to life imprisonment in 2007.

Sentence: life imprisonment, four consecutive life terms at a prison in Israel.

Active in: Iraq DECEASED

Ali Asghar Borujerdi

Asghar the Murderer, Ashare Qatel

BIRTH: | **YEARS ACTIVE:** 1907 - 1934 | **ARRESTED:** 03-10-1933
GENDER: Male | **AGES ACTIVE:** - | **CONVICTED:** 06-06-1934
ZODIAC: | **LIFE SPAN:** - 1934 | **DEATH:** 07-06-1934

33 VICTIMS

SERIAL KILLER RAPIST

Active for **28 years** known to have killed at least **33 victims** between **1907** and **1934**.

previous crimes: ✓ weapon: ✗ gun: ✗ rob: ✗ bound: ✗ strangle: ✗ mutilate: ✓ W M

Ali Asghar Borujerdi an Iranian serial killer and rapist known as Asghar the Murderer, Ashare Qatel. Borujerdi was the son of a famous road thief, Ali Miza Borujerdi. As as a child, he started assaulting, raping, and later murdering, adolescent boys in Baghdad when he was fourteen years old. Borujerdi was convicted of killing thirty-three young boys in Iraq and Iran, eight in Tehran and twenty-five in Baghdad. Borujerdi was convicted and after an unsuccessful appeal, he was sentenced to death. In 1934, Ali Asghar Borujerdi was executed by public hanging in front of a crowd in Tehran's Sepah Square.

Sentence: death by hanging at a prison in Tehran, Iran. **Death:** cause of death: capital punishment, executed by public hanging at Tehran's Sepah Square in Toopkhaneh, Tehran, Iran.

Active in: United States

Lucious Boyd

Lucilous Boyd, Lucifer

BIRTH: 03-22-1959 **YEARS ACTIVE:** 1993 - 1999 **ARRESTED:** 03-26-1999 (Age 40)
GENDER: Male **AGES ACTIVE:** 33/34 - 39/40 **CONVICTED:** 06-21-2002 (Age 43)
ZODIAC: Aries **LIFE SPAN:** 1959 - **DEATH:**

1-10 VICTIMS

SERIAL KILLER RAPIST

Active for **7 years** known to have killed at least **1 victims** between **1993** and **1999**.
previous crimes: ✔ weapon: ✔ gun: ✖ rob: ✖ bound: ✖ strangle: ✖ mutilate: ✖ W M

Lucious Boyd a suspected American serial killer and rapist also known as Lucilous Boyd and Lucifer. Boyd was convicted and sentenced to death for a 1998 murder. He was known to kidnap, rape, stab and murder his victims. The victim from 1998 had been raped and stabbed thirty-six times with a screwdriver. Authorities recovered blood while searching his apartment, the blood was matched to one of his victims. Authorities suspect Boyd of at least ten other homicides or disappearances. Lucious Boyd was sentenced to death in 2002. He is currently on death row awaiting execution at the Union Correctional Institution in Raiford, Florida.

Sentence: death at Union Correctional Institution in Raiford, Florida, US.

Active in: United Kingdom DECEASED

Ian Brady

The Moors murders

BIRTH: 01-02-1938 **YEARS ACTIVE:** 1963 - 1965 **ARRESTED:** 10-07-1965 (Age 27)
GENDER: Male **AGES ACTIVE:** 24/25 - 26/27 **CONVICTED:** 05-06-1966 (Age 28)
ZODIAC: Capricorn **LIFE SPAN:** 1938 - 2017 **DEATH:** 05-15-2017 (Age 79)

5 VICTIMS

SERIAL KILLER RAPIST TORTURER STRANGLER

Active for **3 years** known to have killed at least **5 victims** between **1963** and **1965**.
previous crimes: ✔ weapon: ✔ gun: ✖ rob: ✖ bound: ✔ strangle: ✔ mutilate: ✖ W M

Ian Brady (born Ian Duncan Stewart) a Scottish rapist and serial killer who along with his girlfriend, Myra Hindley, are known for committing the Moors murders. The Moors murders were carried out in England between 1963 and 1965. Five children were abducted and at least four were sexually assaulted. The victims were male and female children aged between 10 and 17. Brady was sentenced to three terms of life imprisonment in 1966. Ian Brady was the longest-serving prisoner in British legal history until the record was broken by fellow serial killer John Straffen.

Sentence: life imprisonment, three life terms at HM Prison Durham in the Elvet area of Durham, County Durham, England. **Death:** cause of death: natural causes, restrictive pulmonary disease at Ashworth Hospital, a high-security psychiatric hospital at Maghull in Merseyside, England.

Active in: United States DECEASED

Jerome Jerry Brudos

The Lust Killer, The Shoe Fetish Slayer

BIRTH: 01-31-1939 YEARS ACTIVE: 1968 - 1969 ARRESTED: 05-25-1969 (Age 30)
GENDER: Male AGES ACTIVE: 28/29 - 29/30 CONVICTED: 06-27-1969 (Age 30)
ZODIAC: Aquarius LIFE SPAN: 1939 - 2006 DEATH: 03-28-2006 (Age 67)

4 VICTIMS

SERIAL KILLER | RAPIST | NECROPHILIAC | STALKER | STRANGLER

Active for **2 years** known to have killed at least **4 victims** between **1968** and **1969**.

previous crimes: ✓ weapon: ✗ gun: ✗ rob: ✗ bound: ✗ strangle: ✓ mutilate: ✓ W M R F

Jerome Jerry Brudos an American serial killer who was known as the Lust Killer and the Shoe Fetish Slayer. Brudos was as electronics technician who bludgeoned and strangled four young women while dressed up in women's clothing. Brudos charged with three counts of first degree murder for the murders of Jan Whitney, Linda Salee, and Karen Sprinker. Brudos decided to revoke his plea of NGRI and plead guilty. Brudos was sentenced to three consecutive life sentences (no death penalty in Oregon). Brudos was one of six killers (Edmund Kemper, Ted Bundy, Ed Gein, Gary M. Heidnik, Gary Ridgway and Brudos) who served as an inspiration for the character of Buffalo Bill in Thomas Harris' 1988 novel The Silence of the Lambs and its film adaptation.

Sentence: life imprisonment at Oregon State Penitentiary in Salem, Oregon, US. **Death:** cause of death: natural causes, liver cancer at Oregon State Penitentiary in Salem, Oregon, US.

Active in: United States DECEASED

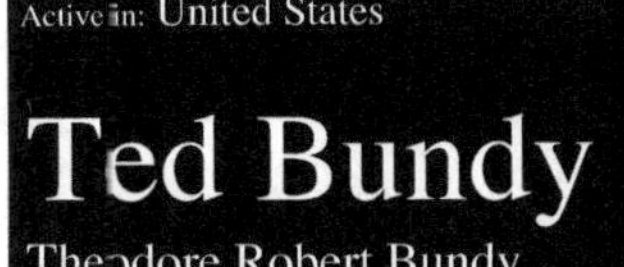

Ted Bundy

Theodore Robert Bundy

BIRTH: 11-24-1946 YEARS ACTIVE: 1974 - 1978 ARRESTED: 08-16-1975 (Age 28)
GENDER: Male AGES ACTIVE: 27/28 - 31/32 CONVICTED: 07-24-1979 (Age 32)
ZODIAC: Sagittarius LIFE SPAN: 1946 - 1989 DEATH: 01-24-1989 (Age 42)

30-36 VICTIMS

SERIAL KILLER | RAPIST | NECROPHILIAC | STRANGLER

Active for **5 years** known to have killed at least **30 victims** between **1974** and **1978**.

previous crimes: ✓ weapon: ✓ gun: ✗ rob: ✓ bound: ✓ strangle: ✓ mutilate: ✓ W M R F

Ted Bundy (born Theodore Robert Cowell) an American serial killer, kidnapper, burglar, rapist and necrophile known for his charisma and good looks. Bundy officially confessed to thirty homicides, some estimates run upwards of a hundred or more, he eventually confessed to thirty-six murders. Infamous for escaping from prison twice and murdering multiple victims in one day. Bundy was one of six killers (Edmund Kemper, Jerome Jerry Brudos, Ed Gein, Gary Heidnik, Gary Ridgway and Bundy) who served as an inspiration for the character of Buffalo Bill in Thomas Harris' 1988 novel The Silence of the Lambs and its film adaptation. In 1989, Ted Bundy was executed in the electric chair at the Florida State Prison in Raiford, Florida.

Sentence: death by electrocution at Florida State Prison, Raiford Prison in Raiford, Florida, US.

Death: cause of death: capital punishment, executed by electrocution via electric chair at Florida State Prison, Raiford Prison in Raiford, Florida, US.

Active in: United States

DECEASED

Angelo Buono

The Hillside Stranglers

BIRTH: 10-05-1934 YEARS ACTIVE: 1977 - 1979 ARRESTED: 10-22-1979 (Age 45)
GENDER: Male AGES ACTIVE: 42/43 - 44/45 CONVICTED: 11-18-1983 (Age 49)
ZODIAC: Libra LIFE SPAN: 1934 - 2002 DEATH: 09-21-2002 (Age 67)

10 VICTIMS

SERIAL KILLER RAPIST TORTURER STRANGLER

Active for **3 years** known to have killed at least **10 victims** between **1977** and **1979**.
previous crimes: ✓ weapon: ✗ gun: ✗ rob: ✗ bound: ✓ strangle: ✓ mutilate: ✗ W M R F

Angelo Buono (Angelo Anthony Buono Jr.) an American serial killer, kidnapper and rapist who was convicted of strangling ten females in Los Angeles, California between October 1977 and February 1978. Buono is one of the Hillside Stranglers, the other is his cousin, Kenneth Alessio Bianchi. Buono and Bianchi would abduct girls 12 to 28 years of age and sexually abuse them before strangling them to death. He was sentenced to life in prison in 1983. In 2002, Angelo Buono died from a heart attack while still in prison.

Sentence: life imprisonment at Calipatria State Prison in Calipatria, California, US. **Death:** cause of death: natural causes, myocardial infarction at Calipatria State Prison in Calipatria, California, US.

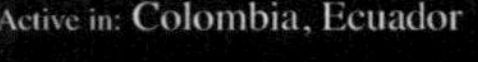

Active in: Colombia, Ecuador

DECEASED

Daniel Camargo

The Sadist of Chanquito, Manuel Bulgarin Solis

BIRTH: 01-22-1930 YEARS ACTIVE: 1974 - 1986 ARRESTED: 05-03-1974 (Age 44)
GENDER: Male AGES ACTIVE: 43/44 - 55/56 CONVICTED: 12-24-1977 (Age 47)
ZODIAC: Aquarius LIFE SPAN: 1930 - 1994 DEATH: 11-13-1994 (Age 64)

72-150 VICTIMS

SERIAL KILLER RAPIST STRANGLER

Active for **13 years** known to have killed at least **72 victims** between **1974** and **1986**.
previous crimes: ✓ weapon: ✓ gun: ✗ rob: ✓ bound: ✗ strangle: ✓ mutilate: ✓ W M

Daniel Camargo (Daniel Camargo Barbosa) a Colombian serial killer known as The Sadist of Chanquito and Manuel Bulgarin Solis. Camargo a child-murderer, believed to have raped and killed over one hundred and fifty victims. He is believed to have been motivated to kill from his stepmother abusing him as a child. He strangled young girls in Colombia and confessed to killing seventy-two victims. He escaped from prison and started killing in Ecuador, rearrested in 1989. In 1994, Camargo was stabbed to death in prison by a nephew of one of his victims.

Sentence: twenty-five years plus sixteen years in prison at Gorgona prison (Colombian Alcatraz) on a Colombian island in the Pacific Ocean. **Death:** cause of death: homicide, murdered in prison by Geovanny Noguera at Garcia Moreno prison in Quito, Ecuador.

Active in: United States

Harvey Carignan

The Want-Ad Killer, Harv the hammer

BIRTH: 05-18-1927 **YEARS ACTIVE:** 1949 - 1973 **ARRESTED:** 09-24-1974 (Age 47)
GENDER: Male **AGES ACTIVE:** 21/22 - 45/46 **CONVICTED:** 05-05-1975 (Age 47)
ZODIAC: Taurus **LIFE SPAN:** 1927 - **DEATH:**

5 VICTIMS

SERIAL KILLER RAPIST

Active for **25 years** known to have killed at least **5 victims** between **1949** and **1973**.
previous crimes: ✓ weapon: ✓ gun: ✗ rob: ✗ bound: ✓ strangle: ✗ mutilate: ✓ W M R F

Harvey Carignan (Harvey Louis Carignan) an American serial killer known as The Want-Ad Killer and Harv the hammer. Carignan raped and beat four young women to death between 1972 and 1973. He escaped hanging for a 1949 killing due to a technicality that claimed his confession was unlawfully obtained. The Supreme Court overruled Carignan's death sentence due to the officers' violations of the McNabb rule. Harvey Carignan (Prisoner AZ935) served a sentence at the Alcatraz Federal Penitentiary between 1951 and 1960. Carignan was sentenced to a total of 150 years in prison which he is currently serving at the Minnesota Correctional Facility in Faribault, Minnesota.
Sentence: life imprisonment at the Minnesota Correctional Facility in Faribault, Minnesota, US.

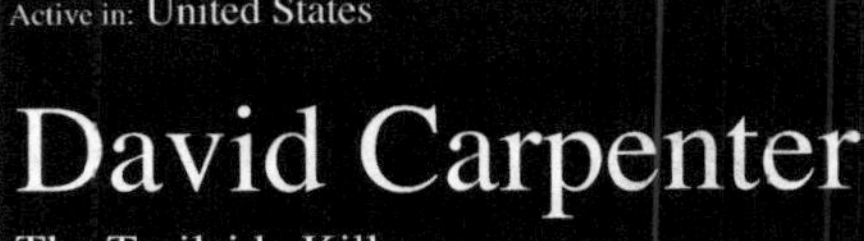

Active in: United States

David Carpenter

The Trailside Killer

BIRTH: 05-06-1930 **YEARS ACTIVE:** 1979 - 1981 **ARRESTED:** 05-14-1981 (Age 51)
GENDER: Male **AGES ACTIVE:** 48/49 - 50/51 **CONVICTED:** 05-10-1988 (Age 58)
ZODIAC: Taurus **LIFE SPAN:** 1930 - **DEATH:**

7-11 VICTIMS

SERIAL KILLER RAPIST STALKER

Active for **3 years** known to have killed at least **7 victims** between **1979** and **1981**.
previous crimes: ✓ weapon: ✓ gun: ✓ rob: ✗ bound: ✗ strangle: ✗ mutilate: ✗ W M R F

David Carpenter (David Joseph Carpenter) an American serial killer known as The Trailside Killer. Carpenter murdered women hikers on San Francisco-area hiking trails between 1979 and 1981. He would stalk, rape and kill hikers by shooting the victims in state parks near San Francisco, California. He was convicted of an attempted murder in 1960. In 1970, Carpenter was convicted for kidnapping. After his release, he was a suspect in the Zodiac murders, although he was eventually cleared. In 1984, Carpenter was sentenced to death, he received a second death sentence in 1988. David Carpenter remains on death row at the San Quentin State Prison in San Quentin, California.
Sentence: death by gas chamber at San Quentin State Prison, San Francisco, California, US.

Active in: Ecuador, Spain

Gilberto Chamba

The Monster of Machala

BIRTH:
YEARS ACTIVE: 1988 - 2004
ARRESTED: 12-01-2004
GENDER: Male
AGES ACTIVE: -
CONVICTED: 11-05-2006
ZODIAC:
LIFE SPAN: -
DEATH:

9
VICTIMS

SERIAL KILLER RAPIST STRANGLER

Active for **17 years** known to have killed at least **9 victims** between **1988** and **2004**.

previous crimes: ✓ weapon: ✓ gun: ✗ rob: ✗ bound: ✗ strangle: ✓ mutilate: ✗ W M

Gilberto Chamba (Gilberto Antonio Chamba Jaramillo) an Ecuadorian serial killer, rapist and taxi driver known as The Monster of Machala. Chamba abducted ten of his passengers, all lone female students, killing eight of them between 1988 and 1993. Chamba skewered some of his victims with an instrument similar to a cane. Chamba was sentenced to sixteen years in prison and later benefitted from an amnesty campaign that cleared his criminal record. He moved to Spain where he was arrested for the murder of another student and the attempted murder of a prostitute in 2004. In 2005, Gilberto Chamba was sentenced to forty-five years in prison.

Sentence: forty-five years in prison at Module 6, Center Penitenciari de Quatre Camins in Spain.

Active in: United States DECEASED

Richard Trenton Chase

Vampire of Sacramento

BIRTH: 05-23-1950
YEARS ACTIVE: 1977 - 1977
ARRESTED: 01-27-1978 (Age 27)
GENDER: Male
AGES ACTIVE: 26/27 - 26/27
CONVICTED: 05-08-1979 (Age 28)
ZODIAC: Gemini
LIFE SPAN: 1950 - 1980
DEATH: 12-26-1980 (Age 30)

6
VICTIMS

SERIAL KILLER RAPIST CANNIBAL NECROPHILIAC TORTURER

Active for **1 year** known to have killed at least **6 victims** in **1977**.

previous crimes: ✓ weapon: ✓ gun: ✓ rob: ✓ bound: ✗ strangle: ✗ mutilate: ✓ W M R F

Richard Trenton Chase an American schizophrenic serial killer necrophile and cannibal who was known as The Vampire of Sacramento, he was convicted of six murders performed in the span of a month after being released of a psychiatric hospital where he had been committed for killing and eating the raw meat of several animals. In addition to killing his victims, he often raped the women's bodies and sometimes drank their blood, or took their organs home and ate them.

Sentence: death by gas chamber at San Quentin prison, California, US. **Death:** cause of death: suicide, overdose of anti-depressants at San Quentin prison, California, US.

Active in: China

DECEASED

Gao Chengyong

the Chinese Jack the Ripper, the Silver City serial killer

BIRTH: 11-10-1964 | YEARS ACTIVE: 1988 - 2002 | ARRESTED: 08-26-2016 (Age 51)
GENDER: Male | AGES ACTIVE: 23/24 - 37/38 | CONVICTED: 03-30-2018 (Age 53)
ZODIAC: Scorpio | LIFE SPAN: 1964 - 2019 | DEATH: 01-03-2019 (Age 54)

11 VICTIMS

SERIAL KILLER | RAPIST | NECROPHILIAC

Active for **15 years** known to have killed at least **11 victims** between **1988** and **2002**.

previous crimes: ✗ weapon: ✓ gun: ✗ rob: ✓ bound: ✓ strangle: ✗ mutilate: ✓ W

Gao Chengyong a Chinese serial killer and rapist known as the Chinese Jack the Ripper and the Silver City serial killer. In China, Gao's crime spree has been labeled the Silver City serial killing case. Gao raped, murdered and mutilated the corpses of his victims. He confessed to murdering eleven women between 1988 and 2002. He committed acts of necrophilia on at least one of his victims. He removed the reproductive organs, cut the hands off multiple victims and a breast off at least one victim. He was arrested in 2016 and sentenced to death in 2018. Gao Chengyong was executed on January 3rd 2019.

Sentence: death at a prison in Baiyin, Gansu China. **Death:** cause of death: capital punishment, executed at Baiyin, prefecture-level city in Gansu, China.

Active in: Russia

DECEASED

Andrei Chikatilo

The Butcher of Rostov, The Red Ripper, The Rostov Ripper, Citizen X

BIRTH: 10-16-1936 | YEARS ACTIVE: 1978 - 1990 | ARRESTED: 11-20-1990 (Age 54)
GENDER: Male | AGES ACTIVE: 41/42 - 53/54 | CONVICTED: 10-14-1992 (Age 55)
ZODIAC: Libra | LIFE SPAN: 1936 - 1994 | DEATH: 02-14-1994 (Age 57)

52-56 VICTIMS

SERIAL KILLER | RAPIST | CANNIBAL | VAMPIRE | STRANGLER

Active for **13 years** known to have killed at least **52 victims** between **1978** and **1990**.

previous crimes: ✓ weapon: ✓ gun: ✗ rob: ✗ bound: ✓ strangle: ✓ mutilate: ✓ W M R

Andrei Chikatilo (Andrei Romanovich Chikatilo) a Soviet serial killer known as The Butcher of Rostov, The Red Ripper, The Rostov Ripper and Citizen X. Chikatilo sexual assaulted, murdered and mutilated the corpses of at least fifty-two women and children between 1978 and 1990. Chikatilo often tasted the blood of his victims and committed acts of cannibalism on some of the body parts including nipples, testicles and a uterus. Andrei Chikatilo was executed in 1994. One man was previously convicted and executed for his first murder. Chikatilo's case inspired the killer in movie Child 44 starring Tom Hardy, a secret policeman tasked with snaring a Stalinist-era monster who preyed on young children.

Sentence: death by gunshot to the head at Novocherkassk prison in Novocherkassk, Rostov oblast, Russia. **Death:** cause of death: capital punishment, executed by single gunshot behind the right ear at Novocherkassk prison in Novocherkassk, Rostov oblast, Russia.

Active in: United States

DECEASED

Thor Nis Christiansen

The Hitchhiker Slayer

BIRTH: 12-28-1957 YEARS ACTIVE: 1976 - 1979 ARRESTED: 07-07-1979 (Age 21)
GENDER: Male AGES ACTIVE: 18/19 - 21/22 CONVICTED: 06-18-1980 (Age 22)
ZODIAC: Capricorn LIFE SPAN: 1957 - 1981 DEATH: 03-30-1981 (Age 23)

4 VICTIMS

SERIAL KILLER RAPIST NECROPHILIAC

Active for **4 years** known to have killed at least **4 victims** between **1976** and **1979**.
previous crimes: ✗ weapon: ✓ gun: ✓ rob: ✗ bound: ✗ strangle: ✗ mutilate: ✗ W M F

Thor Nis Christiansen a Danish-American serial killer, necrophile and rapist known as The Hitchhiker Slayer. Christiansen shot and committed acts of necrophilia on four young women in Isla Vista, California between 1976 and 1979. In 1979, An additional intended victim escaped with a bullet in her head, and later identified him in a Los Angeles bar which led to his arrest. Christiansen was sentenced to life in prison in 1980. In 1981, Thor Nis Christiansen was stabbed to death by an unidentified fellow inmate at Folsom State Prison.

Sentence: life imprisonment at Folsom State Prison, Folsom, California, U.S. **Death:** cause of death: homicide, Stabbed to death by unidentified fellow inmate at Folsom State Prison, Folsom, California, U.S.

Active in: United Kingdom

DECEASED

John Christie

The Rillington Place Strangler

BIRTH: 04-08-1899 YEARS ACTIVE: 1943 - 1953 ARRESTED: 03-31-1953 (Age 53)
GENDER: Male AGES ACTIVE: 43/44 - 53/54 CONVICTED: 07-15-1953 (Age 54)
ZODIAC: Aries LIFE SPAN: 1899 - 1953 DEATH: 07-15-1953 (Age 54)

8 VICTIMS

SERIAL KILLER RAPIST NECROPHILIAC STRANGLER

Active for **11 years** known to have killed at least **8 victims** between **1943** and **1953**.
previous crimes: ✓ weapon: ✗ gun: ✗ rob: ✗ bound: ✗ strangle: ✓ mutilate: ✗ W M R

John Christie (John Reginald Halliday Christie) an English serial killer and necrophile known as The Rillington Place Strangler. Christie was active during the 1940s and early 1950s. Christie gassed, strangled and in some cases raped eight women (one of them his wife) in his flat of Notting Hill, London. Prior to Christie's arrest, one of his victims was attributed to the victim's father, who was hanged after a trial where Christie was declared as a witness. The controversy generated led to the abolition of the death penalty in the United Kingdom. John Christie was executed by hanging in1953 at the Pentonville Prison in London, England.

Sentence: death, execution by hanging at Pentonville Prison in London, England. **Death:** cause of death: capital punishment, executed by hanging at Pentonville Prison in London, England.

Active in: Turkey

Adnan Colak

Artvin Monster, The Beast of Artvin, Artvin Canavari

BIRTH: 09-05-1952 **YEARS ACTIVE:** 1992 - 1995 **ARRESTED:** 07-01-1995 (Age 42)
GENDER: Male **AGES ACTIVE:** 39/40 - 42/43 **CONVICTED:** 06-23-2000 (Age 47)
ZODIAC: Virgo **LIFE SPAN:** 1952 - **DEATH:**

11 VICTIMS

SERIAL KILLER RAPIST

Active for **4 years** known to have killed at least **11 victims** between **1992** and **1995**.

previous crimes: ✓ weapon: ✓ gun: ✓ rob: ✓ bound: ✗ strangle: ✗ mutilate: ✗ W M

Adnan Colak a Turkish serial killer and rapist known as the Artvin Monster, The Beast of Artvin and Artvin Canavari. Colak killed eleven elderly women aged 68 to 95 and raped six others. After his arrest in 1995, Colak's trial in the Zonguldak 1 Heavy Criminal Court lasted for more than five years. He was sentenced to death but changed to life in prison after Turkey abolished the death penalty in 2004. Adnan Colak was released on May 28, 2005, under the Conditional Release Act, which the media called "Rahsan amnesty".

Sentence: six death sentences plus forty years commuted to life imprisonment at a prison in Artvin, Turkey.

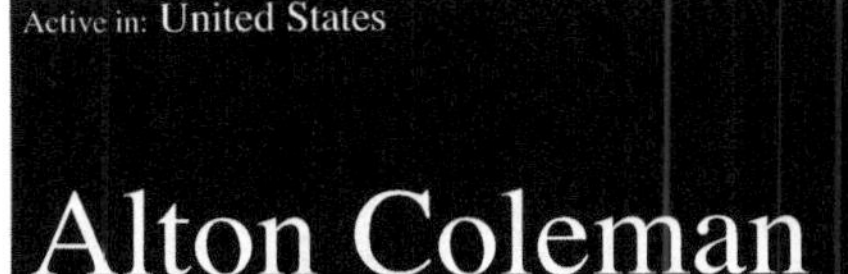

Active in: United States DECEASED

Alton Coleman

BIRTH: 11-06-1955 **YEARS ACTIVE:** 1984 - 1984 **ARRESTED:** 07-20-1984 (Age 28)
GENDER: Male **AGES ACTIVE:** 28/29 - 28/29 **CONVICTED:** 08-03-1994 (Age 38)
ZODIAC: Scorpio **LIFE SPAN:** 1955 - 2002 **DEATH:** 04-26-2002 (Age 46)

8 VICTIMS

SERIAL KILLER RAPIST TORTURER STALKER STRANGLER

Active for **1 year** known to have killed at least **8 victims** in **1984**.

previous crimes: ✓ weapon: ✓ gun: ✓ rob: ✓ bound: ✓ strangle: ✓ mutilate: ✓ W M R F

Alton Coleman an American serial killer, along with accomplice Debra Brown, who committed a crime spree across six states in the Midwest where eight people were murdered between May and July 1984. Coleman was already awaiting trial on a charge of rape when he fled and began his killing spree. Coleman was arrested three days after he made the FBI's Ten Most Wanted List in 1984. On April 26th 2002, Alton Coleman was executed by lethal injection in the death chamber at the Southern Ohio Correctional Facility in Lucasville, Ohio.

Sentence: death by electrocution at Southern Ohio Correctional Facility in Lucasville, Ohio, US.

Death: cause of death: executed by electrocution via electric chair at Southern Ohio Correctional Facility in Lucasville, Ohio, US.

Active in: United States

Daniel Conahan

Hog Trails Killer

BIRTH: 05-11-1954 | **YEARS ACTIVE:** 1994 - 1996 | **ARRESTED:** 07-03-1996 (Age 42)
GENDER: Male | **AGES ACTIVE:** 39/40 - 41/42 | **CONVICTED:** 08-17-1999 (Age 45)
ZODIAC: Taurus | **LIFE SPAN:** 1954 - | **DEATH:**

1-12
VICTIMS

SERIAL KILLER | RAPIST | TORTURER | STRANGLER

Active for **3 years** known to have killed at least **1 victims** between **1994** and **1996**.
previous crimes: ✘ weapon: ✔ gun: ✘ rob: ✘ bound: ✔ strangle: ✔ mutilate: ✔ W M

Daniel Conahan (Daniel Owen Conahan Jr.) a suspected American serial killer and convicted murderer known as the Hog Trails Killer. Conahan targeted mostly homosexual men in Charlotte County, Florida area between 1994 and 1996. Conahan surgically removed one victims genitals after death. He would lured victims, some by offering them money to pose nude in bondage photographs. Conahan was convicted of only one murder but has been linked to over a dozen murders. He was sentenced to death in 1999. Daniel Conahan is currently serving his sentence at Union Correctional Institution in Raiford, Florida.

Sentence: death at Union Correctional Institution, Florida State Prison, Raiford Prison in Raiford, Florida, US.

Active in: United States

Rory Enrique Conde

The Tamiami Trail Strangler

BIRTH: 06-14-1965 | **YEARS ACTIVE:** 1994 - 1995 | **ARRESTED:** 06-26-1995 (Age 30)
GENDER: Male | **AGES ACTIVE:** 28/29 - 29/30 | **CONVICTED:** 03-07-2000 (Age 34)
ZODIAC: Gemini | **LIFE SPAN:** 1965 - | **DEATH:**

6
VICTIMS

SERIAL KILLER | RAPIST | NECROPHILIAC | TORTURER | STRANGLER

Active for **2 years** known to have killed at least **6 victims** between **1994** and **1995**.
previous crimes: ✔ weapon: ✘ gun: ✘ rob: ✘ bound: ✔ strangle: ✔ mutilate: ✘ W M R

Rory Enrique Conde a Colombian serial killer active in the United States who was known as The Tamiami Trail Strangler. Conde killed six prostitutes in Florida, he strangled his victims to death and would have anal sex with the corpses afterward. After killing his third victim Conde left a note reading: "Third, I will call Dwight Channel 10, see if you can catch me". Conde was arrested in 1995 when a surviving victim was found bound head to toe at Conde's Condo. Rory Enrique Conde was sentenced to death in 2000 for the murder of Rhonda Dunn. He later pleaded guilty to the murder of five others and was sentenced to five consecutive life terms without the possibility of parole in 2001.

Sentence: death at Union Correctional Institution, Florida State Prison, Raiford Prison in Raiford, Florida, US.

Active in: Australia

DECEASED

Eric Edgar Cooke

The Night Caller

BIRTH: 02-25-1931 **YEARS ACTIVE:** 1959 - 1963 **ARRESTED:** 09-01-1963 (Age 32)
GENDER: Male **AGES ACTIVE:** 27/28 - 31/32 **CONVICTED:** 11-28-1963 (Age 32)
ZODIAC: Pisces **LIFE SPAN:** 1931 - 1964 **DEATH:** 10-26-1964 (Age 33)

8 VICTIMS

SERIAL KILLER RAPIST NECROPHILIAC STRANGLER

Active for **5 years** known to have killed at least **8 victims** between **1959** and **1963**.

previous crimes: ✓ weapon: ✓ gun: ✓ rob: ✓ bound: ✗ strangle: ✓ mutilate: ✗ W M

Eric Edgar Cooke an Australian serial killer known as the Night Caller. Cooke terrorized the city of Perth assaulting twenty-two people at random with various means, killing eight of them. His behavior was inconsistent and bizarre, Cooke was known to shoot, stab or strangle his victims. Cooke was arrested after authorities waited for him to return and retrieve a rifle he hid in a bush. In 1963, Eric Edgar Cooke was sentenced to death by hanging which was carried out in 1964 at Fremantle Prison in Fremantle, Western Australia.

Sentence: death by hanging at Fremantle Prison in Fremantle, Western Australia, Australia. **Death:** cause of death: capital punishment, executed by hanging at Fremantle Prison in Fremantle, Western Australia, Australia.

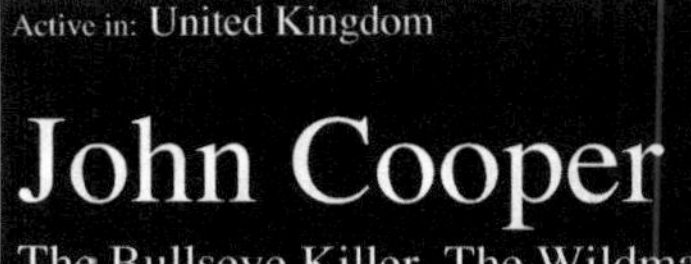

Active in: United Kingdom

John Cooper

The Bullseye Killer, The Wildman

BIRTH: 09-03-1944 **YEARS ACTIVE:** 1985 - 1989 **ARRESTED:** 05-13-2009 (Age 64)
GENDER: Male **AGES ACTIVE:** 40/41 - 44/45 **CONVICTED:** 05-26-2011 (Age 66)
ZODIAC: Virgo **LIFE SPAN:** 1944 - **DEATH:**

4 VICTIMS

SERIAL KILLER RAPIST

Active for **5 years** known to have killed at least **4 victims** between **1985** and **1989**.

previous crimes: ✓ weapon: ✓ gun: ✓ rob: ✓ bound: ✓ strangle: ✗ mutilate: ✗ W M

John Cooper (John William Cooper) a British armed robber, rapist and serial killer known as The Bullseye Killer and The Wildman. He murdered four victims in Pembrokeshire, Wales between 1985 and 1989. In 1989, Cooper participated in the ITV gameshow Bullseye which later led to his arrest. He was sentenced to fourteen years in 1998 and released in 2009. He was a diagnosed psychopath that would bound victims demanding their bank cards and pin numbers along with other valuables. He shot at least two victims in the face with a sawed-off shotgun. In 2011, John Cooper was sentenced to life imprisonment. Cooper is not the only serial killer to appear on a gameshow during their crime spree, Rodney Alcala, appeared as a contestant on The Dating Game in 1978.

Sentence: life imprisonment at an undisclosed prison in Wales, United Kingdom.

Active in: United States

DECEASED

Dean Corll

Candy Man, Pied Piper

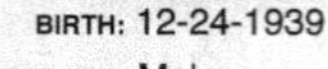

BIRTH: 12-24-1939 YEARS ACTIVE: 1970 - 1973 ARRESTED:

GENDER: Male AGES ACTIVE: 30/31 - 33/34 CONVICTED:

ZODIAC: Capricorn LIFE SPAN: 1939 - 1973 DEATH: 08-08-1973 (Age 33)

28-29 VICTIMS

SERIAL KILLER RAPIST TORTURER STRANGLER

Active for **4 years** known to have killed at least **28 victims** between **1970** and **1973**.

previous crimes: ✗ weapon: ✓ gun: ✓ rob: ✓ bound: ✓ strangle: ✓ mutilate: ✓ W M R F

Dean Corll (Dean Arnold Corll) an American serial killer and rapist known as the Candy Man and the Pied Piper. Corll along with two teenaged accomplices named David Owen Brooks and Elmer Wayne Henley, abducted, raped, tortured and murdered at least twenty-eight young men between 1970 and 1973 in Houston, Texas. The crimes are known as the Houston Mass Murders. Corll and his family owned and operated a candy factory in Houston Heights, Texas. Dean Corll was murdered by his accomplice, Elmer Wayne Henley, after Corll had turned on him.

Sentence: never sentenced, shot by his accomplice before he could be arrested. **Death:** cause of death: homicide, ballistic trauma, he was murdered by his accomplice, Elmer Wayne Henley at 2020 Lamar Drive in Pasadena, Texas, US.

Active in: United States

DECEASED

Juan Vallejo Corona

The Machete Murderer

BIRTH: 01-01-1934 YEARS ACTIVE: 1970 - 1971 ARRESTED: 05-26-1971 (Age 37)

GENDER: Male AGES ACTIVE: 36/36 - 37/37 CONVICTED: 01-18-1973 (Age 39)

ZODIAC: Capricorn LIFE SPAN: 1934 - 2019 DEATH: 03-04-2019 (Age 85)

25 VICTIMS

SERIAL KILLER RAPIST

Active for **2 years** known to have killed at least **25 victims** between **1970** and **1971**.

previous crimes: ✗ weapon: ✓ gun: ✓ rob: ✗ bound: ✗ strangle: ✗ mutilate: ✓ W M R F

Juan Vallejo Corona a Mexican serial killer and rapist known as The Machete Murderer. Corona was convicted of murdering ranch laborers and burying them in orchards near the Feather River in Sutter County, California. He killed victims by inflicting multiple stab wounds and massive head injuries caused by a machete, some of his victims had been shot. In 1973, Corona was convicted of twenty-five counts of first degree murder. He served his life sentence at Corcoran State Prison. Corona was denied parole eight times, most recently in November 2016. Juan Vallejo Corona died of natural causes in 2019.

Sentence: life imprisonment, twenty-five terms at California State Prison in Corcoran, California, US.

Death: cause of death: natural causes at a unnamed hospital in California, US.

Active in: United States

DECEASED

Tony Costa

Antone Charles Costa

BIRTH: 08-02-1944	YEARS ACTIVE: 1968 - 1969	ARRESTED: 03-06-1969 (Age 24)	4-7
GENDER: Male	AGES ACTIVE: 23/24 - 24/25	CONVICTED: 05-29-1969 (Age 24)	VICTIMS
ZODIAC: Leo	LIFE SPAN: 1944 - 1974	DEATH: 05-12-1974 (Age 29)	

SERIAL KILLER RAPIST NECROPHILIAC

Active for **2 years** known to have killed at least **4 victims** between **1968** and **1969**.

previous crimes: ✓ weapon: ✓ gun: ✓ rob: ✗ bound: ✓ strangle: ✗ mutilate: ✓ W M R F

Tony Costa (Antone Charles Costa) an American serial killer known as The Tony Costa Cape Cod murders. Costa murdered mutilated, committed acts of necrophilia and dismembered four women in Cape Cod between 1968 and 1969. Additionally, Costa is linked to at least three other deaths or disappearances. He buried some of his victims body parts in a forest clearing that Costa had used for growing marijuana. He was sentenced to life in prison in 1969. In 1974, Tony Costa committed suicide by hanging himself in his cell at Massachusetts Correctional Institution in South Walpole, Massachusetts.

Sentence: life imprisonment at Massachusetts Correctional Institution in South Walpole, Massachusetts, US. **Death:** cause of death: suicide, committed suicide by hanging himself in his prison cell at Massachusetts Correctional Institution in South Walpole, Massachusetts, US.

Active in: United States

Andre Crawford

South Side killings

BIRTH: 03-20-1962	YEARS ACTIVE: 1993 - 1999	ARRESTED: 01-28-2000 (Age 37)	11
GENDER: Male	AGES ACTIVE: 30/31 - 36/37	CONVICTED: 12-17-2009 (Age 47)	VICTIMS
ZODIAC: Aries	LIFE SPAN: 1962 -	DEATH:	

SERIAL KILLER RAPIST NECROPHILIAC STRANGLER

Active for **7 years** known to have killed at least **11 victims** between **1993** and **1999**.

previous crimes: ✓ weapon: ✗ gun: ✗ rob: ✗ bound: ✗ strangle: ✓ mutilate: ✗ W M F

Andre Crawford an American serial killer and rapist known as the South Side killings. Crawford committed acts of necrophilia after murdering eleven women between 1993 and 1999. On Thanksgiving 1997, a twelfth woman was attacked and left for dead, she survived the attack. He was a transient who lived in vacant buildings in Chicago. Hubert Geralds was previously convicted and sentenced to death for Crawford's eleventh victim. Crawford was arrested in 2000 when DNA was used to link him to his crimes. He eventually confessed to all eleven murders. Andre Crawford was sentenced to life in prison in 2009.

Sentence: life imprisonment at Menard Correctional Center in Randolph County, Illinois.

Active in: Canada

John Martin Crawford

The Lady Killer

BIRTH: 03-29-1962 **YEARS ACTIVE:** 1981 - 1992 **ARRESTED:**
GENDER: Male **AGES ACTIVE:** 18/19 - 29/30 **CONVICTED:**
ZODIAC: Aries **LIFE SPAN:** 1962 - **DEATH:**

4 VICTIMS

SERIAL KILLER RAPIST TORTURER STRANGLER

Active for **12 years** known to have killed at least **4 victims** between **1981** and **1992**.
previous crimes: ✓ weapon: ✓ gun: ✗ rob: ✗ bound: ✗ strangle: ✓ mutilate: ✓ W M R

John Martin Crawford a Canadian serial killer known as The Lady Killer. In 1981, Crawford was sentenced to ten years imprisonment and released in 1989. Crawford raped, tortured and killed three native Saskatoon women in 1992. At least one victim had been mutilated by deep bite marks on her breasts. He was arrested in 1995 and later convicted for the three murders in 1996. In 2001, Warren Goulding wrote a book about Crawfords crimes titled: Just Another Indian - A Serial Killer and Canada's Indifference. In 2006, Jeremy Torrie wrote and directed a movie about his crimes titled: Mr. Soul, a serial killer whose murder of Aboriginal women went unreported and ignored by police and media. The movie is based on Goulding's 2001 book.

Sentence: life imprisonment, three terms at Saskatchewan Federal Penitentiary in Prince Albert, Saskatchewan, Canada.

Active in: United Kingdom DECEASED

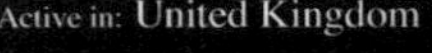

Gordon Cummins

The Blackout Ripper, The Blackout Killer

BIRTH: 02-18-1914 **YEARS ACTIVE:** 1942 - 1942 **ARRESTED:** 02-16-1942 (Age 27)
GENDER: Male **AGES ACTIVE:** 27/28 - 27/28 **CONVICTED:** 04-27-1942 (Age 28)
ZODIAC: Aquarius **LIFE SPAN:** 1914 - 1942 **DEATH:** 06-25-1942 (Age 28)

4-6 VICTIMS

SERIAL KILLER RAPIST STRANGLER

Active for **1 year** known to have killed at least **4 victims** in **1942**.
previous crimes: — weapon: ✓ gun: ✗ rob: ✓ bound: ✗ strangle: ✓ mutilate: ✓ W M

Gordon Cummins (Gordon Frederick Cummins) a British serial killer and rapist known as The Blackout Ripper and The Blackout Killer. Cummins was a serviceman in the Royal Air Force. The murders took place over a six-day period in February 1942, during the Blackout in the Second World War. Cummins raped three of his victims and robbed the remaining victim. He also attacked two other women. He left behind his gas mask container marked with his service number 525987, identifying Cummins as the attacker. Cummins was sentenced to death by hanging. In 1942, Gordon Cummins was executed by hanging at Wandsworth Prison in London, England.

Sentence: death by hanging at HM Wandsworth Prison in London, England. **Death:** cause of death: executed by hanging at HM Wandsworth Prison in London, England.

Active in: Greece

DECEASED

Antonis Daglis

The Athens Ripper

BIRTH: **YEARS ACTIVE:** 1992 - 1995 **ARRESTED:**

GENDER: Male **AGES ACTIVE:** - **CONVICTED:** 01-23-1997

ZODIAC: **LIFE SPAN:** - 1997 **DEATH:** 08-02-1997

3 VICTIMS

SERIAL KILLER RAPIST STALKER STRANGLER

Active for **4 years** known to have killed at least **3 victims** between **1992** and **1995**.

previous crimes: ✓ weapon: ✓ gun: ✗ rob: ✓ bound: ✗ strangle: ✓ mutilate: ✓ W M

Antonis Daglis a Greek serial killer known as the The Athens Ripper. Daglis was a serial rapist with antecedents for violence, upgraded to raping, strangling and dismembering three prostitutes with a hacksaw in 1992, and tried to kill six more women. Daglis, a truck driver who preyed on Athens prostitutes between 1992 and 1995. In his trial he claimed to hate all prostitutes. He was convicted and sentenced to thirteen terms of life imprisonment, plus twenty-five years. In 1997, Antonis Daglis committed suicide in prison.

Sentence: life imprisonment, thirteen life terms plus twenty-five years at an unnamed prison in Athens, Greece. **Death:** cause of death: suicide at an unnamed prison in Athens, Greece, republic in Southeast Europe.

Active in: United States

DECEASED

Jeffrey Dahmer

Milwaukee Cannibal, Milwaukee Murderer

BIRTH: 05-21-1960 **YEARS ACTIVE:** 1978 - 1991 **ARRESTED:** 07-22-1991 (Age 31)

GENDER: Male **AGES ACTIVE:** 17/18 - 30/31 **CONVICTED:** 05-01-1992 (Age 31)

ZODIAC: Gemini **LIFE SPAN:** 1960 - 1994 **DEATH:** 11-28-1994 (Age 34)

17 VICTIMS

SERIAL KILLER RAPIST CANNIBAL NECROPHILIAC STRANGLER

Active for **14 years** known to have killed at least **17 victims** between **1978** and **1991**.

previous crimes: ✓ weapon: ✓ gun: ✗ rob: ✗ bound: ✓ strangle: ✓ mutilate: ✓ W M R

Jeffrey Dahmer (Jeffrey Lionel Dahmer) an American serial killer and sex offender known as the Milwaukee Cannibal and the Milwaukee Murderer. Dahmer committed the rape, murder and dismemberment of seventeen men and boys from 1978 to 1991. Dahmer would drug, rape, strangle and murder his victims. Dahmer also ate some of his victims and kept some of their body parts in his freezer. Jeffrey Dahmer was sentenced to life imprisonment in 1992 and later murdered in 1994 by a fellow inmate Christopher Scarver at the Columbia Correctional Institution in Portage, Wisconsin.

Sentence: life imprisonment, fifteen life terms, a total of 957 years at Columbia Correctional Institution, Portage, Wisconsin, US. **Death:** cause of death: homicide, murdered in prison by fellow inmate Christopher Scarver at Columbia Correctional Institution in Portage, Wisconsin, US.

Active in: United States

Joseph James DeAngelo

EARONS, The East Area Rapist, Original Night Stalker

BIRTH: 11-08-1945 YEARS ACTIVE: 1975 - 1986 ARRESTED: 04-24-2018 (Age 72)
GENDER: Male AGES ACTIVE: 29/30 - 40/41 CONVICTED:
ZODIAC: Scorpio LIFE SPAN: 1945 - DEATH:

13 VICTIMS

SERIAL KILLER RAPIST

Active for **12 years** known to have killed at least **13 victims** between **1975** and **1986**.
previous crimes: ✓ weapon: ✓ gun: ✓ rob: ✓ bound: — strangle: — mutilate: — W

Joseph James DeAngelo (Joseph James DeAngelo Jr.) an American serial killer, rapist, burglar and former police officer known as EARONS, The East Area Rapist, The Original Night Stalker, The Golden State Killer, The Visalia Ransacker and the Diamond Knot Killer, who committed at least thirteen murders, more than fifty rapes, and over a hundred burglaries in California from 1974 to 1986. DeAngelo is suspected of being the Golden State Killer who terrorised residents of six counties during the 1970s and '80s. DeAngelo was arrested in 2018 after authorities linked him to the cold case homicides using DNA from his 4th cousin which was submitted to gedmatch.com. DeAngelo is being kept in isolation in the Sacramento County Jail.

BIRTH: 09-03-1931 YEARS ACTIVE: 1962 - 1964 ARRESTED: 10-27-1964 (Age 33)
GENDER: Male AGES ACTIVE: 30/31 - 32/33 CONVICTED: 01-09-1967 (Age 35)
ZODIAC: Virgo LIFE SPAN: 1931 - 1973 DEATH: 11-25-1973 (Age 42)

13 VICTIMS

SERIAL KILLER RAPIST STRANGLER

Active for **3 years** known to have killed at least **13 victims** between **1962** and **1964**.
previous crimes: ✓ weapon: ✓ gun: ✗ rob: ✗ bound: ✗ strangle: ✓ mutilate: ✗ W M

Albert DeSalvo an American serial killer known as the Boston Strangler. Although Albert DeSalvo is widely thought to be the Boston Strangler, police and others analysing the case have long doubted the truth of his confession. George Nassar also a suspect in the case, claims that DeSalvo confessed the crimes to him while they were both in prison. In 1973, Albert DeSalvo was found stabbed to death in the prison infirmary at the Cedar Junction Correctional Institution in Norfolk, Massachusetts. In 2013 a DNA match confirmed his involvement in at least one of the cases connected to the Boston Strangler.

Sentence: life imprisonment at Bridgewater State Hospital in Bridgewater, Massachusetts, US. **Death:** cause of death: homicide, multiple stab wounds at Cedar Junction Correctional Institution in Norfolk, Massachusetts, US.

Active in: United States DECEASED

Westley Allan Dodd

The Vancouver Child Killer

BIRTH: 07-03-1961 YEARS ACTIVE: 1989 - 1989 ARRESTED: 11-13-1989 (Age 28)
GENDER: Male AGES ACTIVE: 27/28 - 27/28 CONVICTED: 07-15-1990 (Age 29)
ZODIAC: Cancer LIFE SPAN: 1961 - 1993 DEATH: 01-05-1993 (Age 31)

3 VICTIMS

SERIAL KILLER RAPIST TORTURER STRANGLER

Active for **1 year** known to have killed at least **3 victims** in **1989**.
previous crimes: ✓ weapon: ✓ gun: ✗ rob: ✗ bound: ✓ strangle: ✓ mutilate: ✗ W M R

Westley Allan Dodd an American serial killer and rapist known as The Vancouver Child Killer. In 1989, Dodd raped and murdered three young boys in Vancouver, Washington. Dodd had an extensive arrest record for molesting children by the time his behavior escalated to include murder. Dodd refused to appeal his death sentence, he stated that he should be punished to the full extent of the law, as should all sex offenders and murderers, and that if he ever escaped, he would immediately return to killing and raping kids. Westley Allan Dodd was executed by hanging in 1993, his hanging was the first in the United States in twenty-eight years.

Sentence: death by hanging at the Washington State Penitentiary in Walla Walla, Washington, US.

Death: cause of death: capital punishment, executed by hanging at the Washington State Penitentiary in Walla Walla, Washington, US.

Active in: United States

Ronald Dominique

The Bayou Strangler

BIRTH: 01-09-1964 YEARS ACTIVE: 1997 - 2006 ARRESTED: 12-01-2006 (Age 42)
GENDER: Male AGES ACTIVE: 32/33 - 41/42 CONVICTED: 09-23-2008 (Age 44)
ZODIAC: Capricorn LIFE SPAN: 1964 - DEATH:

23 VICTIMS

SERIAL KILLER RAPIST STRANGLER

Active for **10 years** known to have killed at least **23 victims** between **1997** and **2006**.
previous crimes: ✓ weapon: ✗ gun: ✗ rob: ✗ bound: ✓ strangle: ✓ mutilate: ✗ W M

Ronald Dominique (Ronald Joseph Dominique) an American serial killer and rapist known as the Bayou Strangler. Dominique raped and murdered male victims in the Terrebonne Parish, Lafourche Parish, Iberville Parish and Jefferson Parish in Louisiana. Dominique confessed to the rape and murder of at least twenty-three men over a ten-year period beginning in 1997. Ronald Dominique pleaded guilty to eight murders and was sentenced to eight life sentences on September 23rd 2008.

Sentence: life imprisonment at Louisiana State Penitentiary in Angola, West Feliciana, Louisiana, US.

Active in: United Kingdom

John Duffy

The Railway Killers, The Railway Rapists

BIRTH: 11-29-1958 YEARS ACTIVE: 1985 - 1986 ARRESTED: 11-23-1986 (Age 27)
GENDER: Male AGES ACTIVE: 26/27 - 27/28 CONVICTED:
ZODIAC: Sagittarius LIFE SPAN: 1958 - DEATH:

3
VICTIMS

SERIAL KILLER RAPIST STALKER STRANGLER

Active for **2 years** known to have killed at least **3 victims** between **1985** and **1986**.
previous crimes: ✓ weapon: ✗ gun: ✗ rob: ✗ bound: ✓ strangle: ✓ mutilate: ✓ W M

John Duffy (John Francis Duffy) a British rapist and serial killer who along with his accomplice, David Mulcahy, are known as the Railway Rapist and the Railway Killers. Duffy and Mulcahy attacked numerous women and children at railway stations in the south of England between 1985 and 1986. Both are suspected of other sexual attacks, while Mulcahy is also suspected of attacks which took place after Duffy was in prison. In 1988, John Duffy was sentenced to life imprisonment.

Sentence: life imprisonment at HM Prison Whitemoor in March, Cambridgeshire, England.

Active in: United States

Brian Dugan

BIRTH: 09-23-1956 YEARS ACTIVE: 1983 - 1985 ARRESTED: 06-03-1985 (Age 28)
GENDER: Male AGES ACTIVE: 26/27 - 28/29 CONVICTED: 11-19-1985 (Age 29)
ZODIAC: Virgo LIFE SPAN: 1956 - DEATH:

3-5
VICTIMS

SERIAL KILLER RAPIST STRANGLER

Active for **3 years** known to have killed at least **3 victims** between **1983** and **1985**.
previous crimes: ✓ weapon: ✓ gun: ✗ rob: ✗ bound: ✓ strangle: ✓ mutilate: ✗ W M R

Brian Dugan (Brian James Dugan) an American serial killer and rapist active between 1983 and 1985. Dugan claimed to have been sexually abused by John Wayne Gacy at the age of 15. In 1974, Dugan was accused of trying to abduct a 10-year-old girl. The charges were later dropped on a legal technicality. In 1983, Dugan sexually assaulted and bludgeoned to death another 10-year-old girl. In 1984, Dugan beat, raped and drowned a nurse. In 1985, Dugan abducted, raped and killed a 7-year-old girl. Brian Dugan was sentenced to death, his sentence was commuted to life imprisonment in 2011.

Sentence: life sentences, two terms plus 215 years and a pending trial that could lead to the death penalty at Stateville Correctional Center in Crest Hill, Illinois, US.

Active in: United Kingdom

DECEASED

Martin Dumollard

The Maid Killer

BIRTH: 04-21-1810
GENDER: Male
ZODIAC: Aries

YEARS ACTIVE: 1855 - 1861
AGES ACTIVE: 44/45 - 50/51
LIFE SPAN: 1810 - 1862

ARRESTED: 06-02-1861 (Age 51)
CONVICTED: 02-01-1862 (Age 51)
DEATH: 03-08-1862 (Age 51)

3 VICTIMS

SERIAL KILLER | RAPIST | STRANGLER

Active for **7 years** known to have killed at least **3 victims** between **1855** and **1861**.

previous crimes: ✓ weapon: ✗ gun: ✗ rob: ✓ bound: ✗ strangle: ✓ mutilate: ✗ W M

Martin Dumollard a French serial killer known as the Maid Killer. Dumollard was arrested and charged with the deaths of three maids from 1855 to 1861. His wife, Marie-Anne Martinet, was found guilty of assisting him and sentenced to 20 years of hard labor in a women's prison. She died in 1875 at Auberive prison, in Haute-Marne, France. Martin Dumollard was publicly executed by guillotine in 1862.

Sentence: death by beheading via guillotine at a prison in Bourg-en-Bresse, Ain, France. **Death:** cause of death: executed by beheading via guillotine at Bourgeat Square (Place Carnot) in Montluel, commune in Ain, France.

Active in: United States

Joseph Edward Duncan

The Fifth Nail

BIRTH: 02-25-1963
GENDER: Male
ZODIAC: Pisces

YEARS ACTIVE: 1996 - 2005
AGES ACTIVE: 32/33 - 41/42
LIFE SPAN: 1963 -

ARRESTED: 07-02-2005 (Age 42)
CONVICTED: 12-03-2007 (Age 44)
DEATH:

5-7 VICTIMS

SERIAL KILLER | RAPIST | TORTURER

Active for **10 years** known to have killed at least **5 victims** between **1996** and **2005**.

previous crimes: ✓ weapon: ✓ gun: ✓ rob: ✗ bound: ✓ strangle: ✗ mutilate: ✗ W M

Joseph Edward Duncan (Joseph Edward Duncan III) an American serial killer and child rapist known as The Fifth Nail. He was a child molester active between 1996 and 2005. Duncan was convicted of killing a California boy in 1997 and four members of an Idaho family in 2005. He confessed to two 1996 murders in Washington state, but has not been formally charged. Ducan would kidnap, rape and murder victims. Duncan maintained a personal website, entitled The Fifth Nail. He killed at least one victim by hitting them with a hammer. Joseph Duncan is currently on death row at USP Terre Haute in Terre Haute, Indiana.

Sentence: death at United States Penitentiary, Terre Haute, Indiana, US.

Active in: United States

Paul Durousseau

The Jacksonville Strangler

BIRTH: 08-11-1970 **YEARS ACTIVE:** 1997 - 2003 **ARRESTED:** 06-17-2003 (Age 32)
GENDER: Male **AGES ACTIVE:** 26/27 - 32/33 **CONVICTED:** 12-13-2007 (Age 37)
ZODIAC: Leo **LIFE SPAN:** 1970 - **DEATH:**

7-9
VICTIMS

SERIAL KILLER RAPIST STRANGLER

Active for **7 years** known to have killed at least **7 victims** between **1997** and **2003**.
previous crimes: ✓ weapon: ✗ gun: ✗ rob: ✗ bound: ✓ strangle: ✓ mutilate: ✗ W M R

Paul Durousseau an American serial killer and rapist known as The Jacksonville Strangler. Durousseau murdered seven young women, including two who were pregnant, in the southeastern United States. He would gain entrance to the victim's home, bound, rape and strangle the victims to death. Durousseau's DNA was found at one of the crime scenes. Witnesses reported seeing the last two victims with a taxi driver that fit Durousseau's description on the night they disappeared. Paul Durousseau was arrested and charged with five counts of murder in 2003 and sentenced to death in 2007. Paul Durousseau's death sentence was overturned in 2017.

Sentence: death by lethal injection at Union Correctional Institution, Florida State Prison, Raiford Prison in Raiford, Florida, US.

Active in: Belgium

Marc Dutroux

Dutroux murders

BIRTH: 11-06-1956 **YEARS ACTIVE:** 1995 - 1996 **ARRESTED:** 08-13-1996 (Age 39)
GENDER: Male **AGES ACTIVE:** 38/39 - 39/40 **CONVICTED:** 06-22-2004 (Age 47)
ZODIAC: Scorpio **LIFE SPAN:** 1956 - **DEATH:**

5-11
VICTIMS

SERIAL KILLER RAPIST TORTURER

Active for **2 years** known to have killed at least **5 victims** between **1995** and **1996**.
previous crimes: ✓ weapon: ✓ gun: ✓ rob: ✗ bound: ✓ strangle: ✗ mutilate: ✗ W M

Marc Dutroux (Marc Paul Alain Dutroux) a Belgian rapist and serial killer known as the Dutroux murders. Dutroux was convicted of kidnapping, torturing and raping six girls ranging in age from 8 to 19, four of whom he murdered. He also tortured and murdered one of his accomplices, Bernard Weinstein. He was arrested along with his remaining accomplices Michel Lelièvre and Michelle Martin. Throughout the trial, Dutroux insisted that he was part of a sex ring with accomplices among police officers, businessmen, doctors, and even high-level Belgian politicians. Marc Dutroux was sentenced to life imprisonment in 2004.

Sentence: life imprisonment at Jamioulx prison, Nivelles prison in Nivelles, Belgium.

Active in: Russia

Nikolai Dzhumagaliev

Metal Fang, Kolya the Maneater

BIRTH: 11-15-1952 YEARS ACTIVE: 1980 - 1980 ARRESTED: 12-19-1980 (Age 28)
GENDER: Male AGES ACTIVE: 27/28 - 27/28 CONVICTED: 12-03-1981 (Age 29)
ZODIAC: Scorpio LIFE SPAN: 1952 - DEATH:

9-100 VICTIMS

SERIAL KILLER RAPIST CANNIBAL

Active for **1 year** known to have killed at least **9 victims** in **1980**.
previous crimes: ✗ weapon: ✓ gun: ✓ rob: ✗ bound: ✗ strangle: ✗ mutilate: ✓ W M

Nikolai Dzhumagaliev a Soviet serial killer and rapist known as the Metal Fang and Kolya the Maneater. Dzhumagaliev was convicted for the killing seven people between 1979 and 1980. He is known as Metal Fang, due to his false metal teeth. Dzhumagaliev lured women prostitutes who were working local parks during the nighttime hours. He would lure, attack and hack his victims with an axe as part of a plan to rid the world of prostitution. Dzhurmongaliev claimed to have cooked parts of his victims to eat himself or serve them to other people as part of ethnic dishes. Nikolai Dzhumagaliev as found innocent for reason of insanity and interned in a mental institution.

Sentence: not guilty by reason of insanity, involuntary commitment, compulsory treatment at Tashkent mental institution, a closed mental hospital in Tashkent, Uzbekistan.

Active in: United States DECEASED

Mack Ray Edwards

BIRTH: 10-17-1918 YEARS ACTIVE: 1953 - 1970 ARRESTED: 03-06-1970 (Age 51)
GENDER: Male AGES ACTIVE: 34/35 - 51/52 CONVICTED:
ZODIAC: Libra LIFE SPAN: 1918 - 1971 DEATH: 10-30-1971 (Age 53)

6-18 VICTIMS

SERIAL KILLER RAPIST STRANGLER

Active for **18 years** known to have killed at least **6 victims** between **1953** and **1970**.
previous crimes: ✓ weapon: ✓ gun: ✓ rob: ✗ bound: ✗ strangle: ✓ mutilate: ✗ W M

Mack Ray Edwards an American serial killer and child molester who murdered at least six children in Los Angeles County, California between 1953 and 1970. Edwards murdered at least two young girls and four young boys. He claimed at one point to have killed as many as eighteen victims. Edwards pleaded guilty to three counts of murder and was sentenced to death. In 1971, Mack Ray Edwards committed suicide by hanging himself with a television cord in his cell at San Quentin State Prison in San Quentin, California.

Sentence: death by electrocution at San Quentin State Prison in Marin County, California, US. **Death:** cause of death: suicide, committed suicide by hanging himself with a television cord in his prison cell at San Quentin State Prison in Marin County, California, US.

Active in: United States DECEASED

Edward Edwards

Sweetheart Murders

BIRTH: 06-14-1933	**YEARS ACTIVE:** 1977 - 1996	**ARRESTED:** 07-30-2009 (Age 76)	5
GENDER: Male	**AGES ACTIVE:** 43/44 - 62/63	**CONVICTED:** 03-11-2011 (Age 77)	VICTIMS
ZODIAC: Gemini	**LIFE SPAN:** 1933 - 2011	**DEATH:** 04-07-2011 (Age 77)	

SERIAL KILLER RAPIST STRANGLER

Active for **20 years** known to have killed at least **5 victims** between **1977** and **1996**.

previous crimes: ✔ weapon: ✔ gun: ✔ rob: ✔ bound: ✖ strangle: ✔ mutilate: ✖ W M

Edward Edwards (Edward Wayne Edwards) an American serial killer known for committing the Sweetheart Murders. Edwards shot a young couple in 1977. He stabbed and strangled another couple in 1980. In 1955, Edwards escaped from a jail in Akron, Ohio. He robbed gas stations around the country and was on the FBI's Ten Most Wanted Fugitives list in 1961. He was imprisoned and later paroled in 1967, arrested in Louisville, Kentucky, for the 1980 murders. Edwards died on April 7th 2011, months prior to execution for shooting his foster son in a 1996 insurance murder.

Sentence: death by lethal injection at a prison in Columbus, Ohio, US. **Death:** cause of death: natural causes at Corrections Medical Center in Columbus, Ohio, US.

BIRTH:	**YEARS ACTIVE:** 1996 - 1997	**ARRESTED:** 12-22-2016	3
GENDER: Male	**AGES ACTIVE:** -	**CONVICTED:**	VICTIMS
ZODIAC:	**LIFE SPAN:** -	**DEATH:**	

SERIAL KILLER RAPIST STALKER

Active for **2 years** known to have killed at least **3 victims** between **1996** and **1997**.

previous crimes: ✔ weapon: — gun: — rob: — bound: ✔ strangle: — mutilate: — W

Bradley Robert Edwards a suspected Australian serial killer known as the Claremont killer, Codename Macro and Bogsy. The Claremont serial murders refers to a case involving the murder of two Australian women in 1996 and 1997 in Claremont, a suburb of Perth, Australia. All three women disappeared in similar circumstances after attending night spots in Claremont. In 2016, Edwards was arrested and charged with the abduction and murder of Jane Rimmer, 23, and Ciara Glennon, 27. A third victim, Sarah Spiers, remains missing. DNA tests on a kimono found nearly thirty years ago matched samples found on the body of another victim. Edwards faces additional charges including two counts of deprivation of liberty and two counts of aggravated sexual penetration without consent..

Sentence: awaiting trail at the Hakea Prison in Canning Vale, Western Australia.

Active in: Netherlands

Willem van Eijk

The Beast of Harkstede, Gekke Willempje

BIRTH: 08-13-1941 **YEARS ACTIVE:** 1971 - 2001 **ARRESTED:** 11-12-2001 (Age 60)
GENDER: Male **AGES ACTIVE:** 29/30 - 59/60 **CONVICTED:** 11-05-2002 (Age 61)
ZODIAC: Leo **LIFE SPAN:** 1941 - **DEATH:**

5-8 VICTIMS

SERIAL KILLER | RAPIST | STRANGLER

Active for **31 years** known to have killed at least **5 victims** between **1971** and **2001**.
previous crimes: ✓ weapon: ✓ gun: ✗ rob: ✗ bound: ✗ strangle: ✓ mutilate: ✓ W M

Willem van Eijk a Dutch serial killer known as The Beast of Harkstede and Gekke Willempje (Crazy little William). Eijk was convicted of five murders, all female, mostly prostitutes. He was an outcast from early elementary school, being publicly bullied and showing several acts of animal cruelty. Van Eijk was sentenced to eighteen years imprisonment in 1974 for two murders, released in 1990. He started killing again in 2001 and was re-arrested on November 12th 2001. Eijk was convicted in 2002 of three additional murders. He appealed, and asked for clemency but all attempts were denied.
Sentence: life imprisonment at a prison in the Netherlands.

Active in: United States DECEASED

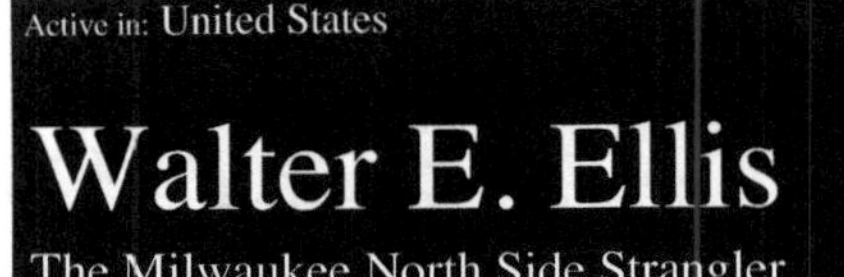

Walter E. Ellis

The Milwaukee North Side Strangler

BIRTH: 07-24-1960 **YEARS ACTIVE:** 1986 - 2007 **ARRESTED:** 09-07-2009 (Age 49)
GENDER: Male **AGES ACTIVE:** 25/26 - 46/47 **CONVICTED:** 02-18-2011 (Age 50)
ZODIAC: Leo **LIFE SPAN:** 1960 - 2013 **DEATH:** 12-01-2013 (Age 53)

7-20 VICTIMS

SERIAL KILLER | RAPIST | STRANGLER

Active for **22 years** known to have killed at least **7 victims** between **1986** and **2007**.
previous crimes: ✓ weapon: ✗ gun: ✗ rob: ✗ bound: ✗ strangle: ✓ mutilate: ✗ W M

Walter E. Ellis an American serial killer known as The Milwaukee North Side Strangler and the North Side Strangler. Ellis was convicted of killing seven prostitutes in Wisconsin between 1986 and 2007. His victims were all African-American women. In 2011, investigators stated they were reviewing the cases of another twenty strangled prostitutes Elis could be connected to. Walter E. Ellis died in prison on December 1st 2013 from apparent natural causes, according to the South Dakota Department of Corrections.
Sentence: life imprisonment, seven life terms, without the possibility of parole at South Dakota State Penitentiary in Sioux Falls, South Dakota, US. **Death:** cause of death: natural causes, apparent natural causes at a hospital in Sioux Falls, South Dakota, US.

Active in: United Kingdom

Kenneth Erskine

The Stockwell Strangler, the heatwave killer

BIRTH: 07-01-1963 YEARS ACTIVE: 1986 - 1986 ARRESTED: 07-28-1986 (Age 23)
GENDER: Male AGES ACTIVE: 22/23 - 22/23 CONVICTED: 01-29-1988 (Age 24)
ZODIAC: Cancer LIFE SPAN: 1963 - DEATH:

7-11
VICTIMS

SERIAL KILLER RAPIST STRANGLER

Active for **1 year** known to have killed at least **7 victims** in **1986**.
previous crimes: ✓ weapon: ✗ gun: ✗ rob: ✓ bound: ✗ strangle: ✓ mutilate: ✗ W M

Kenneth Erskine a British serial killer known as The Stockwell Strangler and the heatwave killer. Erskine, a burglar who raped and strangled at least seven elderly men and women after breaking into their home. Erskine told police he was haunted by a whispering woman's voice, which came out of walls and doors which gave him dizzy spells. Erskine was sentenced to life in prison in 1988. In 2009 the murder convictions were reduced to manslaughter. Erskine is being held at a high-security psychiatric hospital, Broadmoor Hospital at Crowthorne in Berkshire, England.

Sentence: life imprisonment at Broadmoor Hospital a high-security psychiatric hospital at Crowthorne in Berkshire, England.

Active in: United States

Scott Erskine

BIRTH: 12-22-1962 YEARS ACTIVE: 1989 - 1993 ARRESTED:
GENDER: Male AGES ACTIVE: 26/27 - 30/31 CONVICTED: 09-01-2004 (Age 41)
ZODIAC: Sagittarius LIFE SPAN: 1962 - DEATH:

3
VICTIMS

SERIAL KILLER RAPIST TORTURER STRANGLER

Active for **5 years** known to have killed at least **3 victims** between **1989** and **1993**.
previous crimes: ✓ weapon: ✓ gun: ✗ rob: ✗ bound: ✓ strangle: ✓ mutilate: ✓ W M

Scott Erskine (Scott Thomas Erskine) an American serial killer and rapist. Erskine was convicted of raping and murdering a woman in 1989 and the torture-murders of two boys in 1993. Erskine would kidnap, rape and murder his victims. He bound, gagged, strangled and bit the genitals of at least one of his victims. Erskine's DNA was found on two cigarette butts found near one victim and in the mouth of another victim. Authorities suspect he may be linked to other unsolved murders or disappearances. Scott Erskine was sentenced to death in 2004 and is serving his sentence at San Quentin State Prison in San Quentin, California.

Sentence: death at San Quentin State Prison in San Quentin, California, US.

Active in: Spain

DECEASED

Francisco Garcia Escalero

The Killer Beggar

BIRTH: 05-24-1954
GENDER: Male
ZODIAC: Gemini

YEARS ACTIVE: 1987 - 1994
AGES ACTIVE: 32/33 - 39/40
LIFE SPAN: 1954 - 2014

ARRESTED:
CONVICTED:
DEATH: 08-19-2014 (Age 60)

11 VICTIMS

SERIAL KILLER | RAPIST | CANNIBAL | NECROPHILIAC

Active for **8 years** known to have killed at least **11 victims** between **1987** and **1994**.

previous crimes: ✓ weapon: ✓ gun: ✗ rob: ✗ bound: ✗ strangle: ✗ mutilate: ✓ W M

Francisco Garcia Escalero a Spanish serial killer, cannibal, necrophiliac and rapist known as The Killer Beggar. Escalero killed eleven prostitutes and other homeless people between 1987 and 1994. He was a homeless man that was known to go to cemeteries to steal bodies to have sex with them. Escalero committed acts of necrophilia and cannibalism during his crimes. He was known to stab decapitate, crush the skull and burn the remains of his victims. He cut off the penis of one victim and the fingers of another victim. In 1995, Francisco Garcia Escalero was declared insane and preventively detained at a psychiatric hospital.

Sentence: preventively detained at the Fontcalent Prison Psychiatric Hospital in Alacant, Spain.

Death: cause of death: unknown at the Fontcalent Prison Psychiatric Hospital in Alacant, Spain.

Active in: United States

DECEASED

Donald Leroy Evans

Hi Hitler, Heil Hitler

BIRTH: 07-05-1957
GENDER: Male
ZODIAC: Cancer

YEARS ACTIVE: 1985 - 1991
AGES ACTIVE: 27/28 - 33/34
LIFE SPAN: 1957 - 1999

ARRESTED: 08-05-1991 (Age 34)
CONVICTED: 08-16-1993 (Age 36)
DEATH: 01-05-1999 (Age 41)

3-70 VICTIMS

SERIAL KILLER | RAPIST | STRANGLER

Active for **7 years** known to have killed at least **3 victims** between **1985** and **1991**.

previous crimes: ✓ weapon: ✗ gun: ✗ rob: ✗ bound: ✗ strangle: ✓ mutilate: ✗ W M

Donald Leroy Evans an American serial killer convicted for the kidnapping, raping, strangulation and murder of 10-year-old Beatrice Routh in 1993, and the strangulation death of Ira Jean Smith in 1985. Evans is suspected of another dozen murders but recanted confessions to over seventy more. Most of the murders and rapes took place at rest stops and public parks. During the trial Evan's requested a name change to "Hi Hitler." He didn't realize that Hitlers followers addressed their leader with the chant of "Heil Hitler". He escaped from Harrison County jail in 1993, Evans was recaptured about a mile away. In 1999, Donald Leroy Evans was stabbed to death by a fellow inmate at the Mississippi State Penitentiary.

Sentence: death at Mississippi State Penitentiary (Parchman Farm) in Parchman, Mississippi, US.

Death: cause of death: homicide, stabbed in shower by fellow death row inmate Jimmie Mack at Mississippi State Penitentiary.

Active in: United States DECEASED

Richard Evonitz

BIRTH: 07-29-1963 **YEARS ACTIVE:** 1996 - 1997 **ARRESTED:**
GENDER: Male **AGES ACTIVE:** 32/33 - 33/34 **CONVICTED:**
ZODIAC: Leo **LIFE SPAN:** 1963 - 2002 **DEATH:** 06-27-2002 (Age 38)

3 VICTIMS

SERIAL KILLER | RAPIST | STRANGLER

Active for **2 years** known to have killed at least **3 victims** between **1996** and **1997**.
previous crimes: ✓ weapon: ✓ gun: ✓ rob: ✗ bound: ✓ strangle: ✓ mutilate: ✗ W M R

Richard Evonitz (Richard Marc Edward Evonitz) an American serial killer, kidnapper, and rapist responsible for the deaths of three girls in Spotsylvania County, Virginia between 1996 and 1997. An abducted 15-year-old girl escaped and was able to identify Evonitz as her attacker. Evonitz fled after finding the victim gone but police were able to locate him near the waterfront in Sarasota, Florida. Richard Evonitz shot himself while surrounded by police on June 27th 2002. A few days after Evonitz's suicide the police found a lockbox at his residence that linked him to the three Virginia murders.

Sentence: never sentence, committed suicide prior to arrest. **Death:** cause of death: suicide, committed suicide by shooting himself while surrounded by police at near the waterfront in Sarasota, Florida, US.

Active in: United States DECEASED

Albert Fish

Gray Man, Werewolf of Wysteria, The Boogey Man

BIRTH: 03-19-1870 **YEARS ACTIVE:** 1924 - 1932 **ARRESTED:** 12-13-1934 (Age 64)
GENDER: Male **AGES ACTIVE:** 53/54 - 61/62 **CONVICTED:** 03-21-1935 (Age 65)
ZODIAC: Pisces **LIFE SPAN:** 1870 - 1936 **DEATH:** 01-16-1936 (Age 65)

3-9 VICTIMS

SERIAL KILLER | RAPIST | CANNIBAL | TORTURER | STALKER

Active for **9 years** known to have killed at least **3 victims** between **1924** and **1932**.
previous crimes: ✓ weapon: ✓ gun: ✗ rob: ✗ bound: ✓ strangle: ✗ mutilate: ✓ W M R

Albert Fish (born Hamilton Howard Fish) an American serial killer and child rapist who was convicted and executed for the kidnapping, rape, murder and cannibalization of three children in New York, suspected of the deaths of six more children and teenagers. Likely insane (though his insanity plea was denied to make possible his execution), Fish boasted that he "had children in every state" and at one point claimed 100 victims. Fish would drink the blood of his victims. Detective William King believed Fish was a suspect in the Brooklyn vampire case but Fish denied any involvement.

Sentence: death by electrocution at Sing Sing Correctional Facility Ossining, New York, United States. **Death:** cause of death: capital punishment, executed by electrocution via electric chair at Sing Sing Correctional Facility Ossining, New York, United States.

Active in: United States

Wayne Adam Ford

BIRTH: 12-03-1961 **YEARS ACTIVE:** 1997 - 1998 **ARRESTED:** 11-03-1998 (Age 36)
GENDER: Male **AGES ACTIVE:** 35/36 - 36/37 **CONVICTED:** 06-27-2006 (Age 44)
ZODIAC: Sagittarius **LIFE SPAN:** 1961 - **DEATH:**

4 VICTIMS

SERIAL KILLER RAPIST NECROPHILIAC STRANGLER

Active for **2 years** known to have killed at least **4 victims** between **1997** and **1998**.
previous crimes: ✓ weapon: ✓ gun: ✓ rob: ✗ bound: ✓ strangle: ✓ mutilate: ✓ W M R

Wayne Adam Ford an American serial killer who killed three young prostitutes, and one other female victim in California between 1997 and 1998. Ford was arrested when he walked into the Humboldt County Sheriff Department in Eureka, California in 1998 with a woman's severed breast. He confessed to murdering four women and is believed to have killed others. In 2006, Wayne Adam Ford was convicted on four counts of first-degree murder, and was sentenced to death in 2006.

Sentence: capital punishment at San Quentin State Prison in San Quentin, California, US.

BIRTH: 04-04-1942 **YEARS ACTIVE:** 1987 - 2001 **ARRESTED:** 06-26-2003 (Age 61)
GENDER: Male **AGES ACTIVE:** 44/45 - 58/59 **CONVICTED:** 05-28-2008 (Age 66)
ZODIAC: Aries **LIFE SPAN** 1942 - **DEATH:**

8-11 VICTIMS

SERIAL KILLER RAPIST STRANGLER

Active for **15 years** known to have killed at least **8 victims** between **1987** and **2001**.
previous crimes: ✓ weapon: ✓ gun: ✓ rob: ✓ bound: ✓ strangle: ✓ mutilate: ✗ W M

Michel Fourniret (Michel Paul Fourniret) a French serial killer known as the Ogre and the Beast of Ardennes. Fourniret confessed to killing eleven people in France and Belgium between 1987 and 2001. Fourniret was arrested after a failed kidnapping in 2003. In February 2018, Fourniret confessed to the murders of two more victims. His wife, Monique Pierrette Olivier, was convicted of murder and complicity, she was sentenced to life with a minimum term of forty-eight years in prison. In 2008, Michel Fourniret was sentenced to life imprisonment with a second term in 2018.

Sentence: life imprisonment at Ensisheim, a commune in the Haut-Rhin department in Grand Est in north-eastern France.

Active in: United States, Canada

DECEASED

Bobby Jack Fowler

Project E-Pana, the Highway of Tears

BIRTH: 06-12-1939 **YEARS ACTIVE:** 1973 - 1996 **ARRESTED:** 06-28-1995 (Age 56)
GENDER: Male **AGES ACTIVE:** 33/34 - 56/57 **CONVICTED:** 01-08-1996 (Age 56)
ZODIAC: Gemini **LIFE SPAN:** 1939 - 2006 **DEATH:** 05-15-2006 (Age 66)

1-20 VICTIMS

SERIAL KILLER RAPIST STRANGLER

Active for **24 years** known to have killed at least **1 victims** between **1973** and **1996**.
previous crimes: ✓ weapon: ✗ gun: ✗ rob: ✗ bound: ✓ strangle: ✓ mutilate: ✗ W M

Bobby Jack Fowler an American rapist and alleged serial killer known as Project E-Pana, the Highway of Tears. Fowler is a suspect in at least sixteen murders in Canada and the United States dating as far back as 1969. He was a potential suspect in Project E-Pana, the Highway of Tears cases in British Columbia, geographic profiler Kim Rossmo pointed out that many of these murders occurred after Fowler's imprisonment in 1996. Fowler's DNA was found on the body of at least one of his victims. In 2006, Bobby Jack Fowler died from lung cancer while still in custody at Oregon State Penitentiary.

Sentence: sixteen years and three months imprisonment with the possibility of parole at the Oregon State Penitentiary in Salem, Oregon, US. **Death:** cause of death: natural causes, lung cancer at the Oregon State Penitentiary in Salem, Oregon, US.

Active in: United States

DECEASED

Kendall Francois

The Poughkeepsie Killer

BIRTH: 07-26-1971 **YEARS ACTIVE:** 1996 - 1998 **ARRESTED:** 09-02-1998 (Age 27)
GENDER: Male **AGES ACTIVE:** 24/25 - 26/27 **CONVICTED:** 08-11-2000 (Age 29)
ZODIAC: Leo **LIFE SPAN:** 1971 - 2014 **DEATH:** 09-11-2014 (Age 43)

8-9 VICTIMS

SERIAL KILLER RAPIST STALKER STRANGLER

Active for **3 years** known to have killed at least **8 victims** between **1996** and **1998**.
previous crimes: ✗ weapon: ✗ gun: ✗ rob: ✗ bound: ✗ strangle: ✓ mutilate: ✗ W M R

Kendall Francois an American serial killer known as the Poughkeepsie Killer. Francois confessed to killing eight prostitutes in Poughkeepsie, New York, but denied involvement with the disappearance of a ninth prostitute. In 1995, Francois tested positive for HIV. He hid the bodies of his victims in the house that he shared with his parents. In 2000, he was sentenced to life in prison without the possibility of parole. Kendall Francois died of natural causes on September 11th 2014 while incarcerated at Wende Correctional Facility in Alden, New York.

Sentence: life imprisonment without the possibility of parole at Attica prison in Attica, New York, US. **Death:** cause of death: natural causes, reports of AIDS and cancer at Wende Correctional Facility in Erie County, New York, US.

Active in: United States

Lonnie David Franklin

Grim Sleeper, Southside Slayer murders

BIRTH: 08-30-1952 **YEARS ACTIVE:** 1985 - 2007 **ARRESTED:** 07-07-2010 (Age 57)
GENDER: Male **AGES ACTIVE:** 32/33 - 54/55 **CONVICTED:** 08-10-2016 (Age 63)
ZODIAC: Virgo **LIFE SPAN:** 1952 - **DEATH:**

10-25 VICTIMS

SERIAL KILLER RAPIST STRANGLER

Active for **23 years** known to have killed at least **10 victims** between **1985** and **2007**.
previous crimes: ✓ weapon: ✓ gun: ✓ rob: ✗ bound: ✗ strangle: ✓ mutilate: ✗ W M

Lonnie David Franklin (Lonnie David Franklin, Jr.) an American serial killer known as the Grim Sleeper. During his crime spree Franklin took an alleged 14-year hiatus from murdering between 1988 and 2002. Franklin shot and strangled his victims, mostly women, around South Los Angeles. Franklin committed at least one of the Southside Slayer murders, and Michael Hughes, Chester Turner, Daniel Lee Siebert, Louis Craine, and Ivan Hill committed at least one each. Lonnie David Franklin was convicted in 2016 and sentenced to death.

Sentence: death at San Quentin State Prison in San Quentin, California, US.

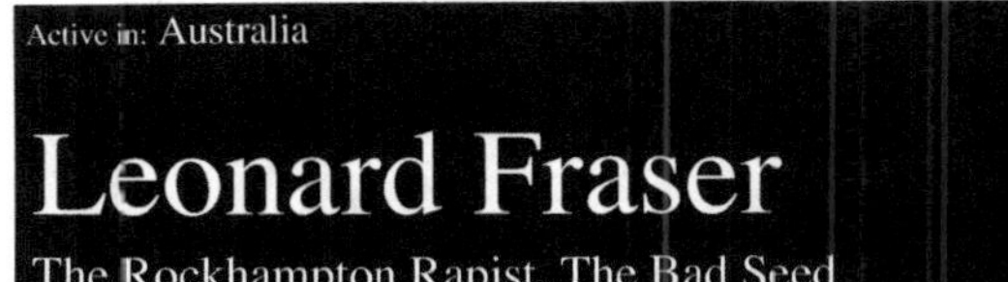

Active in: Australia DECEASED

Leonard Fraser

The Rockhampton Rapist, The Bad Seed

BIRTH: 06-27-1951 **YEARS ACTIVE:** 1998 - 1999 **ARRESTED:** 04-22-1999 (Age 47)
GENDER: Male **AGES ACTIVE:** 46/47 - 47/48 **CONVICTED:** 06-13-2003 (Age 51)
ZODIAC: Cancer **LIFE SPAN:** 1951 - 2007 **DEATH:** 01-01-2007 (Age 55)

4-7 VICTIMS

SERIAL KILLER RAPIST STRANGLER

Active for **2 years** known to have killed at least **4 victims** between **1998** and **1999**.
previous crimes: ✓ weapon: ✓ gun: ✗ rob: ✗ bound: ✗ strangle: ✓ mutilate: ✗ W M R

Leonard Fraser (Leonard John Fraser) an Australian serial killer, rapist and pedophile known as The Rockhampton Rapist and The Bad Seed. Fraser murdered four women in Rockhampton between 1998 and 1999. He was sentenced to five consecutive life sentences plus twenty-five years without the possibility of parole. Leonard Fraser died in prison of a heart attack in 2007.

Sentence: life imprisonment at Wolston Correctional Centre high security prison facility in Wacol, Queensland, Australia.. **Death:** cause of death: natural causes, heart attack, myocardial infarction at Princess Alexandra Hospital in Brisbane, capital city of Queensland, Australia.

Active in: Japan

DECEASED

Sataro Fukiage

Shinshumaro

BIRTH: 02-25-1889 YEARS ACTIVE: 1906 - 1924 ARRESTED: 07-28-1924 (Age 35)
GENDER: Male AGES ACTIVE: 16/17 - 34/35 CONVICTED: 05-17-1925 (Age 36)
ZODIAC: Pisces LIFE SPAN: 1889 - 1926 DEATH: 09-28-1926 (Age 37)

7 VICTIMS

SERIAL KILLER RAPIST STRANGLER

Active for **19 years** known to have killed at least **7 victims** between **1906** and **1924**.
previous crimes: ✓ weapon: ✗ gun: ✗ rob: ✗ bound: ✗ strangle: ✓ mutilate: ✗ W M

Sataro Fukiage a Japanese rapist and serial killer known as Shinshumaro. In 1906, Fukiage raped and murdered an 11-year-old girl. In 1923, Fukiage was arrested for molesting a four-year-old girl, but was later released. He raped and murdered six young girls, aged 11 to 16, between 1923 and 1924. He was arrested on July 28th 1924 and was sentenced to death by hanging in 1925. Fukiage wrote a book titled Shaba (The Street). The Supreme Court of Japan upheld his death sentence in 1926. Sataro Fukiage was executed by hanging on September 28th 1926.

Sentence: death by hanging at a prison in Japan. **Death:** cause of death: capital punishment, executed by hanging at a prison in Japan.

Active in: Canada

William Patrick Fyfe

The Killer Handyman

BIRTH: 02-27-1955 YEARS ACTIVE: 1979 - 1999 ARRESTED: 12-22-1999 (Age 44)
GENDER: Male AGES ACTIVE: 23/24 - 43/44 CONVICTED: 09-21-2001 (Age 46)
ZODIAC: Pisces LIFE SPAN: 1955 - DEATH:

5-9 VICTIMS

SERIAL KILLER RAPIST

Active for **21 years** known to have killed at least **5 victims** between **1979** and **1999**.
previous crimes: — weapon: ✓ gun: ✗ rob: ✗ bound: ✗ strangle: ✗ mutilate: ✗ W M

William Patrick Fyfe a Canadian serial killer and rapist known as The Killer Handyman. Fyfe was convicted of killing five women in the Montreal area of Quebec. He was sentenced to life in prison in 2001. Fyfe made confession to four additional murders in exchange for obtaining a transfer from a Quebec prison to a prison in Western Canada. Authorities say Fyfe will not be tried for the four new murders, because he is already serving a life sentence, the maximum under the law. William Patrick Fyfe is currently serving his sentence at the Saskatoon prison in Western Canada.

Sentence: life imprisonment at the Saskatchewan Federal Penitentiary in Saskatchewan, Canada.

Active in: United States DECEASED

John Wayne Gacy

Pogo the Clown, The Killer Clown

BIRTH: 03-17-1942 **YEARS ACTIVE:** 1972 - 1978 **ARRESTED:** 12-21-1978 (Age 36)
GENDER: Male **AGES ACTIVE:** 29/30 - 35/36 **CONVICTED:** 03-13-1980 (Age 37)
ZODIAC: Pisces **LIFE SPAN:** 1942 - 1994 **DEATH:** 05-10-1994 (Age 52)

33-34 VICTIMS

SERIAL KILLER | RAPIST | TORTURER | STALKER | STRANGLER

Active for **7 years** known to have killed at least **33 victims** between **1972** and **1978**.
previous crimes: ✓ weapon: ✗ gun: ✗ rob: ✗ bound: ✓ strangle: ✓ mutilate: ✗ W M

John Wayne Gacy (John Wayne Gacy Jr.) an American serial killer and rapist known as Pogo the Clown. Gacy was known to have sexually assaulted, tortured and murdered a minimum of thirty-three teenage boys and young men between 1972 and 1978, twenty-six of whom he buried in the crawl space of his Chicago home. He was known as the Killer Clown due to him entertaining children at social events dressed in a self devised clown costume. While in prison, Gacy took up painting as a hobby and means of making money, the paintbox used to create the art is on display at Alcatraz East Crime Museum in Pigeon Forge, Tennessee. John Wayne Gacy was executed by lethal injection In 1994.

Sentence: execution by lethal injection at Stateville Correctional Center in Crest Hill, Illinois, US.

Death: cause of death: capital punishment, executed by lethal injection at Stateville Correctional Center in Crest Hill, Illinois, US.

BIRTH: 07-17-1946 **YEARS ACTIVE:** 1978 - 1980 **ARRESTED:** 11-17-1980 (Age 34)
GENDER: Male **AGES ACTIVE:** 31/32 - 33/34 **CONVICTED:** 06-21-1983 (Age 36)
ZODIAC: Cancer **LIFE SPAN:** 1946 - 2002 **DEATH:** 07-18-2002 (Age 56)

10 VICTIMS

SERIAL KILLER | RAPIST | STRANGLER

Active for **3 years** known to have killed at least **10 victims** between **1978** and **1980**.
previous crimes: ✓ weapon: ✓ gun: ✓ rob: ✓ bound: ✓ strangle: ✓ mutilate: ✗ W M R

Gerald Gallego (Gerald Armond Gallego) an American serial killer, along with his wife Charlene Gallego, were known as The Love Slave Killers and The Gallego Sex Slave Killers. Together they murdered ten victims in Sacramento, California between 1978 and 1980. Some of their victims were kept as sex slaves for the couple before they were murdered. They were known to beat, rape strangle and shoot their victims. They were arrested in 1980 when a witness reported the couples license plate number to authorities. Gerald Gallego was sentenced to death in 1984. In 2002, Gerald Gallego died of cancer in the prison medical center at Ely State Prison in Ely, Nevada while awaiting his execution.

Sentence: death by gas chamber at San Quentin State Prison in San Quentin, California, US. **Death:** cause of death: cancer at the prison medical center inside Ely State Prison in Ely, White Pine County, Nevada, US.

Active in: United States

Charlene Gallego

The Love Slave Killers, The Gallego Sex Slaves Killers

BIRTH: 10-10-1956 **YEARS ACTIVE:** 1978 - 1980 **ARRESTED:** 11-17-1980 (Age 24)
GENDER: Female **AGES ACTIVE:** 21/22 - 23/24 **CONVICTED:**
ZODIAC: Libra **LIFE SPAN:** 1956 - **DEATH:**

10 VICTIMS

SERIAL KILLER RAPIST STRANGLER

Active for **3 years** known to have killed at least **10 victims** between **1978** and **1980**.
previous crimes: ✗ weapon: ✓ gun: ✓ rob: ✓ bound: ✓ strangle: ✓ mutilate: ✗ W M R

Charlene Gallego (Charlene Adell Gallego) (born Charlene Adell Williams) an American serial killer, along with her husband Gerald Gallego, were known as The Love Slave Killers and The Gallego Sex Slave Killers. Together they murdered ten victims in Sacramento, California between 1978 and 1980. Some of their victims were kept as sex slaves for the couple before they were murdered. They were known to beat, rape, strangle and shoot their victims. They were arrested in 1980 when a witness reported the couples license plate number to authorities. Charlene testified against her husband for a plea deal that reduced her prison sentence to sixteen years and eight months. In 1997, Charlene Gallego completed her sentence and was released.

Sentence: sixteen years and eight months imprisonment at Department of Prisons Woman's Center in Carson City, Nevada, US.

Active in: Colombia

Luis Garavito

La Bestia, The Beast

BIRTH: 01-25-1957 **YEARS ACTIVE:** 1992 - 1999 **ARRESTED:** 04-22-1999 (Age 42)
GENDER: Male **AGES ACTIVE:** 34/35 - 41/42 **CONVICTED:** 05-27-2000 (Age 43)
ZODIAC: Aquarius **LIFE SPAN:** 1957 - **DEATH:**

147-300 VICTIMS

SERIAL KILLER RAPIST NECROPHILIAC TORTURER

Active for **8 years** known to have killed at least **147 victims** between **1992** and **1999**.
previous crimes: ✗ weapon: ✓ gun: ✗ rob: ✗ bound: ✓ strangle: ✗ mutilate: ✗ W M

Luis Garavito (Luis Alfredo Garavito Cubillos) a Colombian serial killer child-murderer, torture-killer, and rapist known as La Bestia (The Beast). Garavito targeted boys between the ages of 6 to 16. Confessed to killing 147 children over a five-year period in Colombia. He is suspected of murdering over 300 victims, mostly street children. Luis Garavito was sentenced to 1853 years and 9 days in jail.

Sentence: 1853 years and nine days imprisonment, reduced to twenty-two years at a Colombian prison, the exact location is unavailable to the public.

Active in: Spain

DECEASED

Juan Díaz de Garayo

The Fat Extractor

BIRTH: 10-17-1821 **YEARS ACTIVE:** 1870 - 1879 **ARRESTED:** 09-09-1879 (Age 57)

GENDER: Male **AGES ACTIVE:** 48/49 - 57/58 **CONVICTED:** 11-11-1879 (Age 58)

ZODIAC: Libra **LIFE SPAN:** 1821 - 1881 **DEATH:** 05-11-1881 (Age 59)

6 VICTIMS

SERIAL KILLER RAPIST

Active for **10 years** known to have killed at least **6 victims** between **1870** and **1879**.

previous crimes: ✗ weapon: ✓ gun: ✗ rob: ✗ bound: ✗ strangle: ✗ mutilate: ✓ W

Juan Díaz de Garayo a Spanish serial killer known as El Sacamantecas (The fat extractor). Garayo strangled six victims and attacked four others between 1870 and 1879. Garayo first killed prostitutes after hiring and sleeping with them consensually, but grew more violent, attacking, raping and murdering his victims. Juan Díaz de Garayo was executed in 1881 by garroted at the Polvorín Viejo prison in Vitoria, Álava, Spain.

Sentence: death by garrote at Polvorín Viejo prison in Vitoria, Álava, Spain. **Death:** cause of death: capital punishment, executed by garrote at Polvorín Viejo prison in Vitoria, Álava, Spain.

BIRTH: 09-24-1950 **YEARS ACTIVE:** 1975 - 1978 **ARRESTED:** 05-03-1984 (Age 33)

GENDER: Male **AGES ACTIVE:** 24/25 - 27/28 **CONVICTED:** 08-27-1986 (Age 35)

ZODIAC: Libra **LIFE SPAN:** 1950 - 2018 **DEATH:** 03-15-2018 (Age 67)

7 VICTIMS

SERIAL KILLER RAPIST STRANGLER

Active for **4 years** known to have killed at least **7 victims** between **1975** and **1978**.

previous crimes: ✓ weapon: ✗ gun: ✗ rob: ✓ bound: ✗ strangle: ✓ mutilate: ✗ W M

Carlton Gary (Carlton Michael Gary) an American serial killer known as The Stocking Strangler and the Steakhouse Bandit. Gary would beat, sexually assault and strangle elderly victims, mostly using stockings. An eighth elderly women was beat and sexually assaulted but survived the attack. Gary was convicted of the murders of seven elderly women in Georgia and sentenced to death on August 27th 1986. On March 15th 2018, Carlton Gary was executed by lethal injection at Georgia Diagnostic and Classification State Prison in Jackson, Georgia.

Sentence: death by lethal injection at Georgia Diagnostic and Classification State Prison in Jackson, Butts County, Georgia, US. **Death:** cause of death: capital punishment, executed by lethal injection at Georgia Diagnostic and Classification State Prison in Jackson, Butts County, Georgia, US.

Active in: France

Guy Georges

The Beast of the Bastille, the killer of eastern Paris

BIRTH: 10-15-1962 YEARS ACTIVE: 1991 - 1997 ARRESTED: 03-26-1998 (Age 35)
GENDER: Male AGES ACTIVE: 28/29 - 34/35 CONVICTED: 04-05-2001 (Age 38)
ZODIAC: Libra LIFE SPAN: 1962 - DEATH:

7 VICTIMS

SERIAL KILLER RAPIST

Active for **7 years** known to have killed at least **7 victims** between **1991** and **1997**.
previous crimes: ✓ weapon: ✓ gun: ✗ rob: ✓ bound: ✓ strangle: ✗ mutilate: ✗ W M

Guy Georges (born Guy Rampillon) a French serial killer and rapist known as the Beast of the Bastille and the killer of eastern Paris. Georges assaulted, stabbed, tortured, raped and killed seven women in the neighborhood of the Bastille between 1991 and 1997. His mother abandoned him to state custody at the age of six, he was adopted by a family and grew up in a family of twelve adopted children. Georges' DNA matched evidence found at all four crime scenes, as well as at one attempted rape. In 1998, Georges was arrested and confessed to seven murders. In 2001, Guy Georges was sentenced to life imprisonment without the possibility of parole for twenty-two years.

Sentence: life imprisonment without the possibility of parole for twenty-two years at central house of Ensisheim a prison in Ensisheim, France.

Active in: United States

William Clyde Gibson

BIRTH: 10-10-1957 YEARS ACTIVE: 2002 - 2012 ARRESTED: 04-19-2012 (Age 54)
GENDER: Male AGES ACTIVE: 44/45 - 54/55 CONVICTED: 11-26-2013 (Age 56)
ZODIAC: Libra LIFE SPAN: 1957 - DEATH:

3 VICTIMS

SERIAL KILLER RAPIST TORTURER STRANGLER

Active for **11 years** known to have killed at least **3 victims** between **2002** and **2012**.
previous crimes: ✓ weapon: ✓ gun: ✗ rob: ✗ bound: ✓ strangle: ✓ mutilate: ✓ W M

William Clyde Gibson (William Clyde Gibson III) an American serial killer and rapist. Gibson was convicted of three murders in New Albany from 2002 to 2012. Gibson was known to rape, strangle and stab his victims before mutilating their bodies and burying them in his back yard in New Albany, Indiana. Police found the third body while excavating Gibson's back yard, the victim was identified as a woman who had disappeared in 2012. William Clyde Gibson was sentenced to death in 2013, an additional sixty-five years in 2014 and a second death sentence on August 15th 2014. At sentencing, Gibson responded "I deserve what I'm getting. It ain't no big deal."

Sentence: death at Indiana State Prison in Michigan City, Indiana, US.

Active in: United States

Bernard Giles

BIRTH: 04-09-1953 **YEARS ACTIVE:** 1973 - 1973 **ARRESTED:** 12-12-1973 (Age 20)
GENDER: Male **AGES ACTIVE:** 19/20 - 19/20 **CONVICTED:** 02-17-1977 (Age 23)
ZODIAC: Aries **LIFE SPAN:** 1953 - **DEATH:**

5 VICTIMS

SERIAL KILLER RAPIST NECROPHILIAC STRANGLER

Active for **1 year** known to have killed at least **5 victims** in **1973**.

previous crimes: ✗ weapon: ✓ gun: ✓ rob: ✓ bound: ✓ strangle: ✓ mutilate: ✗ M

Bernard Giles (Bernard Eugene Giles) an American serial killer. Giles raped, strangled and shot to death five young women victims over the span of twelve weeks between September and November 1973. He confessed to killing five Titusville-area women, whose partially decomposed bodies were found in orange groves near Titusville. He was arrested after two young girls escaped after being kidnapped and told authorities his identity. Giles was declared a mentally disturbed sex offender and confined to a state hospital for treatment. Bernard Giles was sentenced to life in prison in 1977. In 2019, Giles was interviewed by Piers Morgan as part of a documentary series on ITV called Confessions Of A Serial Killer With Piers Morgan.

Sentence: life imprisonment at the Okeechobee Correctional Institution in Okeechobee, Florida, US.

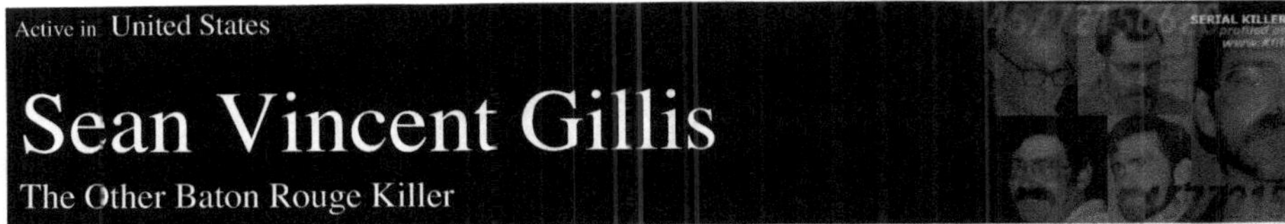

Active in United States

Sean Vincent Gillis

The Other Baton Rouge Killer

BIRTH: 06-24-1962 **YEARS ACTIVE:** 1994 - 2003 **ARRESTED:** 04-29-2004 (Age 41)
GENDER: Male **AGES ACTIVE:** 31/32 - 40/41 **CONVICTED:** 07-31-2008 (Age 46)
ZODIAC: Cancer **LIFE SPAN:** 1962 - **DEATH:**

8 VICTIMS

SERIAL KILLER RAPIST STALKER STRANGLER

Active for **10 years** known to have killed at least **8 victims** between **1994** and **2003**.

previous crimes: ✓ weapon: ✓ gun: ✗ rob: ✓ bound: ✗ strangle: ✓ mutilate: ✓ W M R

Sean Vincent Gillis an American serial killer known as The Other Baton Rouge Killer. The Other Baton Rouge Killer nickname is used because Derrick Todd Lee is known as the Baton Rouge Serial Killer. Gillis kidnapped, raped and mutilated the corpses of women between 1994 and 2003. The three victims to which Gillis has been linked by DNA, were all beaten, strangled, mutilated and found in remote areas of the Parish. Gillis confessed to committing other unsolved local murders After his arrest, police found digital pictures on his computer one of a victims mutilated body, as well as photos of a corpse in the trunk of his car. In 2008, Sean Vincent Gillis was convicted and sentenced to life imprisonment.

Sentence: life imprisonment without the possibility of parole at Louisiana State Penitentiary in Angola, West Feliciana, Louisiana, US.

Active in: United States

Lorenzo Gilyard

The Kansas City Strangler

BIRTH: 05-24-1950 YEARS ACTIVE: 1977 - 1993 ARRESTED: 04-18-2004 (Age 53)
GENDER: Male AGES ACTIVE: 26/27 - 42/43 CONVICTED: 04-13-2007 (Age 56)
ZODIAC: Gemini LIFE SPAN: 1950 - DEATH:

13 VICTIMS

SERIAL KILLER RAPIST STRANGLER

Active for **17 years** known to have killed at least **13 victims** between **1977** and **1993**.
previous crimes: ✓ weapon: ✗ gun: ✗ rob: ✗ bound: ✓ strangle: ✓ mutilate: ✗ W M R

Lorenzo Gilyard (Lorenzo Jerome Gilyard, Jr.) an American serial killer known as The Kansas City Strangler. Gilyard is alleged to have raped and murdered thirteen women and girls from 1977 to 1993. Most, if not all, of Gilyard's victims were sex workers. Gilyard was known to abuse women as early as his teens. In 2007, Lorenzo Gilyard was convicted on six counts of murder and sentenced to life imprisonment. He is serving his life sentence in Crossroads Correctional Center in Cameron, Missouri.

Sentence: life imprisonment without the possibility of parole at Crossroads Correctional Center in Cameron, DeKalb County, Missouri, US.

Active in: United States DECEASED

Harvey Glatman

The Lonely Hearts Killer, Glamour Girl Slayer

BIRTH: 12-10-1927 YEARS ACTIVE: 1957 - 1958 ARRESTED: 10-31-1958 (Age 30)
GENDER: Male AGES ACTIVE: 29/30 - 30/31 CONVICTED: 12-15-1958 (Age 31)
ZODIAC: Sagittarius LIFE SPAN: 1927 - 1959 DEATH: 09-18-1959 (Age 31)

3-4 VICTIMS

SERIAL KILLER RAPIST STRANGLER

Active for **2 years** known to have killed at least **3 victims** between **1957** and **1958**.
previous crimes: ✓ weapon: ✗ gun: ✗ rob: ✗ bound: ✓ strangle: ✓ mutilate: ✗ W M R

Harvey Glatman (Harvey Murray Glatman) an American serial killer and rapist who was known as The Lonely Hearts Killer and the Glamour Girl Slayer. He posed as a professional photographer to lure his victims with the promise of a modeling career. Glatman convinced women to pose for bondage photographs instead he would tie them up and sexually assault them. In 1958, a patrolman saw him struggling with a woman on the side of the road and arrested him. Harvey Glatman was executed in the gas chamber of San Quentin State Prison in San Quentin, California on September 18th 1959.

Sentence: death by gas chamber at San Quentin State Prison in San Quentin, California, US. **Death:** cause of death: capital punishment, executed by gas chamber at San Quentin State Prison in San Quentin, California, US.

Active in: United States DECEASED

Billy Glaze

Butcher Knife Billy, Jesse Sitting Crow

BIRTH: 01-01-1944 YEARS ACTIVE: 1986 - 1987 ARRESTED: 08-31-1987 (Age 43)
GENDER: Male AGES ACTIVE: 42/42 - 43/43 CONVICTED: 02-14-1989 (Age 45)
ZODIAC: Capricorn LIFE SPAN: 1944 - 2015 DEATH: 12-22-2015 (Age 71)

3-20 VICTIMS

SERIAL KILLER RAPIST

Active for **2 years** known to have killed at least **3 victims** between **1986** and **1987**.
previous crimes: ✓ weapon: ✓ gun: ✗ rob: ✗ bound: ✗ strangle: ✗ mutilate: ✗ W M

Billy Glaze (Billy Richard Glaze) an American serial killer known as Butcher Knife Billy and Jesse Sitting Crow. Glaze was convicted of raping and murdering three Native American prostitutes in Minneapolis in 1986 and 1987. In 1987, Glaze was arrested for drunk driving and a violation of parole in a 1974 Texas rape conviction. Authorities found evidence in his vehicle including a bloody shirt and hair samples which were used at his trial. Later DNA testing failed to match Glaze to the crimes, instead it implicated another suspect. In 2014, Glaze filed a motion for a new trial based on the DNA findings. In 2015, Glaze died from lung cancer after spending more than twenty-five years in prison.

Sentence: life imprisonment, three terms at James T. Vaughn Correctional Center in Smyrna, Delaware, US. **Death:** cause of death: natural causes, stage four lung cancer at James T. Vaughn Correctional Center in Smyrna, Delaware, US.

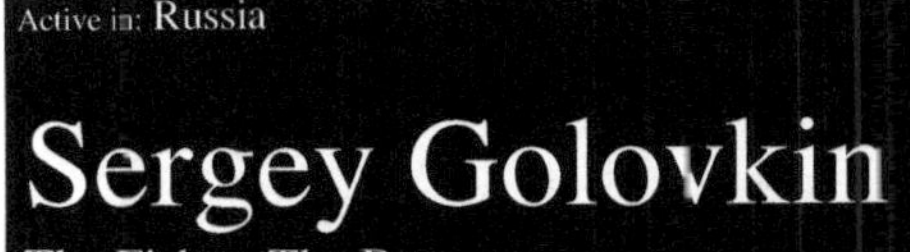

Active in: Russia DECEASED

Sergey Golovkin

The Fisher, The Boa

BIRTH: 11-26-1959 YEARS ACTIVE: 1986 - 1992 ARRESTED: 10-19-1992 (Age 32)
GENDER: Male AGES ACTIVE: 26/27 - 32/33 CONVICTED: 10-19-1994 (Age 34)
ZODIAC: Sagittarius LIFE SPAN: 1959 - 1996 DEATH: 08-02-1996 (Age 36)

11-40 VICTIMS

SERIAL KILLER RAPIST NECROPHILIAC TORTURER STRANGLER

Active for **7 years** known to have killed at least **11 victims** between **1986** and **1992**.
previous crimes: ✓ weapon: ✓ gun: ✗ rob: ✗ bound: ✓ strangle: ✓ mutilate: ✓ W M

Sergey Golovkin a Soviet-Russian serial killer known as The Fisher and The Boa. Golovkin tortured, raped and killed at least eleven young boys in the Moscow area between 1986 and 1992. Golovkin would rape and sodomize the boys while cutting their genitals, torso and throats. He was sentenced to death and was the last person executed in Russia before the death penalty was abolished in 1996. On August 2nd 1996, Sergey Golovkin was executed by a single gunshot to the back of the head in Moscow, Russia.

Sentence: death by gunshot to the head at a prison in Soviet Union, Russia. **Death:** cause of death: capital punishment, execution by gunshot to the head at a prison in Soviet Union, Russia.

Active in: United States

Mark Goudeau

The Baseline Killer

BIRTH: 09-06-1964 YEARS ACTIVE: 2005 - 2006 ARRESTED: 09-04-2006 (Age 41)
GENDER: Male AGES ACTIVE: 40/41 - 41/42 CONVICTED: 09-07-2007 (Age 43)
ZODIAC: Virgo LIFE SPAN: 1964 - DEATH:

9 VICTIMS

SERIAL KILLER RAPIST

Active for **2 years** known to have killed at least **9 victims** between **2005** and **2006**.

previous crimes: ✓ weapon: ✓ gun: ✓ rob: ✓ bound: ✗ strangle: ✗ mutilate: ✗ W M

Mark Goudeau an American serial killer and rapist known as The Baseline Killer and The Baseline Rapist. Goudeau would kidnap, rape, rob and murder victims in Phoenix, Arizona between 2005 and 2006. He murdered nine victims, eight female and one male. He would wear disguises such as a Halloween mask or dress as a homeless man. Ballistics and DNA evidence was used to convict Goudeau. Some of his victims were thought to have been originally committed by the Serial Shooters, Dale Hausner and Samuel Dieteman. In 2007, Goudeau was convicted of the nine murders. He has several other felony convictions including fifteen rapes and eleven kidnappings. In 2011, Mark Goudeau was sentenced to death and is currently being held on death row.

Sentence: death at Arizona State Prison Complex, Florence State Prison, Florence, Arizona, US.

Active in: United States

Kwauhuru Govan

murder of Rashawn Brazell

BIRTH: 07-20-1978 YEARS ACTIVE: 2004 - 2017 ARRESTED: 11-14-2016 (Age 38)
GENDER: Male AGES ACTIVE: 25/26 - 38/39 CONVICTED: 09-07-2018 (Age 40)
ZODIAC: Cancer LIFE SPAN: 1978 - DEATH:

2-4 VICTIMS

SERIAL KILLER RAPIST STRANGLER

Active for **14 years** known to have killed at least **2 victims** between **2004** and **2017**.

previous crimes: ✓ weapon: ✓ gun: ✗ rob: ✗ bound: ✓ strangle: ✓ mutilate: ✓ W

Kwauhuru Govan (Kwauhuru John Govan) a suspected American serial killer who has been arrested for two murders and two murders still under investigation. Govan's DNA was matched with evidence beneath the nails of one of his victims. Govan was arrested at Northwest Florida Reception Center in Chipley, as he was being released from prison in 2016. Govan's previous arrests in Brooklyn include robbery, assault, burglary and weapons possession from 1996 to 2010. Authorities later found a journal in his possession that contained a sketch of a chair designed to restrain women during sexual encounters. Govan called the chair a "sex pod" in his journal entries. Govan is still awaiting trial for the 2005 murder and dismemberment of 19-year-old relative Rashawn Brazell..

Sentence: twenty-five years to life in prison, awaiting one sentencing and one trial for a murder from 2005 at Attica Correctional Facility in Attica, New York, US.

Active in: United States

Shawn Grate

BIRTH: 08-08-1976 **YEARS ACTIVE:** 2005 - 2016 **ARRESTED:** 09-13-2016 (Age 40)
GENDER: Male **AGES ACTIVE:** 28/29 - 39/40 **CONVICTED:** 05-07-2018 (Age 41)
ZODIAC: Leo **LIFE SPAN:** 1976 - **DEATH:**

4-5 VICTIMS

SERIAL KILLER RAPIST STRANGLER

Active for **12 years** known to have killed at least **4 victims** between **2005** and **2016**.
previous crimes: ✓ weapon: ✓ gun: ✗ rob: ✗ bound: ✓ strangle: ✓ mutilate: ✗ W

Shawn Grate (Shawn Michael Grate) an American serial killer, rapist and kidnapper. Grate was convicted on two counts of aggravated murder in 2018. He was arrested after a victim who was kidnapped and raped multiple times escaped and called 911. Grate wrote two letters to a news station in Cleveland, Ohio confessing to the murders of all five victims. He was indicted on twenty-three charges including the two counts of murder. In 2018, Grate was found guilty of fifteen charges and sentenced to death. In 2019, Grate pleaded guilty to two additional murders in Richland County. The City of Ashland is pursuing a federal grant with the intention of demolishing the house Grate committed his crimes in.

Sentence: death at Chillicothe Correctional Institution in Ross County, Ohio, US.

Active in: Germany DECEASED

Fritz Haarmann

Butcher of Hannover, the Vampire of Hannover

BIRTH: 10-25-1879 **YEARS ACTIVE:** 1918 - 1924 **ARRESTED:** 06-22-1924 (Age 44)
GENDER: Male **AGES ACTIVE:** 38/39 - 44/45 **CONVICTED:** 12-19-1924 (Age 45)
ZODIAC: Scorpio **LIFE SPAN:** 1879 - 1925 **DEATH:** 04-15-1925 (Age 45)

24-27 VICTIMS

SERIAL KILLER RAPIST VAMPIRE STRANGLER

Active for **7 years** known to have killed at least **24 victims** between **1918** and **1924**.
previous crimes: ✓ weapon: ✗ gun: ✗ rob: ✗ bound: ✓ strangle: ✓ mutilate: ✓ W M

Fritz Haarmann (Friedrich Heinrich Karl "Fritz" Haarmann) a German serial killer known as the Butcher of Hannover and the Vampire of Hannover. Haarmann confessed to raping, killing and dismembering many young men between 1918 and 1924. Haarmann's preferred method of killing was biting through his victim's throat, sometimes while sodomizing them. He would then dump the bodies in the nearby river Leine. He is believed to have been responsible for the murder of twenty-seven boys and young men. He was convicted of twenty-four murders in 1924. In 1925, Fritz Haarmann was beheaded by guillotine in the grounds of Hanover prison.

Sentence: execution by beheading via guillotine at Hanover Prison in Hanover, Germany. **Death:** cause of death: capital punishment, executed by beheading via guillotine at Hanover Prison in Hanover, Germany.

Active in: Germany DECEASED

Erwin Hagedorn

Hans Erwin Hagedorn

BIRTH: 01-30-1952 YEARS ACTIVE: 1969 - 1971 ARRESTED: 11-12-1971 (Age 19)
GENDER: Male AGES ACTIVE: 16/17 - 18/19 CONVICTED: 05-15-1972 (Age 20)
ZODIAC: Aquarius LIFE SPAN: 1952 - 1972 DEATH: 09-15-1972 (Age 20)

3 VICTIMS

SERIAL KILLER RAPIST STALKER

Active for **3 years** known to have killed at least **3 victims** between **1969** and **1971**.
previous crimes: ✓ weapon: ✓ gun: ✗ rob: ✗ bound: ✗ strangle: ✗ mutilate: ✓ W

Erwin Hagedorn (Hans Erwin Hagedorn) a German serial killer and sex offender. Hagedorn killed three boys ages 9 to 12 in a forest in Eberswalde, Germany. In 1969, Hagedorn killed two nine-year-old boys. The Ministry for State Security matched the case of West German child murderer Jürgen Bartsch while assembling a psychological offender profile, the investigation was unsuccessful. In 1971, Hagedorn stabbed an eleven-year-old boy, dismembered him, and tried to hide the body. Hagedorn was convicted and sentenced to death. Erwin Hagedorn was executed by a single gunshot to the head in 1972.

Sentence: death by gunshot to the head at Leipzig Prison in the southern suburbs of Leipzig, Germany. **Death:** cause of death: execution by shooting at Leipzig Prison in the southern suburbs of Leipzig, Germany.

Active in: United States

Rodney Halbower

Gypsy Hill killings, San Mateo slasher

BIRTH: 06-27-1948 YEARS ACTIVE: 1976 - 1976 ARRESTED: 11-20-2017 (Age 69)
GENDER: Male AGES ACTIVE: 27/28 - 27/28 CONVICTED: 09-19-2018 (Age 70)
ZODIAC: Cancer LIFE SPAN: 1948 - DEATH:

5 VICTIMS

SERIAL KILLER RAPIST

Active for **1 year** known to have killed at least **5 victims** in **1976**.
previous crimes: ✓ weapon: ✓ gun: ✗ rob: ✗ bound: ✗ strangle: ✗ mutilate: ✗ W

Rodney Halbower (Rodney Lynn Halbower) an American serial killer known as the Gypsy Hill killings and the San Mateo slasher. The Gypsy Hill killings refers to five unsolved killings, of young women in San Mateo County, California during early 1976. In 2014, the FBI named Halbower as a person of interest in the Gypsy Hill killings; as of 2015, he was charged with two of the murders based on DNA taken from cigarette butts saved from the scene of a 1976 killing. Halbower is already in prison serving a life sentence with charges of attempted murder, assault, rape and robbery. With the exception of two brief periods when he had escaped, Halbower has been in prison for the past 38 years. In 2018, Halbower was sentenced to two additional life sentences.

Sentence: life imprisonment, without the possibility of parole at the Maguire Correctional Facility in Redwood City, California, US.

Active in: United States

Larry DeWayne Hall

The Springfield Three

BIRTH: 12-11-1962 YEARS ACTIVE: 1987 - 1994 ARRESTED: 11-15-1994 (Age 31)
GENDER: Male AGES ACTIVE: 24/25 - 31/32 CONVICTED: 12-21-1994 (Age 32)
ZODIAC: Sagittarius LIFE SPAN: 1962 - DEATH:

14-54 VICTIMS

SERIAL KILLER RAPIST NECROPHILIAC TORTURER STALKER

Active for **8 years** known to have killed at least **14 victims** between **1987** and **1994**.
previous crimes: ✓ weapon: ✓ gun: ✗ rob: ✗ bound: ✓ strangle: ✓ mutilate: ✓ W R

Larry DeWayne Hall a suspected American serial killer known as The Springfield Three. Hall is suspected of murdering between thirty-nine and fifty-four women, mostly prostitutes, fourteen of which he either confessed to or the body has been found and Hall is the main suspect. He had an I.Q. of 80, from the book Urges, Martin (2010, Page 11). Hall is serving a life sentence on a federal kidnapping charge from eastern Illinois, his murder confessions were made after this conviction. Hall remains a suspect in several open cases, one was reopened as recently as 2016. The Springfield Three refers to an unsolved missing persons case from 1992. The case remains unsolved but similarities match that of Hall's.

Sentence: life imprisonment without the possibility of parole at United States Penitentiary (USP Marion) in Williamson County, Illinois, US.

Active in: United States DECEASED

William Henry Hance

Chairman of the Forces of Evil

BIRTH: 01-01-1952 YEARS ACTIVE: 1977 - 1978 ARRESTED: 04-04-1978 (Age 26)
GENDER: Male AGES ACTIVE: 25/25 - 26/26 CONVICTED: 03-11-1980 (Age 28)
ZODIAC: Capricorn LIFE SPAN: 1952 - 1994 DEATH: 03-31-1994 (Age 42)

4 VICTIMS

SERIAL KILLER RAPIST STRANGLER

Active for **2 years** known to have killed at least **4 victims** between **1977** and **1978**.
previous crimes: ✓ weapon: ✓ gun: ✗ rob: ✓ bound: ✗ strangle: ✓ mutilate: ✓ W M

William Henry Hance an American soldier and serial killer who called himself the Chairman of the Forces of Evil. Hance was convicted of killing four women around military bases in 1977 and 1978. He was a suspect in the Stocking Strangler murders, until the capture of Carlton Gary. In 1984 psychiatrists determined that Mr. Hance was borderline retarded, with an I.Q. of 76. In another evaluation in 1987, psychiatrists said he had an I.Q. of 91, within the average range of intelligence. He was executed by the state of Georgia on March 31st 1994, via the electric chair.

Sentence: death by electrocution at a prison in Muscogee County, Georgia, US. **Death:** cause of death: capital punishment, executed by electrocution via electric chair at a prison in Muscogee County, Georgia, US.

Active in: Estonia DECEASED

Johannes-Andreas Hanni

Estonia's Hannibal Lecter, the Nõmme Cannibal

BIRTH: YEARS ACTIVE: 1982 - 1982 ARRESTED: 10-02-1982
GENDER: Male AGES ACTIVE: - CONVICTED:
ZODIAC: LIFE SPAN: - 1982 DEATH: 11-06-1982

3 VICTIMS

SERIAL KILLER RAPIST CANNIBAL

Active for **1 year** known to have killed at least **3 victims** in **1982**.
previous crimes: ✔ weapon: ✔ gun: ✖ rob: ✔ bound: ✖ strangle: ✖ mutilate: ✔ W

Johannes-Andreas Hanni a Soviet-Estonian serial killer known as Estonia's Hannibal Lecter and The Nõmme Cannibal. Hanni killed murdered three people in Estonia in 1982 with the aid of his wife Pille. Johannes-Andreas Hanni later hanged himself in prison before sentencing in November of 1982. He cut out part of one of his victims thigh to eat, claiming he had wished to try eating human flesh for a long time. His wife, Pille Hanni, was convicted on charges of accessory to murder and spent nearly twelve years in Harku women's prison before being released. She later changed her name and moved to Finland.

Sentence: never sentence committed suicide prior to conviction at a prison in Tallinn, Estonia. **Death:** cause of death: committed suicide by hanging himself in his prison cell at a prison in Tallinn, Estonia.

Active in: United States DECEASED

Robert Christian Hansen

The Butcher Baker

BIRTH: 02-15-1939 YEARS ACTIVE: 1971 - 1983 ARRESTED: 06-13-1983 (Age 44)
GENDER: Male AGES ACTIVE: 31/32 - 43/44 CONVICTED: 02-18-1984 (Age 45)
ZODIAC: Aquarius LIFE SPAN: 1939 - 2014 DEATH: 08-21-2014 (Age 75)

15-21 VICTIMS

SERIAL KILLER RAPIST TORTURER STALKER

Active for **13 years** known to have killed at least **15 victims** between **1971** and **1983**.
previous crimes: ✔ weapon: ✔ gun: ✔ rob: ✖ bound: ✔ strangle: ✖ mutilate: ✖ W M R

Robert Christian Hansen an American serial killer known as The Butcher Baker. Hansen kidnapped prostitutes releasing them into the Alaska wilderness, so Hansen could hunt them down like game animals. Rape, torture, and abduction were among his signatures. Based on discovered remains, police suspect him of six murders in addition to the fifteen for which he was convicted. An aviation map with x marks, was found hidden behind Hansen's headboard. Police later learned the x marks were locations of victims bodies. A 2013 movie titled The Frozen Ground starring Nicolas Cage and John Cusack depicts an Alaskan State Trooper seeking to apprehend Hansen by partnering with a young woman, who escaped Hansen's clutches.

Sentence: life imprisonment, plus 461 years without the possibility of parole at the Spring Creek Correctional Center in Seward, Alaska, US. **Death:** cause of death: natural causes at the Anchorage Correctional Complex in Anchorage, Alaska, US.

Active in: United Kingdom

Anthony Hardy

The Camden Ripper

BIRTH: 05-31-1951 YEARS ACTIVE: 2000 - 2002 ARRESTED: 01-02-2003 (Age 51)
GENDER: Male AGES ACTIVE: 48/49 - 50/51 CONVICTED: 11-25-2003 (Age 52)
ZODIAC: Gemini LIFE SPAN: 1951 - DEATH:

3-9 VICTIMS

SERIAL KILLER RAPIST NECROPHILIAC STRANGLER

Active for **3 years** known to have killed at least **3 victims** between **2000** and **2002**.

previous crimes: ✓ weapon: — gun: — rob: — bound: — strangle: ✓ mutilate: ✓ W M

Anthony Hardy (Anthony John Hardy) an English serial killer known as The Camden Ripper. Hardy killed three prostitutes between 2000 and 2002. In January 2002 police found the naked dead body of a woman lying on the bed while searching Hardy's home. He was diagnosed with a personality disorder and preventively detained in a mental institution until November 2002. In 2002 the dismembered remains of two women were found in trash bins. While arresting Hardy, an officer was stabbed in the hand and had his eye dislocated from his eye socket. He took numerous pornographic pictures of his victims after death prior to dismembering the bodies. In 2003, Anthony Hardy was sentenced to life imprisonment. In 2010, his sentence was upgraded to a whole life tariff.

Sentence: life imprisonment without the possibility of parole at a prison in London, England.

BIRTH: 06-11-1945 YEARS ACTIVE 1974 - 1976 ARRESTED:
GENDER: Male AGES ACTIVE 28/29 - 30/31 CONVICTED: 05-02-1978 (Age 32)
ZODIAC: Gemini LIFE SPAN: 1945 - 2012 DEATH: 09-25-2012 (Age 67)

3 VICTIMS

SERIAL KILLER RAPIST CANNIBAL STRANGLER

Active for **3 years** known to have killed at least **3 victims** between **1974** and **1976**.

previous crimes: ✓ weapon: ✓ gun: ✗ rob: ✓ bound: ✗ strangle: ✓ mutilate: ✓ W M

Trevor Hardy an English serial killer known as the Beast of Manchester and The Monster of Manchester. Hardy murdered three teenage girls in the Manchester area between 1974 and 1976. Hardy was known to rob, stab, strangle and rape his victims prior to stripping and mutilating at least two victims. Hardy confessed he had bitten off the nipple of one of his victims, later filing his own teeth to avoid his teeth matching the marks left on the victims body. He buried two of his victims in shallow graves and dumped the last victims body. In 1977, Hardy was found guilty on three charges of murder and was sentenced to life imprisonment. In 2012, Trevor Hardy died of natural causes after thirty-five years of imprisonment.

Sentence: life imprisonment, three life terms at HM Prison Wakefield in West Yorkshire, England.

Death: cause of death: natural causes, myocardial infarction, collapsed from heart attack in his prison cell at HM Prison Wakefield in West Yorkshire, England.

Active in: United States

DECEASED

Charles Ray Hatcher

Crazy Charlie

BIRTH: 07-16-1929 YEARS ACTIVE: 1969 - 1982 ARRESTED: 07-30-1982 (Age 53)
GENDER: Male AGES ACTIVE: 39/40 - 52/53 CONVICTED: 12-03-1984 (Age 55)
ZODIAC: Cancer LIFE SPAN: 1929 - 1984 DEATH: 12-07-1984 (Age 55)

16 VICTIMS

SERIAL KILLER RAPIST STRANGLER

Active for **14 years** known to have killed at least **16 victims** between **1969** and **1982**.
previous crimes: ✓ weapon: ✓ gun: ✗ rob: ✗ bound: ✗ strangle: ✓ mutilate: ✗ W M R

Charles Ray Hatcher an American serial killer and rapist known as Crazy Charlie. Hatcher confessed to having murdered sixteen victims between 1969 and 1982. Hatcher was a habitual criminal who confessed to the rape and murder of sixteen adolescent males. He escaped from prison several times and was declared a manipulative institutionalized sociopath. In 1961, Hatcher was suspected in the rape and murder of a fellow inmate, no charges were filed. On December 3rd 1984, Charles Ray Hatcher committed suicide by hanging himself in his cell at the Missouri State Penitentiary in Jefferson City, Missouri.
Sentence: life imprisonment at Missouri State Penitentiary in Jefferson City, Missouri, US. **Death:** cause of death: suicide, committed suicide by hanging himself in his prison cell at Missouri State Penitentiary in Jefferson City, Missouri, US.

Active in: France

Francis Heaulme

The Criminal Backpacker

BIRTH: 02-25-1959 YEARS ACTIVE: 1984 - 1992 ARRESTED: 01-07-1992 (Age 32)
GENDER: Male AGES ACTIVE: 24/25 - 32/33 CONVICTED:
ZODIAC: Pisces LIFE SPAN: 1959 - DEATH:

11-20 VICTIMS

SERIAL KILLER RAPIST STRANGLER

Active for **9 years** known to have killed at least **11 victims** between **1984** and **1992**.
previous crimes: ✓ weapon: ✓ gun: ✗ rob: ✗ bound: ✗ strangle: ✓ mutilate: ✗ W M

Francis Heaulme a French serial killer known as The Criminal Backpacker. Heaulme was convicted of eleven murders in at least nine French criminal cases. He is suspected in the murder of dozens. He is known as the Criminal Backpacker due to his travels throughout France. Heaulme has Klinefelter's syndrome which can cause infertility and smaller reproductive organs in males. Heaulme has convictions and sentences ranging from 1994 to 2017. On May 17th 2017, Francis Heaulme was sentenced to life imprisonment.
Sentence: life imprisonment at a prison in France.

Active in: Netherlands DECEASED

Jacobus Dirk Hertogs

Koos Hertogs

BIRTH: 12-16-1949 YEARS ACTIVE: 1979 - 1980 ARRESTED: 10-03-1980 (Age 30)

GENDER: Male AGES ACTIVE: 29/30 - 30/31 CONVICTED: 11-07-1982 (Age 32)

ZODIAC: Sagittarius LIFE SPAN: 1949 - 2015 DEATH: 07-19-2015 (Age 65)

3-12 VICTIMS

SERIAL KILLER RAPIST TORTURER

Active for **2 years** known to have killed at least **3 victims** between **1979** and **1980**.

previous crimes: ✔ weapon: ✔ gun: ✔ rob: ✖ bound: ✖ strangle: ✖ mutilate: ✖ W M

Jacobus Dirk Hertogs a Dutch serial killer and rapist also known as Koos Hertogs. Hertogs was convicted of the abduction, torture, rape and murder three girls. He is suspected of killing a further three to nine girls and young women in the 1970s. In 1980, Hertogs was bit on his littler finger by a victim, the bite was used to help identify and lead to his arrest. During a search of his home Authorities found an attic which was provisionally furnished as a torture chamber and blood from two of his victims. Authorities suspect he abused and eventually killed his victims in the chamber. Hertogs was sentenced to life imprisonment in 1982.

Sentence: life imprisonment at the Nieuw Vosseveld prison in Vught, Netherlands. **Death:** cause of death: natural causes at a hospital in Den Bosch, Southern Netherlands.

Active in: United Kingdom DECEASED

Myra Hindley

The Moors murders

BIRTH: 07-23-1942 YEARS ACTIVE: 1963 - 1965 ARRESTED: 10-11-1965 (Age 23)

GENDER: Female AGES ACTIVE: 20/21 - 22/23 CONVICTED: 05-06-1966 (Age 23)

ZODIAC: Leo LIFE SPAN: 1942 - 2002 DEATH: 11-15-2002 (Age 60)

5 VICTIMS

SERIAL KILLER RAPIST TORTURER STRANGLER

Active for **3 years** known to have killed at least **5 victims** between **1963** and **1965**.

previous crimes: ✖ weapon: ✔ gun: ✖ rob: ✖ bound: ✔ strangle: ✔ mutilate: ✖ W M

Myra Hindley an English rapist and serial killer who along with her boyfriend, Ian Brady, are known for committing the Moors murders. The Moors murders were carried out in England between 1963 and 1965. Five children were abducted and at least four were sexually assaulted. The victims were male and female children aged between 10 and 17. Hindley was sentenced to two concurrent life sentences in 1966. In 2002, Myra Hindley died from bronchial pneumonia, caused by heart disease, at West Suffolk Hospital in Suffolk, England.

Sentence: life imprisonment, two concurrent terms at HM Prison Holloway in London, England. **Death:** cause of death: natural causes, cardiovascular disease at West Suffolk Hospital in Bury St Edmunds, Suffolk, England.

Active in: South Korea

Kang Ho-Sun

the gyeongsangnam-do serial killer

BIRTH: 10-10-1969 YEARS ACTIVE: 2006 - 2008 ARRESTED: 01-27-2009 (Age 39)
GENDER: Male AGES ACTIVE: 36/37 - 38/39 CONVICTED: 04-22-2009 (Age 39)
ZODIAC: Libra LIFE SPAN: 1969 - DEATH:

10 VICTIMS

SERIAL KILLER RAPIST STRANGLER

Active for **3 years** known to have killed at least **10 victims** between **2006** and **2008**.
previous crimes: ✓ weapon: ✗ gun: ✗ rob: ✗ bound: ✗ strangle: ✓ mutilate: ✓ W M

Kang Ho-Sun a South Korean serial killer rapist and kidnapper known as the gyeongsangnam-do serial killer. Kang was sentenced to death in 2010 for killing ten women, including his fourth wife and mother-in-law. Kang Ho-Su acknowledged the murder of seven people during the trial, but strongly denied the allegations that he murdered his mother-in-law and fourth wife in a fire in 2005. Kang Ho-Sun was convicted on charges of rape, murder and arson. Kang Ho-Sun was sentenced to death by a court in Ansan in 2009. Kang gained prison notoriety after a fellow inmate and serial killer, Jung Nam-gyu, committed suicide.

Sentence: death by hanging at Seoul Detention Center in Uiwang, Gyeonggi Province, South Korea.

Active in: Czech Republic DECEASED

Ladislav Hojer

Cowardly Cannibal

BIRTH: 03-15-1958 YEARS ACTIVE: 1978 - 1981 ARRESTED: 02-11-1982 (Age 23)
GENDER: Male AGES ACTIVE: 19/20 - 22/23 CONVICTED:
ZODIAC: Pisces LIFE SPAN: 1958 - 1986 DEATH: 08-07-1986 (Age 28)

5-7 VICTIMS

SERIAL KILLER RAPIST CANNIBAL NECROPHILIAC STRANGLER

Active for **4 years** known to have killed at least **5 victims** between **1978** and **1981**.
previous crimes: ✓ weapon: ✓ gun: ✗ rob: ✗ bound: ✗ strangle: ✓ mutilate: ✓ W

Ladislav Hojer a Czech serial killer and rapist known as the Cowardly Cannibal. Hojer murdered at least five women in Czechoslovakia between 1978 and 1981. He cut off the breasts, vulva and genitalia of one of his victims. Hojer later committed acts of necrophilia on the genitalia before cooking the victims body parts in salt water and committed acts of cannibalism on them. In 1982, Hojer was arrested after a mentally-ill friend who Hojer had shown the scene of the crime, mistakingly confessed to the crime even though he was incarcerated at the time. His confession led to Hojer's arrest. Hojer confessed to five murders and is believed to have been responsible for at least two others. In 1986, Ladislav Hojer was executed at the Pankrác prison in Prague.

Sentence: death by hanging at Prague Pankrác Remand Prison in Prague, Czech Republic. **Death:** cause of death: executed by hanging at Prague Pankrác Remand Prison in Prague, Czech Republic.

Active in: India

DECEASED

M. Jaishankar

M. Shankar, Psycho Shankar

BIRTH:
YEARS ACTIVE: 2008 - 2011
ARRESTED: 10-19-2009

GENDER: Male
AGES ACTIVE: -
CONVICTED: 04-24-2013

ZODIAC:
LIFE SPAN: - 2018
DEATH: 02-27-2018

19 VICTIMS

SERIAL KILLER | RAPIST | TORTURER

Active for **4 years** known to have killed at least **19 victims** between **2008** and **2011**.

previous crimes: ✓ weapon: ✓ gun: ✗ rob: ✓ bound: ✗ strangle: ✗ mutilate: ✓ W M

M. Jaishankar (born M. Shankar) an Indian serial killer and rapist known as Psycho Shankar. Jaishankar is accused of killing at least nineteen women in a series of rapes and murders in Tamil Nadu, Karnataka and Andhra Pradesh, India between 2008 and 2011. He would kidnap, rape and torture his victims before murdering them. He was known to stab and mutilate victims by hacking them with a machete that he always carried with him. In 2009, Jaishankar was arrested on thirteen charges of rape. Jaishankar escaped from jail twice and was placed in solitary confinement after a third escape attempt. In 2018, M. Jaishankar committed suicide by slicing his own throat in his solitary confinement prison cell at the Central Prison in Bangalore, India.

Sentence: ten years in prison at a prison in Bangalore, Karnataka, India. **Death:** at Bangalore, city in Karnataka, India.

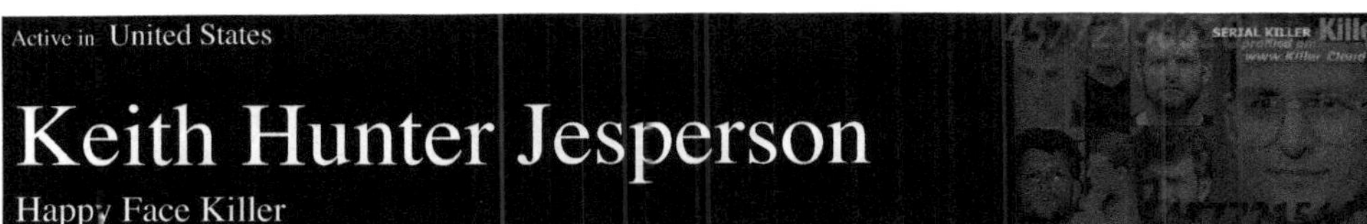

BIRTH: 04-06-1955
YEARS ACTIVE: 1990 - 1995
ARRESTED: 03-30-1995 (Age 39)

GENDER: Male
AGES ACTIVE: 34/35 - 39/40
CONVICTED: 06-03-1998 (Age 43)

ZODIAC: Aries
LIFE SPAN: 1955 -
DEATH:

8-185 VICTIMS

SERIAL KILLER | RAPIST | STRANGLER

Active for **6 years** known to have killed at least **8 victims** between **1990** and **1995**.

previous crimes: ✗ weapon: ✗ gun: ✗ rob: ✗ bound: ✗ strangle: ✓ mutilate: ✗ W M R

Keith Hunter Jesperson a Canadian-American serial killer known as the Happy Face Killer. He murdered at least eight women between 1990 and 1995. Jesperson's victims were sex worker transients who were raped and murdered by strangulation. His eight confirmed victims were killed in California, Florida, Nebraska, Oregon, Washington and Wyoming. Jesperson was known as the Happy Face Killer because he drew smiley faces on his many letters to the media and prosecutors. Jesperson claimed to have killed hundreds of victims, authorities say only eight murders have been confirmed. Keith Hunter Jesperson was ultimately sentenced to four terms of life imprisonment.

Sentence: life imprisonment, four life terms at Oregon State Penitentiary in Salem, Oregon, US.

Active in: United States

Milton Johnson

The Weekend Murderer

BIRTH: 05-15-1950 **YEARS ACTIVE:** 1983 - 1983 **ARRESTED:** 03-09-1984 (Age 33)
GENDER: Male **AGES ACTIVE:** 32/33 - 32/33 **CONVICTED:** 01-28-1986 (Age 35)
ZODIAC: Taurus **LIFE SPAN:** 1950 - **DEATH:**

10-17 VICTIMS

SERIAL KILLER | RAPIST | TORTURER

Active for **1 year** known to have killed at least **10 victims** in **1983**.

previous crimes: ✓ weapon: ✓ gun: ✓ rob: ✗ bound: ✗ strangle: ✗ mutilate: ✗ W M

Milton Johnson an American serial killer known as The Weekend Murderer. In 1983, Johnson killed at least ten victims in Will County, Illinois. In 1983, Johnson murdered two victims on a roadside turn-around, two police officers arrived at the scene and were shot by Johnson. Johnson shot two other motorist, one victim survived suffering six gunshot wounds. A day after the shooting Jackson shot a male victim and abducted his girlfriend. The girlfriend was raped, stabbed and left for death. She later survived, alerted authorities and identified her attacker. He also killed four women in a Joliet ceramics shop in 1983. In 1986, Milton Johnson was sentenced to death and is currently being held at the Menard Correctional Center in Chester, Illinois.

Sentence: death commuted to life in prison at the Menard Correctional Center in Chester, Illinois, US.

Active in: United States

Vincent Johnson

The Brooklyn Strangler, The Williamsburg Strangler

BIRTH: 01-06-1969 **YEARS ACTIVE:** 1999 - 2000 **ARRESTED:** 08-05-2000 (Age 31)
GENDER: Male **AGES ACTIVE:** 29/30 - 30/31 **CONVICTED:** 03-10-2001 (Age 32)
ZODIAC: Capricorn **LIFE SPAN:** 1969 - **DEATH:**

5-6 VICTIMS

SERIAL KILLER | RAPIST | STRANGLER

Active for **2 years** known to have killed at least **5 victims** between **1999** and **2000**.

previous crimes: ✓ weapon: ✗ gun: ✗ rob: ✗ bound: ✓ strangle: ✓ mutilate: ✗

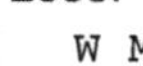

W M R

Vincent Johnson an American serial killer known as The Brooklyn Strangler and The Williamsburg Strangler. His victims were strangled and at least three were sexually assaulted by Johnson. He was described by police as a homeless panhandler and crack addict. His DNA was found on four of the victims, which lead to his arrest for the murders. Johnson confessed to the murders a week before prosecutors were to decide on whether or not to seek the death penalty. Johnson was sentenced to life imprisonment without the possibility of parole on March 10th 2001.

Sentence: life imprisonment without the possibility of parole at Clinton Correctional Facility in Dannemora, New York, US.

Active in: Canada DECEASED

Gilbert Paul Jordan

The Boozing Barber, The Alcohol Murders

BIRTH: 12-12-1931 YEARS ACTIVE: 1965 - 1987 ARRESTED: 10-23-1987 (Age 55)
GENDER: Male AGES ACTIVE: 33/34 - 55/56 CONVICTED:
ZODIAC: Sagittarius LIFE SPAN: 1931 - 2006 DEATH: 07-07-2006 (Age 74)

8-10 VICTIMS

SERIAL KILLER RAPIST

Active for **23 years** known to have killed at least **8 victims** between **1965** and **1987**.
previous crimes: ✓ weapon: ✗ gun: ✗ rob: ✗ bound: ✗ strangle: ✗ mutilate: ✗ W M

Gilbert Paul Jordan (born Gilbert Paul Elsie) a Canadian serial killer and former barber known as The Boozing Barber. Jordan is believed to have committed the Alcohol murders in Vancouver between 1965 and 1988. Jordan would lure, rape and later kill women by alcohol poisoning. In 1994, Jordan was released after his sentence was reduced to nine years, he was placed on probation which restricted him to Vancouver Island. In 2000, Jordan attempted to change his name to Paul Pearce, his application was never approved. He has been in and out of jail more than a dozen times since his original conviction, once for breaching his probation by drinking in the company of women. In 2005, Jordan was released after a public warning was issued by the police.

Sentence: fifteen years in prison, reduced to nine years, released in 1994 at a prison in Vancouver, Canada. **Death:** cause of death: natural causes at Victoria, British Columbia, Canada.

Active in: United States DECEASED

Buddy Earl Justus

BIRTH: 12-25-1952 YEARS ACTIVE: 1978 - 1978 ARRESTED: 10-11-1978 (Age 25)
GENDER: Male AGES ACTIVE: 25/26 - 25/26 CONVICTED: 11-05-1980 (Age 27)
ZODIAC: Capricorn LIFE SPAN: 1952 - 1990 DEATH: 12-13-1990 (Age 37)

3-4 VICTIMS

SERIAL KILLER RAPIST

Active for **1 year** known to have killed at least **3 victims** in **1978**.
previous crimes: ✓ weapon: ✓ gun: ✓ rob: ✓ bound: ✗ strangle: ✗ mutilate: ✗ M

Buddy Earl Justus an American serial killer and rapist. In 1978, Justus raped and murdered an eight and a half month pregnant nurse by shooting her three times in the head. In 1978, Justus and a hitchhiker named Dale Dean Goins, kidnapped raped and murdered two victims before dumping the bodies. Goins was sentenced to life in prison for his part in the Florida and Georgia murders. In 1980, Justus confessed and was sentenced to life imprisonment for kidnapping with bodily injury, armed robbery, rape and to death for murder. Justus also received the death penalty for the murder of a woman in Florida and another woman in Georgia. In 1990, Buddy Earl Justus was executed in the electric chair at Virginia State Penitentiary in Richmond, Virginia.

Sentence: death by electrocution at the Virginia State Penitentiary in Richmond, Virginia, US. **Death:** cause of death: executed by electrocution via electric chair at the Virginia State Penitentiary in Richmond, Virginia, US.

Active in: United States

DECEASED

Joseph Kallinger

The Shoemaker

BIRTH: 12-11-1935 | YEARS ACTIVE: 1974 - 1975 | ARRESTED: 01-17-1975 (Age 39)
GENDER: Male | AGES ACTIVE: 38/39 - 39/40 | CONVICTED: 10-14-1976 (Age 40)
ZODIAC: Sagittarius | LIFE SPAN: 1935 - 1996 | DEATH: 03-26-1996 (Age 60)

3 VICTIMS

SERIAL KILLER | RAPIST | TORTURER

Active for **2 years** known to have killed at least **3 victims** between **1974** and **1975**.
previous crimes: ✓ weapon: ✓ gun: ✓ rob: ✓ bound: ✓ strangle: ✗ mutilate: ✓ W M R

Joseph Kallinger (Joseph Lee Brenner III) an American serial killer and rapist known as The Shoemaker. Kallinger murdered three people, including his teenage son, and tortured four families during 1974 and 1975. Kallinger and his son were charged with kidnapping, murder and rape. Kallinger was sentenced to life in prison in 1976, transferred to a mental hospital on suicide watch in 1979. He spent the last eleven years of his life on suicide watch. Joseph Kallinger died of an epileptic seizure resulting in heart failure in 1996.

Sentence: life imprisonment at State Correctional Institution, Cresson, Pennsylvania, US. **Death:** cause of death: epilepsy, seizure resulting heart failure at State Correctional Institution, Cresson, Pennsylvania, US.

Active in: Japan

DECEASED

Kiyotaka Katsuta

Metropolitan Designated Case 113, Kiyotaka Fujiwara

BIRTH: 08-29-1948 | YEARS ACTIVE: 1982 - 1983 | ARRESTED: 01-31-1983 (Age 34)
GENDER: Male | AGES ACTIVE: 33/34 - 34/35 | CONVICTED: 01-17-1994 (Age 45)
ZODIAC: Virgo | LIFE SPAN: 1948 - 2000 | DEATH: 11-30-2000 (Age 52)

8-22 VICTIMS

SERIAL KILLER | RAPIST | STRANGLER

Active for **2 years** known to have killed at least **8 victims** between **1982** and **1983**.
previous crimes: ✗ weapon: ✓ gun: ✓ rob: ✓ bound: ✗ strangle: ✓ mutilate: ✗ W M

Kiyotaka Katsuta a Japanese firefighter and serial killer known as Metropolitan Designated Case 113 and Kiyotaka Fujiwara. Katsuta shot his victims using a gun he had stolen from a police officer after running him over with his car. He was known to strangle at least one of his victims. Katsuta eluded capture for another two months and was arrested on January 31st 1983. He received two separate death sentences for the eight murders between 1972 and 1982. Kiyotaka Katsuta was executed by hanging on November 30th 2000, nearly seventeen years after his arrest.

Sentence: death by hanging at a prison in Nagoya, Japan. **Death:** cause of death: capital punishment, executed by hanging at a prison in Nagoya, Japan.

Active in: United States

Patrick Wayne Kearney

The Trash Bag Murderer, The Freeway Killer

BIRTH: 09-24-1939 YEARS ACTIVE: 1965 - 1977 ARRESTED: 07-01-1977 (Age 37)
GENDER: Male AGES ACTIVE: 25/26 - 37/38 CONVICTED: 07-15-1977 (Age 37)
ZODIAC: Libra LIFE SPAN: 1939 - DEATH:

21-43
VICTIMS

SERIAL KILLER RAPIST NECROPHILIAC

Active for **13 years** known to have killed at least **21 victims** between **1965** and **1977**.
previous crimes: ✘ weapon: ✓ gun: ✓ rob: ✘ bound: ✓ strangle: ✘ mutilate: ✓ W M R

Patrick Wayne Kearney an American serial killer known as The Trash Bag Murderer and The Freeway Killer. Kearney would pick up young homosexual male hitch-hikers or young men from gay bars near Redondo Beach California, and kill them. All were males, all were nude, all had been shot in the head with a gun. After murdering them, he would take the bodies to a secluded place and engage in acts of necrophilia, then take them home, where they would be sodomized with X-Acto knives. They were then mutilated and dismembered with hacksaws. Some had been dismembered and stuffed into heavy-duty trash bags. Most of the victims were part of a investigation dubbed The Trash Bag Murders.
Sentence: life in prison at Mule Creek State Prison (MCSP), Ione, California.

Active in: United States

Edmund Kemper

The Co-ed Butcher, The Co-ed Killer

BIRTH: 12-18-1948 YEARS ACTIVE: 1964 - 1973 ARRESTED: 04-24-1973 (Age 24)
GENDER: Male AGES ACTIVE: 15/16 - 24/25 CONVICTED: 11-08-1973 (Age 24)
ZODIAC: Sagittarius LIFE SPAN: 1948 - DEATH:

10
VICTIMS

SERIAL KILLER RAPIST CANNIBAL NECROPHILIAC STRANGLER

Active for **10 years** known to have killed at least **10 victims** between **1964** and **1973**.
previous crimes: ✓ weapon: ✓ gun: ✓ rob: ✘ bound: ✓ strangle: ✓ mutilate: ✓ W M

Edmund Kemper (Edmund Emil Kemper III) an American serial killer known as The Co-ed Butcher and The Co-ed Killer. Kemper murdered ten victims, including his paternal grandparents and mother. A victim of Herbert Mullin was attributed to Kemper originally. Kemper was one of six (Jerome Jerry Brudos, Ted Bundy, Ed Gein, Gary M. Heidnik, Gary Ridgway and Kemper) who served as an inspiration for the character of Buffalo Bill in Thomas Harris' 1988 novel The Silence of the Lambs and its film adaptation. In 1973, Kemper was sentenced to life imprisonment. In 2017, Edmund Kemper was procedurally denied parole and is next eligible in 2024.
Sentence: life imprisonment at California Medical Facility in Vacaville, California, US.

Active in: United States DECEASED

Israel Keyes

Izzy

BIRTH: 01-07-1978 YEARS ACTIVE: 1998 - 2012 ARRESTED: 03-13-2012 (Age 34)
GENDER: Male AGES ACTIVE: 19/20 - 33/34 CONVICTED:
ZODIAC: Capricorn LIFE SPAN: 1978 - 2012 DEATH: 12-02-2012 (Age 34)

3-11 VICTIMS

SERIAL KILLER RAPIST STRANGLER

Active for **15 years** known to have killed at least **3 victims** between **1998** and **2012**.
previous crimes: ✓ weapon: ✓ gun: ✓ rob: ✓ bound: ✓ strangle: ✓ mutilate: ✓ W M

Israel Keyes (Israel "Izzy" Keyes) an American serial killer, rapist, arsonist, burglar and bank robber. Keyes murdered three confirmed victims and was linked to another eleven victims in four seperate states. An FBI report said Keyes burglarized twenty to thirty homes and robbed several banks between 2001 and 2012. He may be linked to as many as eleven deaths. Keyes planned murders long ahead of time, usually killed far from home, and never in the same area twice. Keyes committed suicide on December 2nd 2012, via self-inflicted wrist cuts and strangulation at Anchorage Correctional Complex.

Sentence: never sentenced, suicide prior to conviction at Anchorage Correctional Complex in Anchorage, Alaska. **Death:** cause of death: committed suicide via self-inflicted wrist cuts and strangulation at Anchorage Correctional Complex in Anchorage, Alaska.

Active in: United States

Roger Kibbe

The I-5 Strangler

BIRTH: 05-21-1939 YEARS ACTIVE: 1977 - 1987 ARRESTED:
GENDER: Male AGES ACTIVE: 37/38 - 47/48 CONVICTED: 03-18-1991 (Age 51)
ZODIAC: Gemini LIFE SPAN: 1939 - DEATH:

7-38 VICTIMS

SERIAL KILLER RAPIST STRANGLER

Active for **11 years** known to have killed at least **7 victims** between **1977** and **1987**.
previous crimes: ✓ weapon: ✗ gun: ✗ rob: ✗ bound: ✓ strangle: ✓ mutilate: ✗ W M

Roger Kibbe (Roger Reece Kibbe) an American serial killer and rapist known as The I-5 Strangler. Kibbe killed seven women between 1977 and 1987. Six along I-5 near Sacramento, and one in Walnut Creek, California. Kibbe kidnapped his victims, bound, duct taped the mouths and cut open their clothes in irregular shapes with scissors that had belonged to his mother. Kibbe also cut off most of the hair of his victims to remove the duct tape. It took detectives thirty-four years to find the body of one of his victims. Roger Kibbe was sentenced to life imprisonment in 1991.

Sentence: life imprisonment without the possibility of parole at Mule Creek State Prison in Ione, California, US.

Active in: United States

Anthony Kirkland

BIRTH: 09-13-1968 **YEARS ACTIVE:** 1987 - 2009 **ARRESTED:** 03-08-2009 (Age 40)
GENDER: Male **AGES ACTIVE:** 18/19 - 40/41 **CONVICTED:** 05-13-2014 (Age 45)
ZODIAC: Virgo **LIFE SPAN:** 1968 - **DEATH:**

5 VICTIMS

SERIAL KILLER RAPIST STRANGLER

Active for **23 years** known to have killed at least **5 victims** between **1987** and **2009**.
previous crimes: ✓ weapon: ✗ gun: ✗ rob: ✓ bound: ✗ strangle: ✓ mutilate: ✗ W M

Anthony Kirkland an American serial killer who killed his girlfriend and set her body on fire in 1987. Kirkland pleaded guilty to manslaughter and served sixteen years in prison. He was released on parole in 2004. Kirkland murdered four females between 2006 and 2009, three of them children. Kirkland would rape, strangle and then set fire to the bodies of his victims. On August 28th 2018 a Hamilton County judge agreed with the jury and sentenced Kirkland to death. His execution was scheduled for March 7th 2019. Appeals will likely delay that date even further.

Sentence: death by execution at Chillicothe Correctional Institution in Ohio, US.

BIRTH: **YEARS ACTIVE:** 1900 - 1914 **ARRESTED:**
GENDER: Male **AGES ACTIVE:** - **CONVICTED:**
ZODIAC: **LIFE SPAN:** - **DEATH:**

24 VICTIMS

SERIAL KILLER RAPIST VAMPIRE STRANGLER

Active for **15 years** known to have killed at least **24 victims** between **1900** and **1914**.
previous crimes: — weapon: — gun: — rob: ✓ bound: — strangle: ✓ mutilate: — W M

Bela Kiss a Hungarian serial killer known as The Monster of Czinkota. Kiss evaded arrest and conviction after the discovery of twenty-four bodies hidden in large metal drums on his property in 1916. The bodies had puncture marks on their necks and were drained of blood. At the time he was serving in the Austro-Hungarian Army, he deserted when the military was notified of the murders by civilian authorities. His final whereabouts and fate are unknown, as is his final victim count.

Active in: United States

DECEASED

Paul John Knowles

Casanova Killer, Lester Daryl Gates

BIRTH: 04-17-1946 YEARS ACTIVE: 1974 - 1974 ARRESTED: 11-21-1974 (Age 28)
GENDER: Male AGES ACTIVE: 27/28 - 27/28 CONVICTED:
ZODIAC: Aries LIFE SPAN: 1946 - 1974 DEATH: 12-18-1974 (Age 28)

20-35 VICTIMS

SERIAL KILLER RAPIST STRANGLER

Active for **1 year** known to have killed at least **20 victims** in **1974**.

previous crimes: ✓ weapon: ✓ gun: ✓ rob: ✓ bound: ✓ strangle: ✓ mutilate: ✗ W M

Paul John Knowles an American serial killer known as The Casanova Killer. Knowles was convicted of killing twenty victims in 1974. His crimes ranged from petty theft, multiple escapes, kidnapping, abduction, rape and murder. He claimed to have killed thirty-five. He was raised in foster homes, reformatories and later served multiple prison sentences. He was released from prison in 1974, and within two months he was rearrested for stabbing a bartender. He escaped custody by picking the lock to his detention cell at a jail in Jacksonville, Florida. He was later captured, attempted escape again this time ending in three fatal shots issued by Georgia Bureau of Investigation Agent Ronnie Angel.

Sentence: never sentenced killed while attempting escape at a jail in Jacksonville, Florida, US. **Death:** cause of death: ballistic trauma, shot three times in the chest by GBI Agent Ronnie Angel while attempting escape at in-custody transport from Jacksonville Jail to Henry County, Georgia.

Active in: China, Japan

DECEASED

Yoshio Kodaira

the Kodaira case

BIRTH: 01-28-1905 YEARS ACTIVE: 1928 - 1946 ARRESTED: 08-20-1946 (Age 41)
GENDER: Male AGES ACTIVE: 22/23 - 40/41 CONVICTED: 11-16-1948 (Age 43)
ZODIAC: Aquarius LIFE SPAN: 1905 - 1949 DEATH: 10-05-1949 (Age 44)

8-11 VICTIMS

SERIAL KILLER RAPIST NECROPHILIAC STRANGLER

Active for **19 years** known to have killed at least **8 victims** between **1928** and **1946**.

previous crimes: ✓ weapon: ✓ gun: ✗ rob: ✗ bound: ✗ strangle: ✓ mutilate: ✓ W M

Yoshio Kodaira a Japanese serial killer and rapist known as the Kodaira case. Kodaira killed his father-in-law in 1932 and eight to ten women in Japan between 1945 and 1946. In the 1920s, Kodaira was deployed to Northern China as a sailor in the Imperial Japanese Navy to participated in the Jinan incident. Kodaira engaged in acts of necrophilia with the corpse after the fifth murder and stuck a sword into the belly of a pregnant woman. He was sentenced to death by hanging in 1948. Yoshio Kodaira was executed by hanging on October 5th 1949.

Sentence: death by hanging at Miyagi Prison in Wakabayashi-ku, Sendai, Miyagi Prefecture, Japan.
Death: cause of death: capital punishment, executed by hanging at Miyagi Prison in Wakabayashi-ku, Sendai, Miyagi Prefecture, Japan.

Active in: United States

Todd Kohlhepp

Superbike Murders

BIRTH: 03-07-1971 YEARS ACTIVE: 2003 - 2016 ARRESTED: 11-03-2016 (Age 45)
GENDER: Male AGES ACTIVE: 31/32 - 44/45 CONVICTED: 05-26-2017 (Age 46)
ZODIAC: Pisces LIFE SPAN: 1971 - DEATH:

7 VICTIMS

SERIAL KILLER RAPIST

Active for **14 years** known to have killed at least **7 victims** between **2003** and **2016**.
previous crimes: ✓ weapon: ✓ gun: ✓ rob: ✓ bound: ✓ strangle: ✗ mutilate: ✗ W

Todd Kohlhepp (Todd Christopher Sampsell) an American serial killer, convicted of murdering seven people in South Carolina between 2003 and 2016. In 2016, Kohlhepp was named as a person of interest in an unsolved 2003 bank robbery and triple homicide at the local Blue Ridge Savings Bank. In 2017, Kohlhepp pleaded guilty to seven counts of murder, two counts of kidnapping and one count of criminal sexual assault. On August 30th 2018 Kohlhepp's 96-acre property in Woodruff and more than 550 items were sold at a short-sale auction to the general public. The proceeds go to the family members of Kohlhepp's victims.

Sentence: life imprisonment, seven life terms, without the possibility of parole at Broad River Correctional Institute in Columbia, South Carolina, US.

Active in: India

Surinder Koli

Noida serial murders, Nithari serial murders

BIRTH: YEARS ACTIVE: 2005 - 2006 ARRESTED: 12-27-2006
GENDER: Male AGES ACTIVE: - CONVICTED: 02-12-2009
ZODIAC: LIFE SPAN: - DEATH:

19 VICTIMS

SERIAL KILLER RAPIST CANNIBAL NECROPHILIAC STRANGLER

Active for **2 years** known to have killed at least **19 victims** between **2005** and **2006**.
previous crimes: ✓ weapon: ✓ gun: ✗ rob ✗ bound: ✗ strangle: ✓ mutilate: ✓ W M

Surinder Koli an Indian serial killer and rapist known as the Noida serial murders and the Nithari serial murders. The 2006 Noida serial murder investigation began in December 2006 when the skeletal remains of a number of missing children were discovered in the village of Nithari, India on the outskirts of Noida in the Uttar Pradesh near New Delhi. Koli was a domestic servant of Moninder Singh Pandher, both were arrested by the Delhi Police on the suspicion of murdering a call girl named Payal. Charges included rape, murder, kidnapping and criminal conspiracy. In 2009, Pandher and Koli were sentenced to death. Pandher was acquitted in 2009 and re-sentenced to death in 2017. In 2014, Surinder Koli's death sentence was commuted to life imprisonment.

Sentence: death commuted to life in prison at a prison in Meerut, Uttar Pradesh, India.

Active in: Hong Kong

Lam Kor-wan

The Jars Murderer, The Rainy Night Butcher

BIRTH: 03-22-1955 YEARS ACTIVE: 1980 - 1980 ARRESTED: 08-17-1982 (Age 27)
GENDER: Male AGES ACTIVE: 24/25 - 24/25 CONVICTED: 04-08-1983 (Age 28)
ZODIAC: Aries LIFE SPAN: 1955 - DEATH:

4
VICTIMS

SERIAL KILLER RAPIST NECROPHILIAC STRANGLER

Active for **1 year** known to have killed at least **4 victims** in **1980**.
previous crimes: — weapon: ✗ gun: ✗ rob: ✗ bound: ✗ strangle: ✓ mutilate: ✓ W M

Lam Kor-wan a Chinese serial killer known as The Jars Murderer, The Rainy Night Butcher and The Hong Kong Butcher. Lam worked as a taxi driver, he would pick up female passengers, strangle them with electrical wire and take them to his family home to dismember them. Lam Kor-wan was known to commit act of necrophilia with some of the bodies and he kept body parts in his parents' home, including sexual organs in plastic containers found in his room. Lam Kor-wan is one of Hong Kong's only two known serial killers, the other is Lam Kwok-wai. Lam Kor-wan was sentenced to death in 1983, his sentence was commuted to life imprisonment in 1984.

Sentence: death, commuted to life imprisonment at Shek Pik Prison on Lantau Island, Hong Kong.

Active in: United States

Randy Steven Kraft

The Freeway Killer, The Scorecard Killer

BIRTH: 03-19-1945 YEARS ACTIVE: 1971 - 1983 ARRESTED: 05-14-1983 (Age 38)
GENDER: Male AGES ACTIVE: 25/26 - 37/38 CONVICTED: 05-11-1989 (Age 44)
ZODIAC: Pisces LIFE SPAN: 1945 - DEATH:

16-67
VICTIMS

SERIAL KILLER RAPIST TORTURER STRANGLER

Active for **13 years** known to have killed at least **16 victims** between **1971** and **1983**.
previous crimes: ✓ weapon: ✓ gun: ✓ rob: ✗ bound: ✓ strangle: ✓ mutilate: ✓ W M R

Randy Steven Kraft an American serial killer known as The Freeway Killer, The Scorecard Killer and the Southern California Strangler. Kraft murdered a minimum of sixteen young men between 1972 and 1983, the majority of which had been committed in California. Kraft is also believed to have committed the rape and murder of up to fifty-one other boys and young men. He left a cryptic list of sixty-five murders and may have had an accomplice. William Bonin and Patrick Wayne Kearney also share the nickname the Freeway Killer. Randy Steven Kraft was convicted of the sixteen counts of murder and sentenced to death in 1989.

Sentence: death at San Quentin State Prison in Marin County, California, US.

Active in: United States

Timothy Krajcir

the Boogeyman in the blue bandana

BIRTH: 11-28-1944
GENDER: Male
ZODIAC: Sagittarius

YEARS ACTIVE: 1977 - 1982
AGES ACTIVE: 32/33 - 37/38
LIFE SPAN: 1944 -

ARRESTED: 08-29-2007 (Age 62)
CONVICTED: 12-10-2007 (Age 63)
DEATH:

9 VICTIMS

SERIAL KILLER | RAPIST | STALKER | STRANGLER

Active for **6 years** known to have killed at least **9 victims** between **1977** and **1982**.

previous crimes: ✓ weapon: ✓ gun: ✓ rob: ✗ bound: ✓ strangle: ✓ mutilate: ✗ W M R

Timothy Krajcir (Timothy Wayne McBride) an American serial killer known as the Boogeyman in the blue bandana. Krajcir confessed to killing nine women, five in Missouri and four others in Illinois and Pennsylvania. Krajcir would stalk his victims prior to the attack. Krajcir would break into their homes, wait for them to arrive and tie them up. Some victims were kidnapped and transported before they were killed while other victims were found tied up at their residents. Krajcir's victims were killed by a gunshot, stabbing or asphyxiation. Krajcir raped and forced victims to perform sexual acts during his crimes. Timothy Krajcir was sentenced to thirteen terms of life imprisonment.

Sentence: life imprisonment, thirteen terms at Pontiac Correctional Center in Pontiac, Illinois, US.

Active in: Germany

DECEASED

Joachim Georg Kroll

Ruhr Cannibal, The Duisburg Man-Eater, Uncle Joachim

BIRTH: 04-17-1933
GENDER: Male
ZODIAC: Aries

YEARS ACTIVE: 1955 - 1976
AGES ACTIVE: 21/22 - 42/43
LIFE SPAN: 1933 - 1991

ARRESTED: 07-03-1976 (Age 43)
CONVICTED: 04-08-1982 (Age 48)
DEATH: 07-01-1991 (Age 58)

14 VICTIMS

SERIAL KILLER | RAPIST | CANNIBAL | NECROPHILIAC | STRANGLER

Active for **22 years** known to have killed at least **14 victims** between **1955** and **1976**.

previous crimes: ✗ weapon: ✓ gun: ✗ rob: ✗ bound: ✗ strangle: ✓ mutilate: ✓ W M

Joachim Georg Kroll a German child molester and serial killer known as the Ruhr Cannibal, Ruhr Hunter, Uncle Joachim and the Duisburg Man-Eater. In 1982, Kroll was convicted of thirteen murders and one attempted murder. With an IQ of 76, borderline retarded, Kroll was considered the town idiot in Duisburg. Kroll had evidence including body parts in his fridge, a small hand that was cooking in a pan and entrails found stuck in his toilet when police searched his apartment. He confessed saying that he often sliced portions of flesh from his victims to cook and eat, claiming that he did this to save on his grocery bill. He was sentenced to life imprisonment in 1982. In 1991, Joachim Georg Kroll died from a heart attack while in the prison of Rheinbach, Germany.

Sentence: life imprisonment, nine life terms at the Prison of Rheinbach in Rheinbach, Germany.

Death: cause of death: natural causes, heart attack at the Prison of Rheinbach in Rheinbach, Germany.

Active in: India

Sunil Kumar

Gurugram serial killer

BIRTH: **YEARS ACTIVE:** 2011 - 2018 **ARRESTED:** 11-19-2018

GENDER: Male **AGES ACTIVE:** - **CONVICTED:**

ZODIAC: **LIFE SPAN:** - **DEATH:**

15 VICTIMS

SERIAL KILLER RAPIST TORTURER

Active for **8 years** known to have killed at least **15 victims** between **2011** and **2018**.

previous crimes: — weapon: ✔ gun: ✖ rob: ✖ bound: ✖ strangle: ✖ mutilate: ✖

Sunil Kumar an alleged Indian serial killer and rapist known as the Gurugram serial killer. Kumar confessed to killing at least fifteen victims from 2011 to 2018. He would visit community kitchens and offer sweets to lure little girls from poor families. Kumar picked isolated locations prior to the attacks, he would leave the body at the same location. Kumar was arrested in 2018 at his sisters house in a village near Jhansi. He told police he would wear the same shirt while committing the crimes, his Lucky blue shirt. He confessed to crimes in Delhi, Haryana, Uttar Pradesh and Madhya Pradesh. In 2018 police recovered the remains of a five-year-old girl scattered under a Gulmohar tree, the girl was an unfound body Sunil Kumar previously confessed to.

Sentence: awaiting trial at a prison Uttar Pradesh, India.

BIRTH: 11-03-1926 **YEARS ACTIVE:** 1948 - 1952 **ARRESTED:** 01-16-1952 (Age 25)

GENDER: Male **AGES ACTIVE:** 21/22 - 25/26 **CONVICTED:** 08-12-1952 (Age 25)

ZODIAC: Scorpio **LIFE SPAN:** 1926 - 1959 **DEATH:** 10-14-1959 (Age 32)

8 VICTIMS

SERIAL KILLER RAPIST NECROPHILIAC

Active for **5 years** known to have killed at least **8 victims** between **1948** and **1952**.

previous crimes: ✖ weapon: ✔ gun: ✖ rob: ✖ bound: ✖ strangle: ✖ mutilate: ✖ W M

Genzo Kurita a Japanese serial killer and rapist known as Kurita Genzo. Kurita murdered eight victims in Chiba, Tochigi and Shizuoka, Japan between 1948 and 1952. He was a serial rapist engaging in necrophilia during two of his murders. In 1948, Kurita murdered three victims, one was pregnant, he committed acts of necrophilia on her body. In 1951, Kurita threw three children off a cliff, the children of a woman he had murdered, one child survived the fall. In 1952, Kurita murdered two victims and committed acts of necrophilia on one body. In 1952 the district court in Chiba sentenced him to death for the last two murders. In 1953 the district court in Utsunomiya sentenced him to death for six murders. In 1959, Genzo Kurita was executed by hanging.

Sentence: death, execution by hanging at a prison in Japan. **Death:** cause of death: capital punishment, executed by hanging at a prison in Japan.

Active in: German Empire, Germany, German republic DECEASED

Peter Kurten

The Vampire of Düsseldorf, the Düsseldorf Monster

BIRTH: 05-26-1883 **YEARS ACTIVE:** 1913 - 1930 **ARRESTED:** 05-24-1930 (Age 46)

GENDER: Male **AGES ACTIVE:** 29/30 - 46/47 **CONVICTED:** 04-22-1931 (Age 47)

ZODIAC: Gemini **LIFE SPAN:** 1883 - 1931 **DEATH:** 07-02-1931 (Age 48)

9 VICTIMS

SERIAL KILLER RAPIST VAMPIRE STRANGLER

Active for **18 years** known to have killed at least **9 victims** between **1913** and **1930**.

previous crimes: ✓ weapon: ✓ gun: ✗ rob: ✓ bound: ✗ strangle: ✓ mutilate: ✗ W M

Peter Kurten (Peter Kürten) a German serial killer known as The Vampire of Düsseldorf and the Düsseldorf Monster. Kurten stated his primary motive was one of sexual pleasure associated with violent acts and that the sight of blood sexual stimulated him. In 1930, Kürten was arrested and confessed to multiple charges including a total of ten murders. He was charged with nine murders and seven attempted murders. Kürten was found guilty and sentenced to death for the nine murders. In 1932, Peter Kurten was executed at the Klingelputz Prison in Cologne, Germany. Kurten's mummified head is currently on display at the Ripley's Believe It or Not! museum in Wisconsin Dells, Wisconsin.

Sentence: death by beheading via guillotine at Klingelputz Prison in Cologne, North Rhine-Westphalia, Germany. **Death:** cause of death: capital punishment, executed by beheading via guillotine at Klingelputz Prison in Cologne, North Rhine-Westphalia, Germany.

Active in: Argentina DECEASED

Francisco Antonio Laureana

The Satyr of San Isidro

BIRTH: **YEARS ACTIVE:** 1974 - 1975 **ARRESTED:**

GENDER: Male **AGES ACTIVE:** - **CONVICTED:**

ZODIAC: **LIFE SPAN:** - 1975 **DEATH:** 02-27-1975

13 VICTIMS

SERIAL KILLER RAPIST STRANGLER

Active for **2 years** known to have killed at least **13 victims** between **1974** and **1975**.

previous crimes: ✓ weapon: ✓ gun: ✓ rob: ✗ bound: ✗ strangle: ✓ mutilate: ✗ W M

Francisco Antonio Laureana an alleged Argentine rapist and serial killer known as the Satyr of San Isidro. Laureana is suspected of the rape of fifteen women, of whom he is suspected of murdering thirteen between 1974 and 1975. Some victims were raped and strangled, while other victims were shot with a .32 caliber revolver. Francisco Antonio Laureana was killed in a shootout with the Buenos Aires police in 1975. After his death police found personal items from his victims in a boot at Laureana's home, connecting him to the crimes.

Sentence: never sentenced, shot during a shootout with police. **Death:** cause of death: ballistic trauma, shot during a shootout with police at an undisclosed location inside a chicken coop in San Isidro, Buenos Aires, Argentina.

Active in: United States DECEASED

Derrick Todd Lee

Baton Rouge Serial Killer, South Louisiana Serial Killer

BIRTH: 11-05-1968 YEARS ACTIVE: 1992 - 2002 ARRESTED: 05-27-2003 (Age 34)
GENDER: Male AGES ACTIVE: 23/24 - 33/34 CONVICTED: 10-14-2004 (Age 35)
ZODIAC: Scorpio LIFE SPAN: 1968 - 2016 DEATH: 01-21-2016 (Age 47)

7-10 VICTIMS

SERIAL KILLER RAPIST NECROPHILIAC STALKER

Active for **11 years** known to have killed at least **7 victims** between **1992** and **2002**.
previous crimes: ✓ weapon: ✓ gun: ✗ rob: ✗ bound: ✗ strangle: ✗ mutilate: ✗ W M R

Derrick Todd Lee an American serial killer and rapist known as the Baton Rouge Serial Killer and the South Louisiana Serial Killer. Lee was linked by DNA evidence to the deaths of seven women in Baton Rouge and Lafayette, Louisiana between 1992 and 2002. Lee is believed to have murdered several other women in Louisiana, Mississippi and Alabama. Fellow serial killer, Sean Vincent Gillis was active in the Baton Rouge area during the same time period as Lee. Lee scored an average of 65 on various standardized IQ tests. Lee was convicted of three of the murders and sentenced to death by lethal injection in 2004. In 2016, Derrick Todd Lee died of heart disease at the Lane Regional Medical Center in Zachary, Louisiana.

Sentence: death by lethal injection at Louisiana State Penitentiary, Angola, Louisiana, US. **Death:** cause of death: heart disease at Lane Regional Medical Center, Zachary, Louisiana, US.

Active in: Canada

Cody Legebokoff

The Country Boy Killer

BIRTH: 01-21-1990 YEARS ACTIVE: 2009 - 2010 ARRESTED: 11-28-2010 (Age 20)
GENDER: Male AGES ACTIVE: 18/19 - 19/20 CONVICTED: 09-11-2014 (Age 24)
ZODIAC: Aquarius LIFE SPAN: 1990 - DEATH:

4 VICTIMS

SERIAL KILLER RAPIST

Active for **2 years** known to have killed at least **4 victims** between **2009** and **2010**.
previous crimes: ✓ weapon: ✗ gun: ✗ rob: ✗ bound: ✗ strangle: ✗ mutilate: ✗ W M

Cody Legebokoff (Cody Alan Legebokoff) a Canadian serial killer and rapist known as The Country Boy Killer. Legebokoff murdered three women and a teenage girl between 2009 and 2010 in British Columbia, Canada. One victim was included as a suspected victim in the Highway of Tears murders. He used the handle 1CountryBoy on a Canadian social-networking site named Nexopia. He is one of Canada's youngest serial killers, the youngest was Peter Woodcock who was only 17 years old when he was active in Canada. In 2014, Legebokoff was sentenced to life in prison with no parole for twenty-five years. In 2019, Cody Legebokoff was transferred from the maximum security Kent Institution in British Columbia to the medium security Warkworth Institution in Ontario.

Sentence: sentenced to life in prison with no parole for twenty-five years at the Warkworth Institution in Ontario, Canada.

Active in: Australia

DECEASED

Eddie Leonski

The Brownout Strangler

BIRTH: 12-12-1917 **YEARS ACTIVE:** 1942 - 1942 **ARRESTED:** 05-22-1942 (Age 24)
GENDER: Male **AGES ACTIVE:** 24/25 - 24/25 **CONVICTED:** 07-17-1942 (Age 24)
ZODIAC: Sagittarius **LIFE SPAN:** 1917 - 1942 **DEATH:** 11-09-1942 (Age 24)

3 VICTIMS

SERIAL KILLER RAPIST STRANGLER

Active for **1 year** known to have killed at least **3 victims** in **1942**.
previous crimes: ✓ weapon: ✗ gun: ✗ rob: ✗ bound: ✗ strangle: ✓ mutilate: ✗ W M

Eddie Leonski (Edward Joseph Leonski) an American soldier and serial killer known as The Brownout Strangler. Leonski confessed to the strangulation, rape and murder of three women in Melbourne, Australia. He was picked from a lineup of American servicemen by the uncle of one of his victims. Leonski claimed he killed to obtain the voices of his victims. Leonski's crimes were committed in Australia, but his trial was conducted under American military law. Leonski confessed to three murders and was sentenced to death. In 1942, Eddie Leonski was executed by hanging at Her Majesty's Prison Pentridge in Coburg, Victoria, Australia.

Sentence: death by hanging at HM Prison Pentridge in Coburg, Victoria, Australia. **Death:** cause of death: capital punishment, executed by hanging at Victoria, state in Australia.

Active in: United States

Samuel Little

Samuel McDowell

BIRTH: 06-07-1940 **YEARS ACTIVE:** 1970 - 2005 **ARRESTED:** 09-05-2012 (Age 72)
GENDER: Male **AGES ACTIVE:** 29/30 - 64/65 **CONVICTED:** 09-25-2014 (Age 74)
ZODIAC: Gemini **LIFE SPAN:** 1940 - **DEATH:**

60-93 VICTIMS

SERIAL KILLER RAPIST STRANGLER

Active for **36 years** known to have killed at least **60 victims** between **1970** and **2005**.
previous crimes: ✓ weapon: ✗ gun: ✗ rob: ✓ bound: ✗ strangle: ✓ mutilate: ✗ W

Samuel Little an American serial killer also known as Samuel McDowell. Little claims to have killed as many as ninety people. He was convicted of three murders in California from 1987 to 1989 and was sentenced to life imprisonment without possibility of parole. In November of 2018 Little confessed to ninety murders across fourteen states between 1970 and 2005. California authorities have confirmed Little as a murder suspect in sixty cases across fourteen states from as early as 1981, and are working to match the remaining confessions to known murders or suspicious deaths.

Sentence: life imprisonment without the possibility of parole at California State Prison in Los Angeles County, Lancaster, California, US.

Active in: United States DECEASED

Michael Lee Lockhart

The Perfect Gentleman

BIRTH: 09-30-1960 YEARS ACTIVE: 1987 - 1988 ARRESTED: 03-22-1988 (Age 27)
GENDER: Male AGES ACTIVE: 26/27 - 27/28 CONVICTED: 10-22-1988 (Age 28)
ZODIAC: Libra LIFE SPAN: 1960 - 1997 DEATH: 12-09-1997 (Age 37)

3-6 VICTIMS

SERIAL KILLER RAPIST TORTURER

Active for **2 years** known to have killed at least **3 victims** between **1987** and **1988**.
previous crimes: ✓ weapon: ✓ gun: ✓ rob: ✓ bound: ✓ strangle: ✗ mutilate: ✓ W M R

Michael Lee Lockhart an American serial killer known as The Perfect Gentleman. Lockhart received death sentences in three separate states Florida, Indiana, and Texas. He would rape, stab and mutilate his victims, he shot at least one of his victims. Lockhart was convicted of the capital murder of police officer Paul Hulsey Jr. in Beaumont, Texas. He was also implicated in the sexual assault, murder and mutilation of 16-year-old Wendy Gallagher in Griffith, Indiana, 14-year-old Jennifer Colhouer in Land O' Lakes, Florida and the sexual assault of Lockhart's former wife in Toled. In 1997, Michael Lee Lockhart was executed by lethal injection at the Texas State Penitentiary at Huntsville, Texas.

Sentence: death, execution by lethal injection at the Texas State Penitentiary in Huntsville, Texas, US. **Death:** cause of death: capital punishment, executed by lethal injection at the Texas State Penitentiary in Huntsville, Texas, US.

Active in: United States DECEASED

Bobby Joe Long

The Classified Ad Rapist, The Adman Rapist

BIRTH: 10-14-1953 YEARS ACTIVE: 1984 - 1984 ARRESTED: 11-16-1984 (Age 31)
GENDER: Male AGES ACTIVE: 30/31 - 30/31 CONVICTED: 07-25-1986 (Age 32)
ZODIAC: Libra LIFE SPAN: 1953 - 2019 DEATH: 05-23-2019 (Age 65)

10 VICTIMS

SERIAL KILLER RAPIST STRANGLER

Active for **1 year** known to have killed at least **10 victims** in **1984**.
previous crimes: ✓ weapon: ✓ gun: ✓ rob: ✓ bound: ✓ strangle: ✓ mutilate: ✗ W M

Bobby Joe Long an American serial killer and rapist known as The Classified Ad Rapist, The Adman Rapist and Robert Joe Long. Long abducted, sexually assaulted, and murdered at least ten women in the Tampa Bay Area in Tampa Bay, Florida in 1984. Long's victims were strangled and/or asphyxiated, one victim died of a knife cut to the throat. He was in possession of a firearm during his crimes and shot at least one of his victims. Long was a distant cousin of fellow serial killer Henry Lee Lucas. Long confessed to the murders and was sentenced to death in1986. In 2019, Bobby Joe Long was executed by lethal injection Union Correctional Institution in Raiford, Florida.

Sentence: death at Union Correctional Institution in Raiford, Florida, US. **Death:** cause of death: executed by lethal injection at Union Correctional Institution, Florida State Prison in Raiford, Florida, US.

Active in: Colombia, Ecuador, Peru

Pedro Lopez

The Monster of the Andes

BIRTH: 10-08-1948 YEARS ACTIVE: 1969 - 2002 ARRESTED: 03-09-1980 (Age 31)
GENDER: Male AGES ACTIVE: 20/21 - 53/54 CONVICTED: 01-25-1981 (Age 32)
ZODIAC: Libra LIFE SPAN: 1948 - DEATH:

110-300 VICTIMS

SERIAL KILLER | RAPIST | STALKER | STRANGLER

Active for **34 years** known to have killed at least **110 victims** between **1969** and **2002**.

previous crimes: ✓ weapon: ✗ gun: ✗ rob: ✗ bound: ✗ strangle: ✓ mutilate: ✗ W M

Pedro Lopez (Pedro Alonso López) a Colombian serial killer and rapist known as The Monster of the Andes. López targeted young girls in Colombia, Ecuador and Peru between 1969 and 2002. He was arrested in 1980 and later convicted in 1983 of killing 110 young girls in Ecuador. López confessed to killing at least 300 victims. In 1994, Lopez was released from an Ecuadorian prison. He was rearrest and sent to a Colombian psychiatric hospital. López was released from the psychiatric hospital in 1998. In 2002, López was suspected of murder by Colombian authorities.

Sentence: sixteen years imprisonment, released, fourteen years preventively detained, released at a psychiatric wing of a hospital in Bogotá, Colombia.

Active in: Sweden DECEASED

John Ingvar Lovgren

Flickmördaren, The Girl Killer

BIRTH: 10-22-1930 YEARS ACTIVE: 1958 - 1963 ARRESTED:
GENDER: Male AGES ACTIVE: 27/28 - 32/33 CONVICTED:
ZODIAC: Libra LIFE SPAN: 1930 - 2002 DEATH: 02-09-2002 (Age 71)

4 VICTIMS

SERIAL KILLER | RAPIST

Active for **6 years** known to have killed at least **4 victims** between **1958** and **1963**.

previous crimes: ✓ weapon: ✓ gun: ✗ rob: ✗ bound: ✗ strangle: ✗ mutilate: ✗ W M

John Ingvar Lovgren (John Ingvar Lövgren) a Swedish serial killer and rapist known as Flickmördaren, The Girl Killer. Lovgren confessed to four murders committed between 1958 and 1963 in the Stockholm region. He would assault, rape and beat his victims to death with a rock. Lovgren was never convicted for one of the murders and the case has since been closed, authorities consider the case solved with Lovgren as the assailant. In 1964, Lovgren was convicted for three of the murders and preventively detained at the Salberga psychiatric hospital, Salberga has been ran as a prison facility since 1997. In 2002, John Ingvar Lovgren died from complications with cancer, he was no longer in threatment because of his poor health.

Sentence: preventively detained, institutionalized at the Salberga psychiatric hospital in Sala, Sweden.

Death: cause of death: cancer at an unknown location in Sweden.

Active in: South Africa

Maoupa Cedric Maake

Wemmer Pan Killer, Hammer Killer

BIRTH: | **YEARS ACTIVE:** 1996 - 1997 | **ARRESTED:** 12-23-1997

GENDER: Male | **AGES ACTIVE:** - | **CONVICTED:** 09-06-2000

ZODIAC: | **LIFE SPAN:** - | **DEATH:**

27-35
VICTIMS

SERIAL KILLER | RAPIST

Active for **2 years** known to have killed at least **27 victims** between **1996** and **1997**.
previous crimes: — weapon: ✓ gun: ✓ rob: ✓ bound: ✗ strangle: ✗ mutilate: ✗ W M

Maoupa Cedric Maake a South African serial killer known as the Wemmer Pan Killer and Hammer Killer. He killed his victims with different instruments such as guns, rocks, a knife, and a hammer. Authorities attributed the murders to two serial killers because of the inconsistent modus operandi. In some cases he killed his victims with a rock, in others he shot them, and in others he murdered with a hammer. Maake was arrested after Moses Sithole was found guilty of thirty-eight killings and sentenced to 1,340 years in prison. In 2000, Maake was convicted of twenty-seven murders, twenty-six attempted murders, fourteen rapes and other less serious offenses. Maoupa Cedric Maake was sentenced to twenty-seven life sentences.

Sentence: 27 life sentences + 1159 years and 3 months imprisonment at Johannesburg, South Africa.

Active in: South Africa

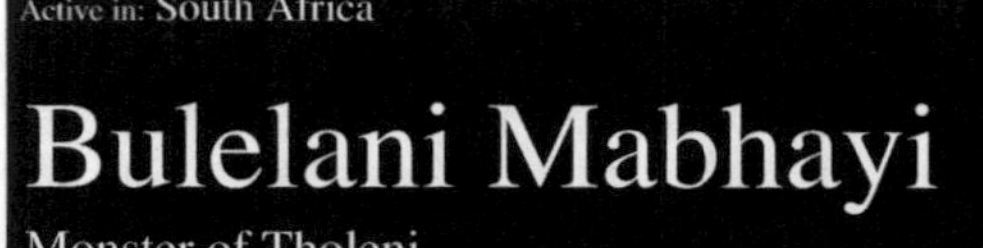

Bulelani Mabhayi

Monster of Tholeni

BIRTH: | **YEARS ACTIVE:** 2007 - 2012 | **ARRESTED:** 08-12-2012

GENDER: Male | **AGES ACTIVE:** - | **CONVICTED:** 09-03-2013

ZODIAC: | **LIFE SPAN:** - | **DEATH:**

20
VICTIMS

SERIAL KILLER | RAPIST | STALKER

Active for **6 years** known to have killed at least **20 victims** between **2007** and **2012**.
previous crimes: — weapon: ✓ gun: ✗ rob: ✓ bound: ✗ strangle: ✗ mutilate: ✓ W M

Bulelani Mabhayi a South African serial killer and rapist known as the Monster of Tholeni. Mabhayi killed eleven women and nine children in the Eastern Cape of South Africa from 2007 to 2012. Nineteen victims were murdered in the village of Tholeni and one victim in another nearby village. Mabhayi would breaking into homes and rape some of his victims killing all of them with an axe or panga. His victims ranged in aged from 14-months-old to 79 years of age. Bulelani Mabhayi was found guilty of twenty counts of murder, six rapes and ten burglaries. In 2013, Bulelani Mabhayi was sentenced to twenty-five years to life imprisonment.

Sentence: life imprisonment, twenty-five life terms at a prison in the Eastern Cape Province, South Africa.

Active in: United States

Michael Madison

BIRTH: 10-15-1977 **YEARS ACTIVE:** 2012 - 2013 **ARRESTED:** 07-19-2013 (Age 35)
GENDER: Male **AGES ACTIVE:** 34/35 - 35/36 **CONVICTED:** 05-05-2016 (Age 38)
ZODIAC: Libra **LIFE SPAN:** 1977 - **DEATH:**

3 VICTIMS

SERIAL KILLER RAPIST NECROPHILIAC STRANGLER

Active for **2 years** known to have killed at least **3 victims** between **2012** and **2013**.
previous crimes: ✓ weapon: ✓ gun: ✓ rob: ✗ bound: — strangle: ✓ mutilate: ✗ W M

Michael Madison an American serial killer from East Cleveland, Ohio who committed at least three murders. He registered as a sex offender in 2002 after serving four years for an attempted rape conviction, he also had previous drug convictions in 2000 and 2001. In 2013, Madison was arrested at his mothers house after a short stand-off. Authorities responded to a report of a foul odor at a garage leased to Madison, a decomposing body was found inside. Two other bodies were located each wrapped in plastic bags. In 2016, Madison was convicted of the three murders along with other charges. In 2016, Michael Madison was sentenced to death, at his sentencing he was attacked by the father of one of his victims.

Sentence: death at the Chillicothe Correctional Institution in Ross County, Ohio, US.

Active in: South Africa

Jimmy Maketta

Jesus Killer

BIRTH: **YEARS ACTIVE:** 2005 - 2005 **ARRESTED:** 12-20-2005
GENDER: Male **AGES ACTIVE:** - **CONVICTED:** 05-03-2007
ZODIAC: **LIFE SPAN:** - **DEATH:**

16 VICTIMS

SERIAL KILLER RAPIST

Active for **1 year** known to have killed at least **16 victims** in **2005**.
previous crimes: — weapon: ✓ gun: ✗ rob: ✓ bound: ✗ strangle: ✗ mutilate: ✗ W M

Jimmy Maketta a South African serial killer and rapist known as the Jesus Killer. Maketta pleaded guilty to and was convicted of sixteen murders and nineteen rapes committed over a nine-month period in 2005. Maketta had called authorities twice to tell where his victim's body could be located. In 2005, Maketta was arrested in Constantia following a reign of terror in the Philippi farmlands in Cape Town. In 2007, Jimmy Maketta was sentenced to life imprisonment at a prison in Cape Town, South Africa.

Sentence: life imprisonment at a prison in Cape Town, South Africa.

Active in: Egypt

Ramadan Abdel Rehim Mansour

al-Tourbini, The Express Train

BIRTH:
GENDER: Male
ZODIAC:
YEARS ACTIVE: 1999 - 2006
AGES ACTIVE: -
LIFE SPAN: -
ARRESTED: 11-29-2006
CONVICTED: 05-23-2007
DEATH:

32 VICTIMS

SERIAL KILLER RAPIST TORTURER

Active for **8 years** known to have killed at least **32 victims** between **1999** and **2006**.
previous crimes: ✓ weapon: ✓ gun: ✓ rob: ✗ bound: ✓ strangle: ✗ mutilate: ✗ W M

Ramadan Abdel Rehim Mansour an Egyptian serial killer and gang leader known as al-Tourbini (The Express Train). Mansour raped and tortured homeless children, mostly boys aged 10 to 14 years old. The murders took place aboard trains between Cairo, Alexandria, Qalyoubeya and Beni Sueif. The some victims were thrown off the moving train, other victims were thrown into the Nile river and at least one victim was buried alive. In 2007, Mansour and fellow gand ringleader, Farag Samir Mahmoud, also known as Hanata, were convicted by the criminal court in Tanta. Both suspects were also found guilty of illegal possession of weapons. Ramadan Abdel Rehim Mansour was executed in 2010.
Sentence: death at a prison in Tanta, Cairo, Egypt.

Active in: United Kingdom DECEASED

Peter Manuel

Beast of Birkenshaw

BIRTH: 03-01-1927
GENDER: Male
ZODIAC: Pisces
YEARS ACTIVE: 1956 - 1958
AGES ACTIVE: 28/29 - 30/31
LIFE SPAN: 1927 - 1958
ARRESTED: 01-13-1958 (Age 30)
CONVICTED: 05-29-1958 (Age 31)
DEATH: 07-11-1958 (Age 31)

7-9 VICTIMS

SERIAL KILLER RAPIST TORTURER

Active for **3 years** known to have killed at least **7 victims** between **1956** and **1958**.
previous crimes: ✓ weapon: ✓ gun: ✓ rob: ✓ bound: ✓ strangle: ✗ mutilate: ✗ W M R

Peter Manuel an American-Scottish serial killer, burglar and rapist known as the Beast of Birkenshaw. Manuel was convicted of murdering seven people across Lanarkshire between 1956 and 1958. He is believed to have killed two other victims. Manuel was the one of the last prisoner to be hanged in Scotland, after a sensational trial in which he conducted his own defense. In 1958, Manuel was convicted of the murders of seven people, one murder case was thrown out of court and another was attributed to him but was never proven. In 1958, Peter Manuel was executed by hanging at Barlinnie prison in Glasgow, Scotland.
Sentence: death by hanging at HM Prison Peterhead, HM Prison Barlinnie, Riddrie, Glasgow, Scotland. **Death:** cause of death: capital punishment, executed by hanging at HM Prison Barlinnie, Riddrie, Glasgow, Scotland.

Active in: United States

Richard Laurence Marquette

Dick Marquette

BIRTH: 12-12-1934 **YEARS ACTIVE:** 1961 - 1975 **ARRESTED:**
GENDER: Male **AGES ACTIVE:** 26/27 - 40/41 **CONVICTED:** 06-11-1975 (Age 40)
ZODIAC: Sagittarius **LIFE SPAN:** 1934 - **DEATH:**

3 VICTIMS

SERIAL KILLER RAPIST STRANGLER

Active for **15 years** known to have killed at least **3 victims** between **1961** and **1975**.

previous crimes: — weapon: ✓ gun: ✗ rob: ✓ bound: ✗ strangle: ✓ mutilate: ✓ W M

Richard Laurence Marquette an American serial killer also known as Dick Marquette. Marquette was known to drain the blood, mutilate, dismember and scatter the remains of his victims. Marquette was the first person ever to be added as an eleventh name on the FBI Ten Most Wanted List for killing, mutilating and dismembering a woman in 1961. Marquette killed two more with victims using the same modus operandi upon his release from prison in 1973. In 1975, Richard Laurence Marquette was sentenced to life imprisonment with no possibility of parole at the Oregon State Correctional Institution in Salem, Oregon.

Sentence: life imprisonment without the possibility of parole at the Oregon State Penitentiary in Salem, Oregon, US.

Active in: United States DECEASED

Lee Roy Martin

The Gaffney Strangler

BIRTH: 04-25-1937 **YEARS ACTIVE:** 1966 - 1967 **ARRESTED:** 02-15-1968 (Age 30)
GENDER: Male **AGES ACTIVE:** 28/29 - 29/30 **CONVICTED:** 05-31-1972 (Age 35)
ZODIAC: Taurus **LIFE SPAN:** 1937 - 1972 **DEATH:** 05-31-1972 (Age 35)

3 VICTIMS

SERIAL KILLER RAPIST STRANGLER

Active for **2 years** known to have killed at least **3 victims** between **1966** and **1967**.

previous crimes: — weapon: ✗ gun: ✗ rob: ✗ bound: ✗ strangle: ✓ mutilate: ✗ W M

Lee Roy Martin an American serial killer known as The Gaffney Strangler. Martin killed two women and two young girls in South Carolina in 1967 and 1968. Martin raped and strangled his victims, multiple victims had cigarette burns and at least one victim was stabbed to death. He was convicted on four charges of first-degree murder and received four life terms. Lee Roy Martin was stabbed to death by fellow inmate, Kenneth Rumsey, while incarcerated at Central Correctional Institution in Columbia in 1972.

Sentence: life imprisonment at Central Correctional Institution in Columbia, South Carolina, US.

Death: cause of death: homicide, stabbed to death by a fellow inmate at Central Correctional Institution in Columbia, South Carolina, US.

Active in: Spain DECEASED

Damaso Rodriguez Martin

El Brujo, The Warlock

BIRTH: 12-11-1944 YEARS ACTIVE: 1981 - 1991 ARRESTED:
GENDER: Male AGES ACTIVE: 36/37 - 46/47 CONVICTED:
ZODIAC: Sagittarius LIFE SPAN: 1944 - 1991 DEATH: 02-19-1991 (Age 46)

3 VICTIMS

SERIAL KILLER RAPIST STRANGLER

Active for **11 years** known to have killed at least **3 victims** between **1981** and **1991**.
previous crimes: ✓ weapon: ✓ gun: ✓ rob: ✓ bound: ✗ strangle: ✓ mutilate: ✗ W

Damaso Rodriguez Martin (Dámaso Rodríguez Martín) a Spanish serial killer known as El Brujo (The Warlock). Martin was charged with murder, rape, theft of a firearm and illegal possession of weapons. He was active in the Canary Islands an autonomous community of Spain located in the Atlantic Ocean. In 1981, Martin was sentenced to fifty-five years in prison for murdering a man and raping his girlfriend. He escaped from prison in 1991 and fled to the Anaga Mountains where he killed two German hikers, the woman was raped. In 1991, Authorities cornered Martin in an abandoned house, Damaso Rodriguez Martin shot himself unsuccessfully and was then shot dead by law enforcement.

Sentence: fifty-five years in prison, Martin escaped in 1991 at a prison in El Solís, Tegueste, Tenerife, Canary Islands, Spain. **Death:** cause of death: homicide, ballistic trauma, shot during a shootout with police at Macizo de Anaga, a mountain range on the island of Tenerife in the Canary Islands.

Active in: Russia

Sergei Martynov

Raschlenytel, Torso killer

BIRTH: 06-02-1962 YEARS ACTIVE: 1992 - 2010 ARRESTED: 11-18-2010 (Age 48)
GENDER: Male AGES ACTIVE: 29/30 - 47/48 CONVICTED: 11-10-2012 (Age 50)
ZODIAC: Gemini LIFE SPAN: 1962 - DEATH:

9 VICTIMS

SERIAL KILLER RAPIST STRANGLER

Active for **19 years** known to have killed at least **9 victims** between **1992** and **2010**.
previous crimes: ✓ weapon: ✓ gun: ✗ rob: ✓ bound: ✗ strangle: ✓ mutilate: ✓ W M

Sergei Martynov a Russian serial killer known as Raschlenytel and the Torso killer. Martynov often mutilated his female victims by removing their breasts and genitalia. In 1984, Martynov was serving in the army and charged for desertion. In 1989, Martynov was released on parole. In 1991, Martynov raped and killed a minor girl and hid her body in a cellar, for which he was sentenced to fifteen years in prison in 1992. He was released on parole in 2004. He was arrested in 2010 at a cafe in where he worked. He was sentenced to life imprisonment for killing eight more women during a violent crime spree between 2005 and 2010. In 2012, Sergei Martynov was sentenced to life imprisonment at the White Swan Colony in Solikamsk, Russia.

Sentence: life imprisonment at the White Swan Colony in Solikamsk, Russia.

Active in: South Africa DECEASED

Johannes Mashiane

The Beast of Atteridgeville

BIRTH: YEARS ACTIVE 1982 - 1989 ARRESTED:
GENDER: Male AGES ACTIVE - CONVICTED:
ZODIAC: LIFE SPAN: - 1989 DEATH: 10-01-1989

13 VICTIMS

SERIAL KILLER RAPIST STRANGLER

Active for **8 years** known to have killed at least **13 victims** between **1982** and **1989**.

previous crimes: ✓ weapon: ✓ gun: ✗ rob: ✗ bound: ✗ strangle: ✓ mutilate: ✗ W M

Johannes Mashiane a South African serial killers and sodomite known as The Beast of Atteridgeville. Mashiane committed thirteen counts of murder and twelve counts of sodomy from 1982 to 1989. In 1977, Mashiane killed his girlfriend and was sentenced to five years in prison, he was released in 1982. Mashiane killed twelve boys by either strangling or stoning them between 1988 and 1989. In 1989, Mashiane committed suicide when he jumped under a bus in Marabastad while being chased by police. Micki Pistorius notes "Mashiane had a droopy eye and a tattoo of a cross and dagger on his left forearm." in his 2012 book Strangers On The Street - Serial homicide in South Africa.

Sentence: five years imprisonment for the first murder at a prison near Atteridgeville, South Africa.

Death: cause of death: suicide, committed suicide when he jumped under a bus in Marabastad while being chased by police in 1989 at the Pretoria suburb of Marabastad in South Africa.

Active in: Germany, United States DECEASED

David Edward Maust

Crazy Dave

BIRTH: 04-05-1954 YEARS ACTIVE: 1974 - 2003 ARRESTED: 12-10-2003 (Age 49)
GENDER: Male AGES ACTIVE: 19/20 - 48/49 CONVICTED: 10-31-2005 (Age 51)
ZODIAC: Aries LIFE SPAN: 1954 - 2006 DEATH: 01-20-2006 (Age 51)

5-9 VICTIMS

SERIAL KILLER RAPIST STRANGLER

Active for **30 years** known to have killed at least **5 victims** between **1974** and **2003**.

previous crimes: ✓ weapon: ✓ gun: ✗ rob: ✗ bound: ✗ strangle: ✓ mutilate: ✗ W M

David Edward Maust an American serial killer known as Crazy Dave. Maust killed and molested teenage boys, he was arrested in 2003 when the bodies of three boys were found in the concrete floor of his basement in Hammond, Indiana. He was previously sentenced to four years for the manslaughter and larceny in the murder of a 13-year-old boy in Germany where Maust was stationed while in the army. Maust made parole in 1977, arrested again in 1979 and later released in 1981. The same year Maust was convicted again and served seventeen years in prison before his release in 1999. In 2006, Maust committed suicide by hanging himself in his jail cell after his latest conviction in 2005.

Sentence: life imprisonment, three terms at Illinois state prison in Illinois, US. **Death:** cause of death: suicide, committed suicide by hanging himself in his jail cell at St. Anthony Medical Center in Crown Point, Indiana, US.

Active in: Canada

Bruce McArthur

Santa, 2010–2017 Toronto serial homicides

BIRTH: 10-08-1951	YEARS ACTIVE: 2010 - 2018	ARRESTED: 01-18-2018 (Age 66)	8
GENDER: Male	AGES ACTIVE: 58/59 - 66/67	CONVICTED: 01-29-2019 (Age 67)	VICTIMS
ZODIAC: Libra	LIFE SPAN: 1951 -	DEATH:	

SERIAL KILLER RAPIST STRANGLER

Active for **9 years** known to have killed at least **8 victims** between **2010** and **2018**.

previous crimes: ✓ weapon: ✓ gun: ✗ rob: ✗ bound: ✓ strangle: ✓ mutilate: ✓ W

Bruce McArthur (Thomas Donald Bruce McArthur) a Canadian serial killer known as the 2010–2017 Toronto serial homicides. The 2010–2017 Toronto serial homicides occurred between 2010 and 2017, there was a series of disappearances of men in Toronto, Canada. He was known as Santa for his seasonal employment at a local shopping mall. Authorities found evidence including photographs of victims in his apartment. Authorities found the dismembered remains of several men in planter boxes at a residence where McArthur stored landscaping equipment. He was arrested in 2018 and convicted of all eight murders in 2019. On February 8th 2019, Bruce McArthur was sentenced to eight concurrent life sentences without the possibility of parole for twenty-five years.

Sentence: life imprisonment without the possibility of parole for twenty-five years at Toronto South Detention Centre in Toronto, Ontario, Canada.

Active in: Russia DECEASED

Gennady Mikhasevich

The Vitebsk Case

BIRTH: 04-07-1947	YEARS ACTIVE: 1971 - 1985	ARRESTED: 12-09-1985 (Age 38)	36-55
GENDER: Male	AGES ACTIVE: 23/24 - 37/38	CONVICTED:	VICTIMS
ZODIAC: Aries	LIFE SPAN: 1947 - 1987	DEATH: 09-25-1987 (Age 40)	

SERIAL KILLER RAPIST STRANGLER

Active for **15 years** known to have killed at least **36 victims** between **1971** and **1985**.

previous crimes: ✓ weapon: ✓ gun: ✗ rob: ✓ bound: ✗ strangle: ✓ mutilate: ✗ W M

Gennady Mikhasevich (Gennady Modestovich Mikhasevich) a Soviet serial killer known as The Vitebsk Case. Mikhasevich raped and strangled at least thirty-six female victims between 1971 and 1985. The murders occurred in Vitebsk, Polotsk and the rural areas in the nearby regions of the Byelorussian SSR. He robbed his victims of money and other valuable items, some of the items were given to his wife as a gift. Mikhasevich confessed to forty-three murders but was only convicted for thirty-six of the murders. Gennady Mikhasevich was executed on September 25th 1987.

Sentence: death by firing squad at a prison in the USSR. **Death:** cause of death: capital punishment, executed by firing squad at a prison in the USSR.

Active in: Japan

DECEASED

Tsutomu Miyazaki

The Otaku Murderer, The Little Girl Murderer

BIRTH: 08-21-1962 YEARS ACTIVE: 1988 - 1989 ARRESTED: 07-23-1989 (Age 26)

GENDER: Male AGES ACTIVE: 25/26 - 26/27 CONVICTED: 04-14-1997 (Age 34)

ZODIAC: Leo LIFE SPAN: 1962 - 2008 DEATH: 06-17-2008 (Age 45)

4 VICTIMS

SERIAL KILLER | RAPIST | CANNIBAL | NECROPHILIAC | VAMPIRE

Active for **2 years** known to have killed at least **4 victims** between **1988** and **1989**.

previous crimes: ✗ weapon: ✗ gun: ✗ rob: ✗ bound: ✓ strangle: ✓ mutilate: ✓ W M

Tsutomu Miyazaki a Japanese serial killer, cannibal, and necrophile known as The Otaku Murderer and The Little Girl Murderer. Miyazaki murdered four girls aged between four and seven. He mutilated and sexually molested the corpse of at least one of his victims. He drank the blood of at least one victim and ate her hands. A premature birth left him with deformed hands, which were permanently fused directly to the wrists. Miyazaki blamed his actions on Rat Man, an alter ego who he claimed forced him to kill. Miyazaki drew pictures of Rat Man during his trial.

Sentence: death by hanging at a prison in Tokyo, Japan. **Death:** cause of death: capital punishment, executed by hanging at a prison in Tokyo, Japan.

Active in: Poland

DECEASED

Stanislaw Modzelewski

The Vampire of Galkowek

BIRTH: 03-15-1929 YEARS ACTIVE: 1952 - 1967 ARRESTED: 09-24-1967 (Age 38)

GENDER: Male AGES ACTIVE: 22/23 - 37/38 CONVICTED: 02-05-1969 (Age 39)

ZODIAC: Pisces LIFE SPAN: 1929 - 1969 DEATH: 11-13-1969 (Age 40)

7-8 VICTIMS

SERIAL KILLER | RAPIST | STALKER | VAMPIRE | STRANGLER

Active for **16 years** known to have killed at least **7 victims** between **1952** and **1967**.

previous crimes: — weapon: ✓ gun: ✓ rob: ✓ bound: ✗ strangle: ✓ mutilate: ✓ W M

Stanislaw Modzelewski a Polish serial killer known as The Vampire of Galkowek. Modzelewski confessed to strangling eight women. He murdered eight and attempted the murder of six other women between 1952 and 1967. Modzelewski's victims were women aged between 18 and 87, he killed victims by strangling with a scarf or with his bare hands. At least one victim had razor blade like cuts on her buttocks. He was only convicted of seven murders because one victims body was never found. Modzelewski took valuable and other useless items from his victims. Stanislaw Modzelewski was sentenced to death by hanging, which was carried out on November 13th 1969, in Warsaw, Poland.

Sentence: death by hanging at Warsaw-Mokotów Investigation Detention Center in Mokotów, Poland. **Death:** cause of death: capital punishment, executed by hanging at Warsaw-Mokotów Investigation Detention Center in Mokotów, Poland.

Active in: South Africa

Jack Mogale

the West-End serial killer

BIRTH: | YEARS ACTIVE: 2008 - 2009 | ARRESTED: 03-27-2009
GENDER: Male | AGES ACTIVE: - | CONVICTED: 02-17-2011
ZODIAC: | LIFE SPAN: - | DEATH:

16 VICTIMS

SERIAL KILLER | RAPIST | STRANGLER

Active for **2 years** known to have killed at least **16 victims** between **2008** and **2009**.

previous crimes: — weapon: ✗ gun: ✗ rob: ✓ bound: ✗ strangle: ✓ mutilate: ✓ W M

Jack Mogale a South African serial killer known as the West-End serial killer. Mogale killed sixteen victims between 2008 and 2009. Mogale raped and strangled females in the Donnybrook area of KwaZulu-Natal. He claimed to be a preacher and prophet of the Zion Christian Church, an African initiated church operating across Southern Africa. Mogale was found guilty of nine kidnappings, nineteen rapes, sixteen murders, an attempted murder, three robberies with aggravating circumstances, a fraud or theft, an assault with intent to cause grievous bodily harm, a sexual assault and an escape from lawful custody.

Sentence: life imprisonment without the possibility of parole at a prison in Westonaria, Gauteng, South Africa.

Active in: United States

Cory Deonn Morris

Huggy Bear, Teddy Bear, Crackhead Killer

BIRTH: 05-10-1978 | YEARS ACTIVE: 2002 - 2003 | ARRESTED: 04-12-2003 (Age 24)
GENDER: Male | AGES ACTIVE: 23/24 - 24/25 | CONVICTED: 07-19-2005 (Age 27)
ZODIAC: Taurus | LIFE SPAN: 1978 - | DEATH:

5-6 VICTIMS

SERIAL KILLER | RAPIST | NECROPHILIAC | STRANGLER

Active for **2 years** known to have killed at least **5 victims** between **2002** and **2003**.

previous crimes: — weapon: ✗ gun: ✗ rob: ✗ bound: ✗ strangle: ✓ mutilate: ✗ M

Cory Deonn Morris an American serial killer known as Huggy Bear, Teddy Bear and the Crackhead Killer. Morris was convicted of luring five women to a camper, strangling them during sex and dumping their bodies. Morris is reported to have kept the victims body for some time, committing act of necrophilia on the lifeless bodies. All five women were killed in a camper behind a house owned by Morris' aunt, and their bodies were dumped in nearby alleys or on sidewalks. Cory Deonn Morris was sentenced to death in 2005.

Sentence: death at Arizona State Prison Complex, Florence State Prison (FSP) in Florence, Arizona, US.

Active in: Czech Republic DECEASED

Vaclav Mrazek

BIRTH: 10-22-1925 **YEARS ACTIVE:** 1951 - 1956 **ARRESTED:** 03-17-1957 (Age 31)
GENDER: Male **AGES ACTIVE:** 25/26 - 30/31 **CONVICTED:**
ZODIAC: Libra **LIFE SPAN:** 1925 - 1957 **DEATH:** 12-29-1957 (Age 32)

7 VICTIMS

SERIAL KILLER RAPIST

Active for **6 years** known to have killed at least **7 victims** between **1951** and **1956**.

previous crimes: ✓ weapon: ✓ gun: ✓ rob: ✓ bound: ✗ strangle: ✗ mutilate: ✗ W

Vaclav Mrazek (Václav Mrázek) a Czech serial killer who killed six women and one man in Chomutov. He would rape, rob, beat, shoot and murder his victims. He had an extensive criminal history prior to his killing spree. In 1951, Mrazekis is thought to have committed his first murder, the murder of a 15-year-old girl. He was convicted and sentenced to death in 1957. In 1957, Vaclav Mrazek was executed at the Prague Pankrác Remand Prison in Prague, Czech Republic.

Sentence: death at the Prague Pankrác Remand Prison in Prague, Czech Republic. **Death:** cause of death: executed at the Prague Pankrác Remand Prison in Prague, Czech Republic.

Active in: Russia

Vladimir Mukhankin

The pupil of Chikatilo

BIRTH: 04-22-1960 **YEARS ACTIVE:** 1995 - 1995 **ARRESTED:** 05-01-1995 (Age 35)
GENDER: Male **AGES ACTIVE:** 34/35 - 34/35 **CONVICTED:**
ZODIAC: Taurus **LIFE SPAN:** 1960 - **DEATH:**

9 VICTIMS

SERIAL KILLER RAPIST TORTURER

Active for **1 year** known to have killed at least **9 victims** in **1995**.

previous crimes: ✓ weapon: ✓ gun: ✗ rob: ✗ bound: ✗ strangle: ✗ mutilate: ✓ W M

Vladimir Mukhankin (Vladimir Anatolyevich Mukhankin) a convicted Russian serial killer and rapist known as The pupil of Chikatilo. Mukhankin murdered at least nine victims in Rostov Oblast in 1995. Mukhankin was known as The pupil of Andrei Chikatilo. He would stab or suffocate his victims some victims were tortured before death. He would dismember and sometimes burn the bodies of his victims. In 1995, Mukhankin was arrested and sentenced to death. His death sentence was later commuted to life imprisonment. Vladimir Mukhankin is currently serving his sentence at the Black Dolphin Prison in Orenburg Oblast, Russia.

Sentence: death, commuted to life imprisonment at the Black Dolphin Prison, Orenburg Oblast, Russia.

Active in: United Kingdom

David Mulcahy

The Railway Killers, The Railway Rapists

BIRTH: YEARS ACTIVE: 1985 - 1986 ARRESTED: 02-03-1999
GENDER: Male AGES ACTIVE: - CONVICTED: 02-01-2001
ZODIAC: LIFE SPAN: - DEATH:

3 VICTIMS

SERIAL KILLER RAPIST STALKER STRANGLER

Active for **2 years** known to have killed at least **3 victims** between **1985** and **1986**.
previous crimes: — weapon: ✗ gun: ✗ rob: ✗ bound: ✓ strangle: ✓ mutilate: ✓ W M

David Mulcahy a British rapist and serial killer who along with his accomplice, John Duffy, are known as the Railway Rapist and the Railway Killers. Mulcahy and Duffy attacked numerous women and children at railway stations in the south of England between 1985 and 1986. Both are suspected of other sexual attacks, while Mulcahy is also suspected of attacks which took place after Duffy was in prison. In 2001, David Mulcah was sentenced to three life terms in prison.

Sentence: life imprisonment, three life terms at HM Prison Full Sutton in the East Riding of Yorkshire, England.

Active in: Japan

Seisaku Nakamura

Hamamatsu Deaf Killer, Hamamatsu serial murder case

BIRTH: YEARS ACTIVE: 1938 - 1942 ARRESTED: 10-12-1942
GENDER: Male AGES ACTIVE: - CONVICTED:
ZODIAC: LIFE SPAN: - DEATH:

9-11 VICTIMS

SERIAL KILLER RAPIST

Active for **5 years** known to have killed at least **9 victims** between **1938** and **1942**.
previous crimes: ✗ weapon: ✓ gun: ✗ rob: ✗ bound: ✗ strangle: ✗ mutilate: ✗ W M

Seisaku Nakamura a Japanese teenage serial killer known as the Hamamatsu Deaf Killer and the Hamamatsu serial murder case. In 1924, Nakamura was born deaf in Shizuoka, Japan. He murdered eleven victims and attacked many others, among them his father, brother and nephew. He committed his first two murder at the age of fourteen and nine more before he turned eighteen. In 1942, Nakamura was arrested and confessed to eleven murders. He was tried as an adult and sentenced to death. In 1943, Seisaku Nakamura was executed by hanging at a prison in Japan.

Sentence: death by hanging at a prison in Japan.

Active in: United Kingdom

Robert Napper

Green Chain Rapist, The Plumstead Ripper

BIRTH: 02-25-1966 **YEARS ACTIVE:** 1992 - 1993 **ARRESTED:**
GENDER: Male **AGES ACTIVE:** 25/26 - 26/27 **CONVICTED:** 12-18-2008 (Age 42)
ZODIAC: Pisces **LIFE SPAN:** 1966 - **DEATH:**

3 VICTIMS

SERIAL KILLER RAPIST STALKER

Active for **2 years** known to have killed at least **3 victims** between **1992** and **1993**.
previous crimes: ✓ weapon: ✓ gun: ✗ rob: ✗ bound: ✗ strangle: ✗ mutilate: ✓ W M

Robert Napper a British serial killer and rapist known as the Green Chain Rapist and The Plumstead Ripper. Napper would rape, smother, stab and mutilate his victims. Napper was suspected of up to seventy other violent sexual attacks in South East London attributed to the unidentified Green Chain Rapist. In 1994, Napper was arrested after his fingerprint was recovered from a 1993 crime scene. One of his victims was so badly mutilated that a police photographer was put into therapy for two years. In 2008, Robert Napper was convicted of the manslaughter and on the grounds of diminished responsibility was preventively detained at the Broadmoor Hospital in Berkshire, England.

Sentence: preventively detained at the Broadmoor Hospital in Berkshire, England.

Active in: United States

Joseph Naso

The Double Initial Killer, Crazy Joe

BIRTH: 01-07-1934 **YEARS ACTIVE:** 1977 - 1994 **ARRESTED:** 04-11-2011 (Age 77)
GENDER: Male **AGES ACTIVE:** 42/43 - 59/60 **CONVICTED:** 08-20-2013 (Age 79)
ZODIAC: Capricorn **LIFE SPAN:** 1934 - **DEATH:**

6-10 VICTIMS

SERIAL KILLER RAPIST STALKER STRANGLER

Active for **18 years** known to have killed at least **6 victims** between **1977** and **1994**.
previous crimes: ✓ weapon: ✗ gun: ✗ rob: ✗ bound: ✗ strangle: ✓ mutilate: ✗ W M

Joseph Naso an American serial killer known as The Double Initial Killer and Crazy Joe. Naso was a freelance photographer who raped and strangled to death at least six women in California. His first four identified victims bore double initials. All four victims were listed by the police as prostitutes. Authorities discovered a handwritten diary in which Naso listed ten unnamed women with geographical locations, the other four women mentioned in the diary remain unidentified. Naso was also a suspect in the Rochester Alphabet murders of 1971–73 case, but was ruled out when DNA found on a victim was not a match to Naso. Joseph Naso was arrested in 2011 and sentenced to death in 2013.

Sentence: death at San Quentin State Prison in San Quentin, California, US.

Active in: United States

William Neal

Wild Bill Cody

BIRTH: 10-07-1955
GENDER: Male
ZODIAC: Libra

YEARS ACTIVE: 1998 - 1998
AGES ACTIVE: 42/43 - 42/43
LIFE SPAN: 1955 -

ARRESTED: 07-09-1998 (Age 42)
CONVICTED: 09-29-1999 (Age 43)
DEATH:

3
VICTIMS

SERIAL KILLER RAPIST

Active for **1 year** known to have killed at least **3 victims** in **1998**.
previous crimes: ✓ weapon: ✓ gun: ✓ rob: ✓ bound: ✓ strangle: ✗ mutilate: ✓ M R

William Neal (William Neal) an American serial killer known as Wild Bill Cody. Neal massacred three women with an ax. He was convicted of the brutal slayings of Rebecca Lynn Holberton, 44, Angela Fite, 28, and Candace Anita Walters, 48. The women, who all had relationships with Neal, were found dead at a gruesome crime scene in Holberton's townhome in 1998. He tied up a fourth victim, forced her to watch one of the murders and then raped her. He said that if he hadn't wanted to get caught, he would have murdered the women in the mountains and disposed of their bodies. By allowing the rape victim to live, he said, he was assured that "her testimony alone could put me to the death-penalty phase".

Sentence: death sentence changed to life in prison. at Jefferson County Detention Center.

Active in: United States DECEASED

Earle Leonard Nelson

Gorilla Killer, the Dark Strangler

BIRTH: 05-12-1897
GENDER: Male
ZODIAC: Taurus

YEARS ACTIVE: 1926 - 1927
AGES ACTIVE: 28/29 - 29/30
LIFE SPAN: 1897 - 1928

ARRESTED: 06-16-1927 (Age 30)
CONVICTED: 11-05-1927 (Age 30)
DEATH: 01-13-1928 (Age 30)

22-29
VICTIMS

SERIAL KILLER RAPIST NECROPHILIAC STRANGLER

Active for **2 years** known to have killed at least **22 victims** between **1926** and **1927**.
previous crimes: ✓ weapon: ✗ gun: ✗ rob: ✗ bound: ✗ strangle: ✓ mutilate: ✓ W M R

Earle Leonard Nelson (born Earle Leonard Ferral) an American serial killer, rapist, and necrophile known as the Gorilla Killer and the Dark Strangler and at least once used the alias Virgil Wilson. He targeted and strangled landladies throughout the West Coast during 1926. Nelson often carried a bible to gain trust with his victims. Nelson's defense at his six-day trial was insanity. Records were presented to show that Nelson had been confined in an insane asylum in Napa, California, during various periods between 1921 and 1925. In 1928, Earle Leonard Nelson was executed by hanging at the Vaughan Street Jail in Winnipeg, Manitoba, Canada.

Sentence: death, execution by hanging at Vaughan Street Jail in Winnipeg, Manitoba, Canada. **Death:** cause of death: capital punishment, executed by hanging at Vaughan Street Jail in Winnipeg, Manitoba, Canada.

Active in: United Kingdom DECEASED

Dennis Nilsen

The Muswell Hill Murderer, the Kindly Killer

BIRTH: 11-23-1945 YEARS ACTIVE: 1978 - 1983 ARRESTED: 02-09-1983 (Age 37)
GENDER: Male AGES ACTIVE: 32/33 - 37/38 CONVICTED: 11-04-1983 (Age 37)
ZODIAC: Sagittarius LIFE SPAN: 1945 - 2018 DEATH: 05-12-2018 (Age 72)

12-16 VICTIMS

SERIAL KILLER RAPIST NECROPHILIAC STRANGLER

Active for **6 years** known to have killed at least **12 victims** between **1978** and **1983**.
previous crimes: ✗ weapon: ✗ gun: ✗ rob: ✗ bound: ✓ strangle: ✓ mutilate: ✓ W M F

Dennis Nilsen a Scottish serial killer and necrophile known as The Muswell Hill Murderer and the Kindly Killer. Nilsen murdered and dismembered young men in London between 1978 and 1983. Nilsen observed a ritual in which he bathed and dressed the victims' bodies before dissecting and disposing of the remains. He kept various body parts around his home for an extended amount of time. Nilsen died at York Hospital in 2018 while still in custody. He had been transferred to the hospital after complaining of stomach pains, during surgery a blood clot ended his life.

Sentence: life imprisonment at HMP Full Sutton in the East Riding of Yorkshire, England. **Death:** cause of death: natural causes, taken to the hospital after complaining of stomach pains, suffered a blood clot as a result of surgery complications at York Hospital in York, England.

Active in: United States DECEASED

Robert Nixon

The Brick Moron, The Brick Bat Murders

BIRTH: YEARS ACTIVE: 1937 - 1938 ARRESTED: 05-28-1938
GENDER Male AGES ACTIVE: - CONVICTED:
ZODIAC: LIFE SPAN: - 1939 DEATH: 06-16-1939

5 VICTIMS

SERIAL KILLER RAPIST

Active for **2 years** known to have killed at least **5 victims** between **1937** and **1938**.
previous crimes: ✓ weapon: ✓ gun: ✗ rob: ✓ bound: ✗ strangle: ✗ mutilate: ✗ W M

Robert Nixon an American serial killer and rapist known as the Brick Moron and the Brick Bat Murders. Nixon killed five women using a brick between 1937 and 1938. The Brick Bat Murders refers to a 1937 case that occurred in Los Angeles. Nixon sometimes had an accomplice named Earl Hicks (a.k.a. Howard Jones Green). Robert Nixon confessed to the five murders and was sentenced to death. In 1939, Robert Nixon was executed in the electric chair at the Cook County Jail. Some of the incidents in the novel Native Son are fictionalized versions of the Robert Nixon case.

Sentence: death by electrocution at Cook County Jail, Chicago, Cook County, Illinois, US. **Death:** cause of death: capital punishment, executed by electrocution via electric chair at Cook County Jail, Chicago, Cook County, Illinois, US.

Active in: United States

Roy Lewis Norris

Tool Box Killers

BIRTH: 02-02-1948 | YEARS ACTIVE: 1979 - 1979 | ARRESTED: 11-20-1979 (Age 31)
GENDER: Male | AGES ACTIVE: 30/31 - 30/31 | CONVICTED: 03-18-1980 (Age 32)
ZODIAC: Aquarius | LIFE SPAN: 1948 - | DEATH:

5 VICTIMS

SERIAL KILLER · RAPIST · TORTURER · STALKER · STRANGLER

Active for **1 year** known to have killed at least **5 victims** in **1979**.

previous crimes: ✔ weapon: ✔ gun: ✘ rob: ✘ bound: ✔ strangle: ✔ mutilate: ✘ W M R F

Roy Lewis Norris Roy Lewis Norris and Lawrence Bittaker are American serial killers and rapists known as the Tool Box Killers, who together committed the kidnap, rape, torture and murder of five teenage girls over a period of five months in southern California in 1979. Bittaker and Norris used standard tools such as pliers, ice picks and sledgehammers to torture and murder their victims. Norris accepted a plea bargain whereby he agreed to testify against Bittaker and was sentenced to life imprisonment in 1980, with possibility of parole after serving thirty years. Roy Lewis Norris is currently incarcerated at Richard J. Donovan Correctional Facility.

Sentence: life imprisonment with out the possibility of parole for thirty years at the Richard J. Donovan Correctional Facility in San Diego County, California, US.

Active in: Germany DECEASED

Paul Ogorzow

S-Bahn murderer

BIRTH: 09-29-1912 | YEARS ACTIVE: 1940 - 1941 | ARRESTED: 07-12-1941 (Age 28)
GENDER: Male | AGES ACTIVE: 27/28 - 28/29 | CONVICTED: 07-24-1941 (Age 28)
ZODIAC: Libra | LIFE SPAN: 1912 - 1941 | DEATH: 07-26-1941 (Age 28)

8 VICTIMS

SERIAL KILLER · RAPIST · STRANGLER

Active for **2 years** known to have killed at least **8 victims** between **1940** and **1941**.

previous crimes: ✔ weapon: ✔ gun: ✘ rob: ✘ bound: ✘ strangle: ✔ mutilate: ✘ W

Paul Ogorzow (born Paul Saga) a German serial killer and rapist known as the S-Bahn murderer. Ogorzow was a Sturmabteilung sergeant convicted of raping and murdering eight women by throwing them off trains in Berlin during wartime blackouts in 1941 and 1942. He worked on The Deutsche Reichsbahn, also known as the German National Railway. Most of his victims were married women whose husbands were away serving in the military. Ogorzow was executed by guillotine at the Plötzensee Prison in Berlin, Nazi Germany on July 26th 1941.

Sentence: death by beheading via guillotine at Plötzensee Prison in Charlottenburg-Wilmersdorf, Berlin, Germany. **Death:** cause of death: executed by beheading via guillotine at Plötzensee Prison, in the Charlottenburg-Nord locality of Berlin, Germany.

Active in: Japan

DECEASED

Kiyoshi Okubo

Watanabe Kyoshi, Tanigawa Ivan

BIRTH: 01-17-1935 | YEARS ACTIVE: 1971 - 1971 | ARRESTED: 05-14-1971 (Age 36)
GENDER: Male | AGES ACTIVE: 35/36 - 35/36 | CONVICTED: 02-22-1973 (Age 38)
ZODIAC: Capricorn | LIFE SPAN: 1935 - 1976 | DEATH: 01-22-1976 (Age 41)

8 VICTIMS

SERIAL KILLER RAPIST STRANGLER

Active for **1 year** known to have killed at least **8 victims** in **1971**.

previous crimes: ✓ weapon: ✗ gun: ✗ rob: ✗ bound: ✗ strangle: ✓ mutilate: ✗ W M

Kiyoshi Okubo a Japanese serial killer known as Watanabe Kyoshi and Tanigawa Ivan. Okubo raped and murdered eight women aged 16 to 21 in 1971. He was recently released from prison for previous rape charges. A brother of one of his victims located and turned Okubo's whereabouts to the police, his arrest followed. Kiyoshi Okubo was sentenced to death by hanging and executed in 1976.

Sentence: death by hanging at Kosuge Detention Center in Katsushika, Tokyo, Japan. **Death:** cause of death: capital punishment, executed by hanging at Kosuge Detention Center in Katsushika, Tokyo, Japan.

BIRTH: 01-01-1940 | YEARS ACTIVE: 1980 - 1981 | ARRESTED: 08-12-1981 (Age 41)
GENDER: Male | AGES ACTIVE: 40/40 - 41/41 | CONVICTED: 01-14-1982 (Age 42)
ZODIAC: Capricorn | LIFE SPAN: 1940 - 2011 | DEATH: 09-30-2011 (Age 71)

11 VICTIMS

SERIAL KILLER RAPIST STRANGLER

Active for **2 years** known to have killed at least **11 victims** between **1980** and **1981**.

previous crimes: ✓ weapon: ✓ gun: ✗ rob: ✗ bound: ✗ strangle: ✓ mutilate: ✗ W M R

Clifford Olson (Clifford Robert Olson, Jr.) a Canadian serial killer known as The Beast of British Columbia. Olson confessed to the rape and murder of eleven children and young adults between the ages of 9 and 18 in the early 1980s. Olson was considered a dangerous offender, and the sentencing judge recommended Olson never be released from prison. He had three parole applications, all were rejected. Clifford Olson died of cancer on September 30th 2011 while still in custody.

Sentence: life imprisonment at Kingston Penitentiary, Archambault Institution, a prison in Sainte-Anne-des-Plaines, Québec. **Death:** cause of death: natural causes, terminal cancer at a hospital in Laval, city & region in Québec, Canada.

Active in: United States DECEASED

Carl Panzram

Jefferson Baldwin

BIRTH: 06-28-1892 YEARS ACTIVE: 1920 - 1929 ARRESTED: 08-30-1928 (Age 36)
GENDER: Male AGES ACTIVE: 27/28 - 36/37 CONVICTED: 06-20-1929 (Age 36)
ZODIAC: Cancer LIFE SPAN: 1892 - 1930 DEATH: 09-05-1930 (Age 38)

5-22 VICTIMS

SERIAL KILLER RAPIST TORTURER STRANGLER

Active for **10 years** known to have killed at least **5 victims** between **1920** and **1929**.
previous crimes: ✓ weapon: ✓ gun: ✓ rob: ✓ bound: ✗ strangle: ✓ mutilate: ✗ W M

Carl Panzram an American serial killer known as Jefferson Baldwin along with various other aliases. Panzram was a rapist, arsonist, robber and burglar who from 1920 to 1928 went on a murder spree along the east coast with a previous crime spree in Oregon. Panzram claimed in his autobiography that he committed over twenty-two killings and sodomy of more than a thousand young men. He was executed by hanging in 1930 for the murder of a prison employee at Leavenworth Federal Penitentiary in Leavenworth, Kansas.

Sentence: death by hanging at Leavenworth Federal Penitentiary in Leavenworth, Kansas, US. **Death:** cause of death: capital punishment, executed by hanging at Leavenworth Federal Penitentiary in Leavenworth, Kansas, US.

Active in: United States

Gerald Parker

The Bedroom Basher

BIRTH: YEARS ACTIVE: 1978 - 1979 ARRESTED:
GENDER: Male AGES ACTIVE: - CONVICTED: 02-22-1999
ZODIAC: LIFE SPAN: - DEATH:

5-6 VICTIMS

SERIAL KILLER RAPIST

Active for **2 years** known to have killed at least **5 victims** between **1978** and **1979**.
previous crimes: ✓ weapon: ✓ gun: ✗ rob: ✗ bound: ✗ strangle: ✗ mutilate: ✗ W M

Gerald Parker an American serial killer and rapist known as The Bedroom Basher. Parker raped and murdered five women and killed the unborn baby of a sixth woman in Orange County, California between 1978 and 1979. Parker bludgeoned victims with a 2x4 or a hammer. Parker was identified by DNA evidence in 1996. Kevin Lee Green, the husband of the woman who survived the attack, was wrongfully convicted of murder and spent sixteen years in prison before he was freed in 1996. Parker was already in prison at the time he confessed to the murders. In 1999, Gerald Parker was sentenced to death by lethal injection, plus life without possibility of parole, plus sixty-four years in prison.

Sentence: death by by lethal injection at the San Quentin State Prison in San Quentin, California, US.

Active in: Brazil

Francisco de Assis Pereira

O Maníaco do Parque, The Park Maniac

BIRTH: 11-29-1967 YEARS ACTIVE: 1997 - 1998 ARRESTED: 08-04-1998 (Age 30)
GENDER: Male AGES ACTIVE: 29/30 - 30/31 CONVICTED:
ZODIAC: Sagittarius LIFE SPAN: 1967 - DEATH:

11 VICTIMS

SERIAL KILLER RAPIST TORTURER STRANGLER

Active for **2 years** known to have killed at least **11 victims** between **1997** and **1998**.

previous crimes: ✓ weapon: ✗ gun: ✗ rob: ✗ bound: ✗ strangle: ✓ mutilate: ✗ W M

Francisco de Assis Pereira a Brazilian rapist and serial killer known as O Maníaco do Parque (The Park Maniac). Pereira was arrested for the torture, rape and death of eleven women and for assaulting nine in a park in São Paulo, Brazil during the 1990s. Pereira found his victims by posing as a talent scout for a modeling agency. Francisco de Assis Pereira was arrested in 1998 and sentenced to a total of 268 years in prison. In 2000, Francisco de Assis Pereira was attacked by inmates at the Taubate House of Custody, including fellow serial killer Pedro Rodrigues Filho, tried to kill Pereira during a prison riot.

Sentence: 268 years in prison at Taubaté House of Custody and Psychiatric Treatment in Taubaté, São Paulo, Brazil.

Active in: Canada

Robert Pickton

The Pig Farmer Killer, The Pigheaded Killer, Pork Chop Rob

BIRTH: 10-24-1949 YEARS ACTIVE: 1995 - 2001 ARRESTED: 02-22-2002 (Age 52)
GENDER: Male AGES ACTIVE: 45/46 - 51/52 CONVICTED: 12-09-2007 (Age 58)
ZODIAC: Scorpio LIFE SPAN: 1949 - DEATH:

6-49 VICTIMS

SERIAL KILLER RAPIST TORTURER STRANGLER

Active for **7 years** known to have killed at least **6 victims** between **1995** and **2001**.

previous crimes: ✓ weapon: ✓ gun: ✓ rob: ✗ bound: ✓ strangle: ✓ mutilate: ✓ W M R

Robert Pickton (Robert William "Willy" Pickton) a Canadian serial killer known as The Pig Farmer Killer, The Pigheaded Killer and Pork Chop Rob. Pickton was convicted in 2007 on six counts of second-degree murder. He was accused of murdering twenty other women, mostly prostitutes. In 1997, Pickton was charged with the attempted murder of a prostitute by handcuffing and stabbing her. Pickton was held at Eagle Ridge Hospital after being stabbed by the victim. The charges were dismissed in 1998 due to the victim being unreliable. Pickton claims his total number of victims was forty-nine. On February 22nd 2002 police arrested Robert Pickton at his farm in Port Coquitlam, British Columbia.

Sentence: life imprisonment without the possibility of parole for twenty-five years at North Fraser Pretrial Centre in Port Coquitlam, British Columbia, Canada.

Active in: Czech Republic

DECEASED

Hubert Pilcik

The Beast

BIRTH: 10-14-1981	**YEARS ACTIVE:** 1948 - 1951	**ARRESTED:** 09-01-1951 (Age 30)	5-10 VICTIMS
GENDER: Male	**AGES ACTIVE:** 33/32 - 30/29	**CONVICTED:**	
ZODIAC: Libra	**LIFE SPAN:** 1981 - 1951	**DEATH:** 09-09-1951 (Age 30)	

SERIAL KILLER RAPIST

Active for **4 years** known to have killed at least **5 victims** between **1948** and **1951**.

previous crimes: — weapon: ✓ gun: ✓ rob: ✓ bound: ✓ strangle: ✗ mutilate: ✗ W M

Hubert Pilcik (Hubert Pilcík) a Czech serial killer known as The Beast. Pilcik made money smuggling people across the Czechoslovakia-Germany border, he killed most of his customers. He would beat, rob, rape and shoot his victims. He was known to burn the remains of at least one of his victims. A 12-year-old girl was found belted to a torture structure constructed at Pilcik's home. Authorities found firearms and numerous other items that being to his victims during the search of his home. In 1951, Hubert Pilcik committed suicide in a prison in Plzen, Czech Republic.

Sentence: never sentence committed suicide prior to conviction at the Veznice Plzen, Bory Prison in Pilsen, Czech Republic. **Death:** cause of death: committed suicide by hanging himself in his prison cell at the Veznice Plzen, Bory Prison in Pilsen, Czech Republic.

Active in: Slovenia, Serbia and Montenegro

DECEASED

Silvo Plut

BIRTH: 05-29-1968	**YEARS ACTIVE:** 1990 - 2006	**ARRESTED:** 02-25-2006 (Age 37)	3 VICTIMS
GENDER: Male	**AGES ACTIVE:** 21/22 - 37/38	**CONVICTED:** 10-02-2006 (Age 38)	
ZODIAC: Gemini	**LIFE SPAN:** 1968 - 2007	**DEATH:** 04-28-2007 (Age 38)	

SERIAL KILLER RAPIST

Active for **17 years** known to have killed at least **3 victims** between **1990** and **2006**.

previous crimes: ✓ weapon: ✓ gun: ✗ rob: ✓ bound: ✓ strangle: ✗ mutilate: ✗ W M

Silvo Plut a Slovenian serial killer. After serving thirteen years in prison in Slovenia for a rape and murder, Plut murdered a second woman in Serbia in 2004 and fled back to Slovenia, where a Serbian petition of extradition was turned down by the government. He was then arrested for attacking a couple, the wife died, the husband survived. Plut's cousin Bojan Plut was also a serial killer. Plut was sentenced to thirty years in prison. In 2007, Silvo Plut committed suicide by overdosing on sleeping pills in his Ljubljana prison cell.

Sentence: thirty years in prison at Ljubljana Prison in Ljubljana, Slovenia. **Death:** cause of death: suicide, committed suicide by overdosing on sleeping pills at Ljubljana Prison in Ljubljana, Slovenia.

Active in: Russia

Mikhail Popkov

The Werewolf, The Angarsk maniac

BIRTH: 03-07-1964 YEARS ACTIVE: 1992 - 2010 ARRESTED: 06-23-2012 (Age 48)
GENDER: Male AGES ACTIVE: 27/28 - 45/46 CONVICTED: 12-10-2018 (Age 54)
ZODIAC: Pisces LIFE SPAN: 1964 - DEATH:

78-81
VICTIMS

SERIAL KILLER RAPIST NECROPHILIAC STRANGLER

Active for **19 years** known to have killed at least **78 victims** between **1992** and **2010**.
previous crimes: ✗ weapon: ✓ gun: ✗ rob: ✗ bound: ✗ strangle: ✓ mutilate: ✓ W M

Mikhail Popkov (Mikhail Viktorovich Popkov) a Russian serial killer, former police officer and rapist known as The Werewolf and the Angarsk maniac. Popkov sexually assaulted and murdered numerous young women between 1992 and 2010. He was convicted of twenty-two murders in 2015 and confessed to fifty-nine additional homicides three years later. He killed and mutilated his victims, while dressed in his police uniform, with weapons including knives, axes, baseball bats and screwdrivers. Popkov contracted syphilis while raping one of his victims. On December 10th 2018, Popkov was convicted of fifty-six additional murders in the regional court of Irkutsk in Siberia.

Sentence: life imprisonment at a prison in Russia.

Active in: United Kingdom

Stephen John Port

The Grindr Killer

BIRTH: 02-22-1975 YEARS ACTIVE: 2014 - 2015 ARRESTED: 10-15-2015 (Age 40)
GENDER: Male AGES ACTIVE: 38/39 - 39/40 CONVICTED: 11-25-2016 (Age 41)
ZODIAC: Pisces LIFE SPAN: 1975 - DEATH:

4
VICTIMS

SERIAL KILLER RAPIST

Active for **2 years** known to have killed at least **4 victims** between **2014** and **2015**.
previous crimes: — weapon: ✗ gun: ✗ rob: ✗ bound: ✗ strangle: ✗ mutilate: ✗ W M

Stephen John Port a convicted British serial killer and rapist known as The Grindr Killer. Port met his victims using online dating services including Grindr and spiked their drinks with fatal amounts of the drug GHB to rape them while they were unconscious. He is responsible for murdering at least four men and committing multiple rapes. Port planted a fake suicide note on one of his victims body, the note suggested he was responsible for the death of another victim, and that he had killed himself out of guilt. In 2016, Port received a life sentence with a whole life order. In response to the Port case, authorities announced they are reviewing at least fifty-eight deaths connected to the use of gamma-Hydroxybutyric acid (GHB) in London as far back as 2012.

Sentence: life imprisonment at HM Prison Belmarsh in Thamesmead, London, England.

Active in: United States

Cleophus Prince

The Clairemont Killer

BIRTH: 07-24-1967 YEARS ACTIVE: 1990 - 1990 ARRESTED: 03-03-1991 (Age 23)
GENDER: Male AGES ACTIVE: 22/23 - 22/23 CONVICTED: 07-15-1993 (Age 25)
ZODIAC: Leo LIFE SPAN: 1967 - DEATH:

6 VICTIMS

SERIAL KILLER RAPIST STALKER

Active for **1 year** known to have killed at least **6 victims** in **1990**.

previous crimes: ✓ weapon: ✓ gun: ✗ rob: ✓ bound: ✗ strangle: ✗ mutilate: ✗ W M R

Cleophus Prince (Cleophus Prince Jr.) a serial killer known as The Clairemont Killer. Prince raped and killed six women in San Diego, California in 1990. He was known to have stalked at least one of his victims. He would break into homes to rape, stab and murder his victims, he stole the wedding rings of some of his victims. In 1991, Prince's license plate number was taken down by a potential victims neighbor which led to his arrest, he was released on bail. In 1991, Prince walked into the precinct with his mother and he was taken into custody after authorities requested he come in to fill out additional paperwork. In 1993, Prince was found guilty on all six counts of first-degree murder along with other felony charges and was sentenced to death.

Sentence: death at the San Quentin State Prison in San Quentin, California, US.

Active in: Argentina

Robledo Puch

The Unisex, The Death Angel, The Black Angel

BIRTH: 01-19-1952 YEARS ACTIVE: 1971 - 1971 ARRESTED: 02-04-1972 (Age 20)
GENDER: Male AGES ACTIVE: 18/19 - 18/19 CONVICTED:
ZODIAC: Capricorn LIFE SPAN: 1952 - DEATH:

11 VICTIMS

SERIAL KILLER RAPIST STRANGLER

Active for **1 year** known to have killed at least **11 victims** in **1971**.

previous crimes: — weapon: ✓ gun: ✓ rob: ✓ bound: ✗ strangle: ✓ mutilate: ✓ W M

Robledo Puch (Carlos Eduardo Robledo Puch) an Argentine serial killer known as the Unisex, the Death Angel and The Black Angel. Puch was convicted of eleven murders and multiple other crimes including attempted murder and sexual assault. He was arrested in 1972 and sentenced to life imprisonment in 1980. Robledo Puch is serving his sentence at the high-security prison of Sierra Chica, near the city of Olavarria, Buenos Aires, Argentina since 1973.

Sentence: life imprisonment at the high-security prison of Sierra Chica near the city of Olavarria in Buenos Aires, Argentina..

Active in: China DECEASED

Wang Qiang

super killer, No. 54

BIRTH: 01-16-1975 **YEARS ACTIVE:** 1995 - 2003 **ARRESTED:** 07-14-2003 (Age 28)
GENDER: Male **AGES ACTIVE:** 19/20 - 27/28 **CONVICTED:** 03-23-2005 (Age 30)
ZODIAC: Capricorn **LIFE SPAN:** 1975 - 2005 **DEATH:** 11-17-2005 (Age 30)

45 VICTIMS

SERIAL KILLER RAPIST NECROPHILIAC

Active for **9 years** known to have killed at least **45 victims** between **1995** and **2003**.
previous crimes: ✓ weapon: ✓ gun: ✗ rob: ✓ bound: ✗ strangle: ✗ mutilate: ✗ W

Wang Qiang a Chinese serial killer, rapist and necrophile known as the super killer and No. 54. He killed forty-five and raped ten from 1995 to 2003 in Budayuan Town, Kuandian County, Liaoning Province, China. Wang Qiang would rob, beat and rape, some post-mortem, his victims. Dadong Public Security Bureau concluded that the various features of Wang Qiang were very similar to those of "No. 54" criminal suspect "super killer". Wang Qiang was arrested by the Shenyang police in 2003, after interrogation, he confessed to murder, rape, robbery and other various crimes. Wang Qiang was sentenced to death and executed in 2005.

Sentence: death by gunshot to the head at Shenyang China. **Death:** cause of death: capital punishment, executed by gunshot to the head at China.

Active in: France DECEASED

Gilles de Rais

Baron de Rais, Bluebeard, Barbe bleue

BIRTH: **YEARS ACTIVE:** 1420 - 1435 **ARRESTED:** 09-15-1440
GENDER: Male **AGES ACTIVE:** - **CONVICTED:** 10-25-1440
ZODIAC: **LIFE SPAN:** - 1440 **DEATH:** 10-26-1440

80-200 VICTIMS

SERIAL KILLER RAPIST TORTURER

Active for **16 years** known to have killed at least **80 victims** between **1420** and **1435**.
previous crimes: ✓ weapon: ✓ gun: ✗ rob: ✗ bound: ✓ strangle: ✗ mutilate: ✓ W

Gilles de Rais (Gilles de Montmorency-Laval) an Breton nobleman and serial killer known as Baron de Rais and Barbe bleue (bluebeard). Rais confessed to an uncertain number of murders, estimates are between eighty and two-hundred. His victims were all children that were sodomized prior to death. Gilles de Rais is believed to be the inspiration for the 1697 fairy tale Bluebeard by Charles Perrault.

Sentence: death by hanging while being burnt alive at a prison on the Island of Nantes in Nantes, France. **Death:** cause of death: capital punishment, executed by hanging while being burnt alive at a prison on the Island of Nantes in Nantes, France.

Active in: United States

DECEASED

Richard Ramirez

The Night Stalker

BIRTH: 02-29-1960 YEARS ACTIVE: 1984 - 1985 ARRESTED: 08-31-1985 (Age 25)
GENDER: Male AGES ACTIVE: 23/24 - 24/25 CONVICTED: 09-20-1989 (Age 29)
ZODIAC: Pisces LIFE SPAN: 1960 - 2013 DEATH: 06-07-2013 (Age 53)

13-20 VICTIMS

SERIAL KILLER RAPIST TORTURER STALKER STRANGLER

Active for **2 years** known to have killed at least **13 victims** between **1984** and **1985**.
previous crimes: ✓ weapon: ✓ gun: ✓ rob: ✓ bound: ✓ strangle: ✓ mutilate: ✓ W M R

Richard Ramirez (Ricardo Leyva Muñoz Ramírez) an American serial killer, burglar and rapist known as the Night Stalker. Ramirez killed thirteen people between 1984 and 1985, in Los Angeles, California. Ramirez used a wide variety of weapons, including handguns, knives, a machete, a tire iron, and a hammer. Richard Ramirez was captured as a crowd of bystanders surrounded him, beat him, and held him until police arrived to arrest him. Ramirez was sentenced to death in 1989, and died of natural causes (complications due to B-cell lymphoma) on June 7th 2013 while still on death row at San Quentin State Prison.
Sentence: death by gas chamber at San Quentin State Prison in San Quentin, California, US. **Death:** cause of death: natural causes, B-cell lymphoma at Marin General Hospital in Greenbrae, California, US.

Active in: South Africa

DECEASED

David Randitsheni

the Modimolle Child Rapist

BIRTH: YEARS ACTIVE: 2004 - 2008 ARRESTED: 05-16-2008
GENDER: Male AGES ACTIVE: - CONVICTED: 08-18-2009
ZODIAC: LIFE SPAN: - 2009 DEATH: 08-30-2009

10 VICTIMS

SERIAL KILLER RAPIST

Active for **5 years** known to have killed at least **10 victims** between **2004** and **2008**.
previous crimes: — weapon: — gun: — rob: — bound: — strangle: — mutilate: ✗ W M

David Randitsheni an African serial killer known as the Modimolle Child Rapist. Randitsheni was arrested in 2008 after a police investigation where over 550 DNA samples were tested before forensic experts identified Randitsheni. He was charged and convicted of kidnapping nineteen, raping seventeen, and the murder of ten people. Sentenced to sixteen consecutive life sentences plus 220 years in prison. In 2009, Randitsheni was found dead hanging by a sheet from a window frame in the Thohoyandou prison.
Sentence: sixteen life sentences plus 220 years imprisonment thirty-five years till parole at Thohoyandou prison, Modimolle, Limpopo South African. **Death:** cause of death: committed suicide by hanging himself in his cell at Thohoyandou prison, Modimolle, Limpopo South African.

Active in: India

Umesh Reddy

Rajulu, Ramesh, Venkatesh, Hrishikesh Malagi

BIRTH: YEARS ACTIVE: 1996 - 2002 ARRESTED: 05-17-2002

GENDER: Male AGES ACTIVE: - CONVICTED: 10-26-2006

ZODIAC: LIFE SPAN: - DEATH:

18 VICTIMS

SERIAL KILLER RAPIST

Active for **7 years** known to have killed at least **18 victims** between **1996** and **2002**.

previous crimes: ✓ weapon: ✓ gun: ✗ rob: ✓ bound: ✓ strangle: ✗ mutilate: ✗ W M

Umesh Reddy (born BA Umesh) a Indian serial killer known as Rajulu, Ramesh, Venkatesh, and Hrishikesh Malagi. Reddy confessed to eighteen rapes and murders. Reddy was sentenced to death by the Supreme Court of India, and is currently on death row. Reddy carefully selected his victims, targeting housewives, threatening them with a knife to undress so he could bound and rape them. He often choked his victims, and raped them while they were unconscious. He was known to take at least one victim's undergarments. Reddy was reported to like wearing women's lingerie under his clothes. In 2006, Umesh Reddy was sentenced to death and is currently on death row.

Sentence: death at a prison in India.

Active in: United States DECEASED

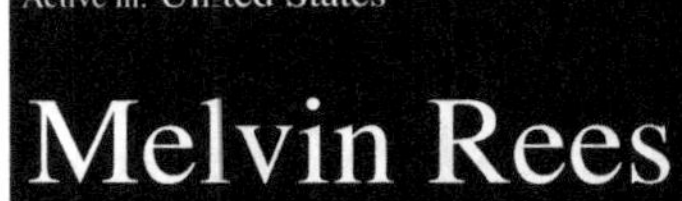

Melvin Rees

The Sex Beast

BIRTH: YEARS ACTIVE: 1957 - 1959 ARRESTED: 06-24-1960

GENDER: Male AGES ACTIVE: - CONVICTED: 02-28-1961

ZODIAC: LIFE SPAN: - 1995 DEATH: 07-10-1995

5-9 VICTIMS

SERIAL KILLER RAPIST TORTURER STRANGLER

Active for **3 years** known to have killed at least **5 victims** between **1957** and **1959**.

previous crimes: ✓ weapon: ✓ gun: ✓ rob: ✗ bound: ✗ strangle: ✓ mutilate: ✗ W M

Melvin Rees (Melvin David Rees Jr.) an American serial killer known as The Sex Beast. Rees shot and defiled a woman in 1957, he tortured and murdered a family of four in 1959 and is suspected in four other killings. Rees would beat, rape, suffocate, strangle, torture, and shoot his victims. In 1960, the FBI arrested and charged Melvin Rees with unlawful flight to avoid prosecution of a murder in Maryland. At the time of his arrest he was living with a woman who was a nightclub stripper and working at a music store in West Memphis, Arkansas. In 1961, Rees was sentenced to life in prison in Maryland, sentenced to death in Virginia in 1961. His death sentence was commuted to life in prison in 1972. Melvin Rees died in prison in 1995.

Sentence: death commuted to life in prison at an unnamed prison in Maryland, US. **Death:** cause of death: heart attack at a federal facility in Missouri, US.

Active in: United States, Mexico DECEASED

Angel Maturino Resendiz

The Railroad Killer

BIRTH: 08-01-1959	YEARS ACTIVE: 1986 - 1999	ARRESTED:	15-18 VICTIMS
GENDER: Male	AGES ACTIVE: 26/27 - 39/40	CONVICTED: 05-18-2000 (Age 40)	
ZODIAC: Leo	LIFE SPAN: 1959 - 2006	DEATH: 06-27-2006 (Age 46)	

SERIAL KILLER RAPIST STRANGLER

Active for **14 years** known to have killed at least **15 victims** between **1986** and **1999**.
previous crimes: ✓ weapon: ✓ gun: ✓ rob: ✓ bound: ✓ strangle: ✓ mutilate: ✗ W M

Angel Maturino Resendiz (born Ángel Leoncio Reyes Recendis) a Mexican serial killer known as the Railroad Killer because his killings were committed near the railroad tracks he used to traverse the country. He was charged with and confessed to fifteen murders occurring from 1986 to 1999 in Texas, Florida, Illinois, Georgia, and Kentucky. He was also suspected in a 1997 California murder case and claimed two additional killings he refused to elaborate on. His mother, Virginia de Maturino, says the real spelling of his surname is Recendis, not Resendez. Other nicknames: The Railway Killer and The Railcar Killer.

Sentence: execution by lethal injection at Texas State Penitentiary in Huntsville, Texas, US. **Death:** cause of death: capital punishment, executed by lethal injection at Texas State Penitentiary in Huntsville, Texas, US.

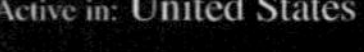

Active in: United States

Robert Ben Rhoades

The Truck Stop Killer

BIRTH: 11-22-1945	YEARS ACTIVE: 1975 - 1990	ARRESTED: 04-01-1990 (Age 44)	3-50 VICTIMS
GENDER: Male	AGES ACTIVE: 29/30 - 44/45	CONVICTED: 09-11-1992 (Age 46)	
ZODIAC: Scorpio	LIFE SPAN: 1945 -	DEATH:	

SERIAL KILLER RAPIST TORTURER STRANGLER

Active for **16 years** known to have killed at least **3 victims** between **1975** and **1990**.
previous crimes: ✓ weapon: ✓ gun: ✓ rob: ✗ bound: ✓ strangle: ✓ mutilate: ✗ W M R

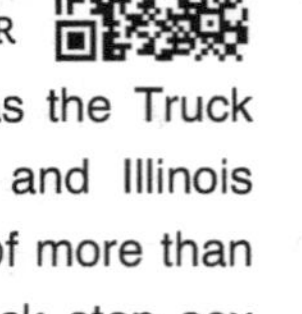

Robert Ben Rhoades an American serial killer and rapist who was known as the Truck Stop Killer. Rhoades was convicted of murdering three women in Texas and Illinois between 1989 and 1990. He is suspected of the torture, rape and the murder of more than fifty women between 1975 and 1990. He would target on hitchhikers and truck stop sex workers. He was known to take photos of some of his victims, he strangled at least one and shot at least one victim. In 1990, Rhodes was arrested in Arizona for the assault, rape, and unlawful imprisonment of an intended victim, the victim survived. In 1992, Rhoades was convicted of first degree murder and sentenced to life without parole at the Menard Correctional Center in Chester, Illinois.

Sentence: life imprisonment without the possibility of parole at the Menard Correctional Center in Chester, Illinois, US.

Active in: United States

Gary Ridgway

The Green River Killer, The Riverman

BIRTH: 02-18-1949 | YEARS ACTIVE: 1982 - 2000 | ARRESTED: 11-30-2001 (Age 52)
GENDER: Male | AGES ACTIVE: 32/33 - 50/51 | CONVICTED: 11-05-2003 (Age 54)
ZODIAC: Aquarius | LIFE SPAN: 1949 - | DEATH:

49-90 VICTIMS

SERIAL KILLER | RAPIST | NECROPHILIAC | STRANGLER

Active for **19 years** known to have killed at least **49 victims** between **1982** and **2000**.

previous crimes: ✓ weapon: ✗ gun: ✗ rob: ✓ bound: ✗ strangle: ✓ mutilate: ✗ W M R

Gary Ridgway (Gary Leon Ridgway) an American serial killer known as The Green River Killer and The Riverman. Ridgway began murdering women in 1982 and was arrested in 2001 when a DNA test revealed a match. He targeted sex workers along Route 99 in south King County, Washington. Ridgway didn't smoke or chew gum, yet he left cigarette butts and gum wrappers near his victims' bodies as confusing clues. Ridgway was suspected of killing over ninety victims, confessed to seventy-one and was convicted of forty-nine. Ridgway was one of six killers (Jerome Jerry Brudos, Ted Bundy, Ed Gein, Gary M. Heidnik, Edmund Kemper and Ridgway) who served as an inspiration for the character of Buffalo Bill in Thomas Harris' 1988 novel The Silence of the Lambs and its film adaptation..

Sentence: life imprisonment, forty-eight life terms plus 480 years at Washington State Penitentiary in Walla Walla, Washington.

Active in: United States

Montie Rissell

Monte

BIRTH: | YEARS ACTIVE: 1976 - 1977 | ARRESTED: 05-18-1977
GENDER: Male | AGES ACTIVE: - | CONVICTED:
ZODIAC: | LIFE SPAN: - | DEATH:

5 VICTIMS

SERIAL KILLER | RAPIST | STRANGLER

Active for **2 years** known to have killed at least **5 victims** between **1976** and **1977**.

previous crimes: ✓ weapon: ✓ gun: ✗ rob: ✓ bound: ✗ strangle: ✓ mutilate: ✗ W M

Montie Rissell (Montie Ralph Rissell) an American serial killer and rapist known as Monte. Rissell raped and murdered five women between 1976 and 1977 in Alexandria, Virginia. He was arrested at fourteen-years-old for the rape and robbery of one of his neighbors, who he attacked at knife point while wearing a mask. Before his nineteenth birthday he had committed and been arrested for the five murders. Rissell was diagnosed with multiple personality disorder and institutionalized prior to adulthood. Rissell stabbed one of his victims more than 100 times and drowned another victim to death. Montie Rissell was sentenced to five life sentences in 1978.

Sentence: life imprisonment, five terms at the Pocahontas State Correctional Center in Pocahontas, Virginia, US.

Active in: United States

John Edward Robinson

The Slavemaster

BIRTH: 12-27-1943 YEARS ACTIVE: 1984 - 2000 ARRESTED: 06-02-2000 (Age 56)
GENDER: Male AGES ACTIVE: 40/41 - 56/57 CONVICTED: 01-21-2003 (Age 59)
ZODIAC: Capricorn LIFE SPAN: 1943 - DEATH:

8 VICTIMS

SERIAL KILLER RAPIST TORTURER

Active for **17 years** known to have killed at least **8 victims** between **1984** and **2000**.
previous crimes: ✓ weapon: ✓ gun: ✗ rob: ✓ bound: ✓ strangle: ✗ mutilate: ✗ W M R

John Edward Robinson (John Edward Robinson Sr.) an American serial killer known as The Slavemaster. Robinson lured his victims through the internet via BDSM online chat rooms. In 1969, Robinson was arrested for the first time in Kansas City after embezzling money from a medical practice. From 1970 to 1979 he had several other charges including embezzlement, check forgery and mail fraud. In 2000, Robinson was arrested after a woman filed a sexual battery complaint against him. He was found guilty of three murders and admitted responsibility for five additional murders. Robinson currently remains on death row at the El Dorado Correctional Facility in El Dorado, Kansas.

Sentence: death at El Dorado Correctional Facility, El Dorado, Kansas, US.

Active in: United States

Harvey Miguel Robinson

BIRTH: 12-06-1974 YEARS ACTIVE: 1992 - 1993 ARRESTED: 07-31-1993 (Age 18)
GENDER: Male AGES ACTIVE: 17/18 - 18/19 CONVICTED: 11-10-1994 (Age 19)
ZODIAC: Sagittarius LIFE SPAN: 1974 - DEATH:

3 VICTIMS

SERIAL KILLER RAPIST STALKER STRANGLER

Active for **2 years** known to have killed at least **3 victims** between **1992** and **1993**.
previous crimes: ✓ weapon: ✓ gun: ✓ rob: ✓ bound: ✗ strangle: ✓ mutilate: ✗ W M

Harvey Miguel Robinson (Harvey Miguelito Robinson) an American serial killer. Robinson stalked, raped and killed three women in Allentown, Pennsylvania in 1992 and 1993. He was seventeen years old when the crimes took place and eighteen when he was apprehended. Harvey Robinson was arrested when he sought medical attention at a hospital after a shoot-out with the police.

Sentence: one death sentence, two terms of life imprisonment at State Correctional Institution, SCI Phoenix in Skippack Township, Montgomery County, Pennsylvania.

Active in: United States

Jose Rodriguez

BIRTH: 01-19-1972 **YEARS ACTIVE:** 2018 - 2018 **ARRESTED:** 07-17-2018 (Age 46)
GENDER: Male **AGES ACTIVE:** 45/46 - 45/46 **CONVICTED:**
ZODIAC: Capricorn **LIFE SPAN:** 1972 - **DEATH:**

3 VICTIMS

SERIAL KILLER RAPIST

Active for **1 year** known to have killed at least **3 victims** in **2018**.
previous crimes: ✓ weapon: ✓ gun: ✓ rob: ✓ bound: ✓ strangle: ✗ mutilate: ✓

Jose Rodriguez (Jose Gilberto Rodriguez) a suspected American serial killer who has been charged with three counts of capital murder and is being held without bond. Rodriguez, a registered sex offender who was on parole, he allegedly clipped off his ankle monitor around July 5th 2018, resulting in a motion to revoke parole. Harris County Sheriff deputy Jorge Reyes arrested Rodriguez on July 17th 2018 in connection with revoking parole and killing at least three people in four days starting on July 9th 2018. Rodriguez's previous convictions include attempted aggravated sexual assault of a 16-year-old girl, auto theft and criminal trespassing. He was just released from prison in 2017, due to a mandatory release date. Rodriguez is due back in court on June 11th 2019..

Sentence: awaiting trial at the Harris County Jail, Houston, Texas, US.

Active in: United States

Dayton Leroy Rogers

Molalla Forest Murderer

BIRTH: 09-30-1953 **YEARS ACTIVE:** 1983 - 1987 **ARRESTED:** 08-07-1987 (Age 33)
GENDER: Male **AGES ACTIVE:** 29/30 - 33/34 **CONVICTED:** 06-09-1989 (Age 35)
ZODIAC: Libra **LIFE SPAN:** 1953 - **DEATH:**

7-8 VICTIMS

SERIAL KILLER RAPIST TORTURER

Active for **5 years** known to have killed at least **7 victims** between **1983** and **1987**.
previous crimes: ✓ weapon: ✓ gun: ✗ rob: ✗ bound: ✓ strangle: ✗ mutilate: ✗ W M

Dayton Leroy Rogers an American serial killer known as the Molalla Forest Murderer. Rogers killed street women, usually addicts, prostitutes and runaways. He picked up prostitutes and took them to secluded areas. He would bound, torture, rape, and murder his victims, leaving the bodies in a forest outside Molalla, Oregon. Authorities found the fingerprint of one of his victims on the door handle of his vehicle. Blood and numerous knife marks were found inside the cab of his vehicle. Rogers was original convicted in 1988, he has received multiple death sentences. He was sentenced to death for the fourth time in 2015. Dayton Leroy Rogers is currently on death row at the Oregon State Penitentiary in Salem, Oregon.

Sentence: death at the Oregon State Penitentiary in Salem, Oregon, US.

Active in: United States

Glen Edward Rogers

The Cross Country Killer, The Casanova Killer

BIRTH: 07-15-1962 YEARS ACTIVE: 1993 - 1995 ARRESTED: 11-13-1995 (Age 33)
GENDER: Male AGES ACTIVE: 30/31 - 32/33 CONVICTED: 07-11-1997 (Age 34)
ZODIAC: Cancer LIFE SPAN: 1962 - DEATH:

2-3 VICTIMS

SERIAL KILLER RAPIST STRANGLER

Active for **3 years** known to have killed at least **2 victims** between **1993** and **1995**.
previous crimes: ✓ weapon: ✓ gun: ✗ rob: ✓ bound: ✓ strangle: ✓ mutilate: ✗ W M R

Glen Edward Rogers an American serial killer known as The Cross Country Killer and The Casanova Killer. Rogers was convicted of two murders and is a suspect in numerous others throughout the United States. Rogers has not been charged, but was a possible alternative suspect in the O.J. Simpson case regarding the murders of Nicole Brown Simpson and Ronald Goldman. He was featured on the FBI Ten Most Wanted Fugitives list after a crime spree that began on September 28th 1995. In 1997, Glen Edward Rogers was sentenced to death in Florida. In 1999, Rogers received a second death sentence in California.

Sentence: death at The Union Correctional Institution, Florida State Prison, Raiford Prison in Raiford, Florida, US.

Active in: United States DECEASED

Danny Rolling

Gainesville Ripper

BIRTH: 05-26-1954 YEARS ACTIVE: 1989 - 1990 ARRESTED: 09-08-1990 (Age 36)
GENDER: Male AGES ACTIVE: 34/35 - 35/36 CONVICTED: 04-20-1994 (Age 39)
ZODIAC: Gemini LIFE SPAN: 1954 - 2006 DEATH: 10-25-2006 (Age 52)

5-8 VICTIMS

SERIAL KILLER RAPIST NECROPHILIAC

Active for **2 years** known to have killed at least **5 victims** between **1989** and **1990**.
previous crimes: ✓ weapon: ✓ gun: ✗ rob: ✓ bound: ✓ strangle: ✗ mutilate: ✓ W M R

Danny Rolling (Danny Harold Rolling) an American serial killer known as the Gainesville Ripper. Rolling murdered five students in 1990. In 1990, Rolling attempted to kill his father during a family argument in which his father lost an eye and an ear. He was executed by lethal injection in 2006. Shortly before his execution, he gave a handwritten confession to authorities for the triple homicide of an elderly man, his daughter, and grandson that occurred years earlier in Rolling's hometown of Shreveport, Louisiana. Rolling was never officially charged or extradited to Louisiana to stand trial for the Grissom Murders, Shreveport Police had confirmed even before the confession that Rolling had long been considered the lone suspect and the case was closed.

Sentence: death by by lethal injection at the Florida State Prison in Raiford, Florida, US. **Death:** cause of death: capital punishment, executed by lethal injection at the Florida State Prison in Raiford, Florida, US.

Active in: United States DECEASED

Michael Bruce Ross

The Roadside Strangler

BIRTH: 07-26-1959 YEARS ACTIVE: 1981 - 1984 ARRESTED: 06-29-1984 (Age 24)

GENDER: Male AGES ACTIVE: 21/22 - 24/25 CONVICTED: 07-06-1987 (Age 27)

ZODIAC: Leo LIFE SPAN: 1959 - 2005 DEATH: 05-13-2005 (Age 45)

8 VICTIMS

SERIAL KILLER RAPIST TORTURER STALKER STRANGLER

Active for **4 years** known to have killed at least **8 victims** between **1981** and **1984**.

previous crimes: ✓ weapon: ✓ gun: ✗ rob: ✗ bound: ✓ strangle: ✓ mutilate: ✗ W M

Michael Bruce Ross an American serial killer known as The Roadside Strangler. Ross murdered at least eight girls and women aged between 14 and 25 in Connecticut and New York. Ross confessed to all of the murders, and was convicted of four of them. He raped seven out of his eight murder victims. Michael Bruce Ross was executed by the state of Connecticut on May 13th 2005 by lethal injection, making it the first execution in Connecticut and the whole of New England since 1960.

Sentence: death by by lethal injection at Osborn Correctional Institution in Somers, Connecticut, US.

Death: cause of death: capital punishment, executed by lethal injection at Osborn Correctional Institution in Somers, Connecticut, US.

Active in: United States

Paul Rowles

disappearance of Tiffany Sessions

BIRTH: 04-28-1948 YEARS ACTIVE: 1972 - 1992 ARRESTED:

GENDER: Male AGES ACTIVE: 23/24 - 43/44 CONVICTED: 07-13-1994 (Age 46)

ZODIAC: Taurus LIFE SPAN: 1948 - DEATH:

2-3 VICTIMS

SERIAL KILLER RAPIST STRANGLER

Active for **21 years** known to have killed at least **2 victims** between **1972** and **1992**.

previous crimes: ✓ weapon: ✓ gun: ✗ rob: ✗ bound: ✓ strangle: ✓ mutilate: ✗ W M

Paul Rowles (Paul Eugene Rowles) an American serial killer known as the prime suspect in the disappearance of Tiffany Sessions. Tiffany Sessions is a missing person from Tampa, Florida, who was last seen on February 9, 1989. As of 2014, police believed that Rowles was responsible for Sessions' disappearance and murder. In 1976, Rowles was sentenced to life in prison, he was later released in 1985. In 1994, Rowles was sentenced to nineteen years in prison for the kidnapping and sexual assault of a Clearwater girl. In 2013, Paul Rowles died from complications with lung cancer while still in prison.

Sentence: nineteen years in prison at the Dade Correctional Institution in Florida City, Florida, US.

Active in: China

DECEASED

Gong Runbo

BIRTH: YEARS ACTIVE: 2005 - 2006 ARRESTED: 02-28-2006
GENDER: Male AGES ACTIVE: - CONVICTED: 12-20-2006
ZODIAC: LIFE SPAN: - 2018 DEATH: 12-31-2018

6-20
VICTIMS

SERIAL KILLER RAPIST NECROPHILIAC

Active for **2 years** known to have killed at least **6 victims** between **2005** and **2006**.
previous crimes: ✓ weapon: ✗ gun: ✗ rob: ✗ bound: — strangle: — mutilate: ✓ W M

Gong Runbo a Chinese serial killer and rapist. Runbo murdered of six children in Jiamusi, China aged between 9 and 16 from 2005 to 2006. He also lured and molested five others aged 12 and 13 in the same area. In 2006, Runbo was arrested after a boy escaped his sexual assault in Jiamusi. The young boy alerted authorities leading them back to the house where remains were found rotting on Gong's bed. The remains were later identified as four missing children. DNA revealed at least two other victims besides the four boys identified. Forensic evidence led police to believe he may have killed over twenty victims. Gong Runbo was executed by firing squad in 2007.

Sentence: death by gunshot to the head at a prison in Heilongjiang Province, China. **Death:** cause of death: capital punishment, executed by gunshot to the head at a prison in Heilongjiang Province, China.

Active in: Russia

DECEASED

Sergei Ryakhovsky

the Balashikha Ripper, The Hippopotamus

BIRTH: 12-29-1962 YEARS ACTIVE: 1988 - 1993 ARRESTED: 04-13-1993 (Age 30)
GENDER: Male AGES ACTIVE: 25/26 - 30/31 CONVICTED:
ZODIAC: Capricorn LIFE SPAN: 1962 - 2005 DEATH: 01-21-2005 (Age 42)

19
VICTIMS

SERIAL KILLER RAPIST NECROPHILIAC TORTURER STRANGLER

Active for **6 years** known to have killed at least **19 victims** between **1988** and **1993**.
previous crimes: ✓ weapon: ✓ gun: ✗ rob: ✓ bound: ✗ strangle: ✓ mutilate: ✓ W M

Sergei Ryakhovsky (Sergei Vasilyevich Ryakhovsky) a Soviet-Russian serial killer known as the Balashikha Ripper and The Hippopotamus. Ryakhovsky was convicted for the killing of nineteen people in the Moscow area between 1988 and 1993. Ryakhovsky's mainly stabbed or strangulated his victims, he mutilated some bodies, mainly in the genital area. Allegedly Ryakhovsky carried out necrophilic acts on his victims and stole their belongings. Ryakhovsky standing 6'5" tall and weighting 286 pounds, gaining him the nickname, The Hippo. Sergei Ryakhovsky died on January 21st 2005 from untreated tuberculosis while serving his life sentence in prison.

Sentence: death by firing squad at a maximum-security penal colony in Solikamsk, Perm Oblast, Russia. **Death:** cause of death: natural causes, untreated tuberculosis at a maximum-security penal colony in Solikamsk, Perm Oblast, Russia.

Active in: France

Issei Sagawa

Pang, The Cannibal Celebrity

BIRTH: 04-26-1949 YEARS ACTIVE: 1981 - 1981 ARRESTED: 06-13-1981 (Age 32)
GENDER: Male AGES ACTIVE: 31/32 - 31/32 CONVICTED:
ZODIAC: Taurus LIFE SPAN: 1949 - DEATH:

1 VICTIMS

SERIAL KILLER RAPIST CANNIBAL NECROPHILIAC

Active for **1 year** known to have killed at least **1 victims** in **1981**.
previous crimes: ✓ weapon: ✓ gun: ✓ rob: ✗ bound: ✗ strangle: ✗ mutilate: ✓ W M

Issei Sagawa a Japanese cannibal known as Pang and The Cannibal Celebrity. In 1981, Sagawa invited a female classmate at the Sorbonne Academy in Paris, France to dinner at his apartment under the pretense of literary conversation. Sagawa shot her in the neck, fainting after the shock of shooting her. He awoke and cannibalized her body, after having sex with the corpse. Sagawa then attempted to dump the mutilated body in a remote lake, but was seen in the act and later arrested by the French police. Sagawa was extradited to Japan where he was released due to missing papers from the French court. As a result, Sagawa checked himself out of the mental institution in 1986, and has been a free man ever since.

Sentence: never sentenced: unfit to stand trial by reason of insanity at a mental institution in Japan, Sagawa checked himself out in 1986.

Active in: United States

Altemio Sanchez

Bike Path Rapist, Bike Path Killer

BIRTH: 01-19-1958 YEARS ACTIVE: 1981 - 2006 ARRESTED: 01-15-2007 (Age 48)
GENDER: Male AGES ACTIVE: 22/23 - 47/48 CONVICTED: 08-15-2007 (Age 49)
ZODIAC: Capricorn LIFE SPAN: 1958 - DEATH:

3 VICTIMS

SERIAL KILLER RAPIST STRANGLER

Active for **26 years** known to have killed at least **3 victims** between **1981** and **2006**.
previous crimes: ✓ weapon: ✓ gun: ✗ rob: ✗ bound: ✗ strangle: ✓ mutilate: ✗ W M R

Altemio Sanchez (Altemio C. Sanchez) an American serial killer known as the Bike Path Rapist and the Bike Path Killer. Sanchez murdered three women and raped at least fourteen others in the Buffalo, New York area between 1981 and 2006. He would beat and raped his victims before using a ligature, wire, or garrote, to strangle and suffocate victims. In 1987, Anthony Capozzi was wrongly convicted of two rapes later linked to Sanchez. In 2007, Capozzi was release from prison after serving twenty-two years. Authorities found DNA evidence at eight crime scenes that matched Sanchez's DNA. In 2007, Altemio Sanchez was sentenced to seventy-five years in prison without the possibility of parole at the Clinton Correctional Facility in Dannemora, New York.

Sentence: seventy-five years in prison at the Clinton Correctional Facility in Dannemora, New York, US.

Active in: India

Satish

Bahadurgarh baby killer

BIRTH: | **YEARS ACTIVE:** 1995 - 1998 | **ARRESTED:** 11-20-1998

GENDER: Male | **AGES ACTIVE:** - | **CONVICTED:** 12-22-1998

ZODIAC: | **LIFE SPAN:** - | **DEATH:**

10 VICTIMS

SERIAL KILLER | RAPIST | STRANGLER

Active for **4 years** known to have killed at least **10 victims** between **1995** and **1998**.

previous crimes: — weapon: ✗ gun: ✗ rob: ✗ bound: ✗ strangle: ✓ mutilate: ✗ W

Satish a Indian serial killer and pedophile rapist known as the Bahadurgarh baby killer. Satish was described as a mentally deranged sex pervert. He raped, cut throats, stabbed and left victims lying to die. He was convicted of the rape and attempted rape of twelve young girls, ten of whom he killed. His victims were between the ages of 5 and 9 years old. Raj Kumar, Ram Babu and Shankar Kumar were all previously prosecuted as the Bahadurgarh baby killer, but the murders did not stop. Satish was captured in 1998, when his last victim, 6-year-old Somani led the police to him after being raped twice by Satish and left for dead in a field. Satish was convicted for twelve sexual assaults and ten murders, sentenced to life imprisonment.

Sentence: life imprisonment at a prison in Haryana, India.

Active in: United States

DECEASED

Charles Schmid

The Pied Piper of Tucson

BIRTH: 07-08-1942 | **YEARS ACTIVE:** 1964 - 1965 | **ARRESTED:** 11-10-1965 (Age 23)

GENDER: Male | **AGES ACTIVE:** 21/22 - 22/23 | **CONVICTED:** 03-01-1966 (Age 23)

ZODIAC: Cancer | **LIFE SPAN:** 1942 - 1975 | **DEATH:** 03-30-1975 (Age 32)

3 VICTIMS

SERIAL KILLER | RAPIST | STRANGLER

Active for **2 years** known to have killed at least **3 victims** between **1964** and **1965**.

previous crimes: ✓ weapon: ✓ gun: ✗ rob: ✗ bound: ✓ strangle: ✓ mutilate: ✗ W M R

Charles Schmid (Charles Howard Schmid Jr.) an American serial killer known as The Pied Piper of Tucson. Schmid murdered three teenage girls in 1964 and 1965 burying their bodies in the desert. He was found guilty of murder and sentenced to death in 1966, commuted to fifty years in prison in 1971. In 1975, Schmid was stabbed by two fellow prisoners at Arizona State Prison, the attack lost Schmid an eye and a kidney. He died on March 30th 1975 at Maricopa County Hospital as a result of wounds suffered in the prison attack.

Sentence: death at Arisona State Prison near Florence, Arisona, US. **Death:** cause of death: capital punishment, multiple stab wounds suffered from an attack by two fellow inmates at Maricopa County Hospital in Phoenix, Arizona, US.

Active in: Germany

Wolfgang Schmidt

Beast of Beelitz, the Pink Giant Beate Schmidt

BIRTH: 10-05-1966 YEARS ACTIVE: 1989 - 1991 ARRESTED: 08-01-1991 (Age 24)
GENDER: Male AGES ACTIVE: 22/23 - 24/25 CONVICTED: 11-30-1992 (Age 26)
ZODIAC: Libra LIFE SPAN 1966 - DEATH:

6 VICTIMS

SERIAL KILLER RAPIST NECROPHILIAC STRANGLER

Active for **3 years** known to have killed at least **6 victims** between **1989** and **1991**.

previous crimes: — weapon: ✓ gun: ✗ rob: ✗ bound: ✗ strangle: ✓ mutilate: ✗ W M

Wolfgang Schmidt a German serial killer known as the Beast of Beelitz, the Pink Giant and Beate Schmidt. Schmidt killed five women and a three-month-old baby from 1989 to 1991. Schmidt legally changed his name to Beate Schmidt in 2001. In 2009, Schmidt underwent a hormone treatment for gender reassignment and is now a trans woman. He was arrested after two joggers found Schmidt masturbating in the woods while wearing a bra. In 1992, Wolfgang Schmidt was sentenced to a fifteen year sentence at a psychiatric hospital in Brandenburg an der Havel, a town in Brandenburg, Germany.

Sentence: fifteen years preventative detention at a psychiatric hospital in Brandenburg an der Havel, a town in Brandenburg, Germany.

Active in: Germany DECEASED

Friedrich Schumann

the Mass Murderer of Falkenhagen Lake, Massenmörder vom Falkenhagener

BIRTH: 02-01-1893 YEARS ACTIVE: 1918 - 1919 ARRESTED: 08-20-1920 (Age 27)
GENDER: Male AGES ACTIVE: 24/25 - 25/26 CONVICTED: 07-13-1920 (Age 27)
ZODIAC: Aquarius LIFE SPAN: 1893 - 1921 DEATH: 08-27-1921 (Age 28)

6 VICTIMS

SERIAL KILLER RAPIST

Active for **2 years** known to have killed at least **6 victims** between **1918** and **1919**.

previous crimes: ✓ weapon: ✓ gun: ✓ rob: ✓ bound: ✗ strangle: ✗ mutilate: ✗ W M

Friedrich Schumann a German serial killer and rapist known as the Massenmörder vom Falkenhagener See (the Mass Murderer of Falkenhagen Lake). Schumann murdered at least six victims in Germany between 1918 and 1919. Schumann would target couples hiking in the Falkenhagener forest near the lake. He would rob and shoot his victims, raping the female victims. Schumann had numerous other charges including multiple charges of rape where the victim was not murdered. In 1921, Schumann was executed by beheading in the courtyard of the Plötzensee Prison by the Prussian executioner Carl Gröpler using an axe.

Sentence: death, decapitation with an axe at Plötzensee Prison, Charlottenburg-Wilmersdorf, Berlin, Germany. **Death:** cause of death: executed by decapitation with an axe at Plötzensee Prison, Charlottenburg-Wilmersdorf, Berlin, Germany.

Active in: United States

DECEASED

Tommy Lynn Sells

The Cross Country Killer

BIRTH: 06-28-1964 YEARS ACTIVE: 1980 - 1999 ARRESTED: 01-02-2000 (Age 35)
GENDER: Male AGES ACTIVE: 15/16 - 34/35 CONVICTED: 09-18-2000 (Age 36)
ZODIAC: Cancer LIFE SPAN: 1964 - 2014 DEATH: 04-03-2014 (Age 49)

3-70 VICTIMS

SERIAL KILLER RAPIST STRANGLER

Active for **20 years** known to have killed at least **3 victims** between **1980** and **1999**.
previous crimes: ✓ weapon: ✓ gun: ✓ rob: ✓ bound: ✗ strangle: ✓ mutilate: ✗ W M R

Tommy Lynn Sells an American serial killer and drifter known as The Cross Country Killer. Sells was active throughout the United States killing children and multiple victims after breaking into their homes. He was arrested when a ten-year-old girl survived his attack and provided his description to the authorities. In 2000, Sells pleaded guilty and was convicted of the capital murder of Kaylene Harris and attempted murder of Krystal Surles. In 2003, Sells was indicted for the 1997 Missouri murder of Stephanie Mahane and pleaded guilty to strangling to death nine-year-old Mary Bea Perez, for which he received a life sentence. In 2014, Tommy Lynn Sells was executed by lethal injection in Texas.

Sentence: death lethal injection at Texas State Penitentiary in Huntsville, Texas, US. **Death:** cause of death: capital punishment, executed by lethal injection at Texas State Penitentiary in Huntsville, Texas, US.

Active in: Afghanistan

DECEASED

Abdullah Shah

Zardads dog

BIRTH: YEARS ACTIVE: 1990 - 2002 ARRESTED: 10-01-2002
GENDER: Male AGES ACTIVE: - CONVICTED: 10-01-2002
ZODIAC: LIFE SPAN: - 2004 DEATH: 04-20-2004

20 VICTIMS

SERIAL KILLER RAPIST

Active for **13 years** known to have killed at least **20 victims** between **1990** and **2002**.
previous crimes: — weapon: — gun: — rob: ✓ bound: — strangle: ✗ mutilate: ✗ W M

Abdullah Shah an Afghan serial killer and rapist known as Zardads dog. Shah killed travelers on the road from Kabul to Jalalabad serving under Zardad Khan, a former Afghan warlord. Shah and Zardad Khan served in the Hezb-i Islami faction of Hekmatyar, although Shah later joined the faction of Abdur Rab Rasoul Sayaf. In 2002, Shah was sentenced to death by a primary court for a series of at least twenty murders, including one of his wives. In 2004, Abdullah Shahwas was executed by a gunshot to the back of the head at the Pul-e-Charkhi prison in Kabul, Afghanistan. Amnesty International protested against the execution claiming Afghanistan avoided basic standards of fairness.

Sentence: death by gunshot to the head at the Pul-e-Charkhi prison in Kabul, Afghanistan. **Death:** cause of death: executed by gunshot to the head at the Pul-e-Charkhi prison in Kabul, Afghanistan.

Active in: United States DECEASED

Arthur Shawcross

Genesee River Killer, Genesee River Strangler

BIRTH: 06-06-1945 YEARS ACTIVE: 1972 - 1989 ARRESTED: 01-05-1990 (Age 44)
GENDER: Male AGES ACTIVE: 26/27 - 43/44 CONVICTED: 12-13-1990 (Age 45)
ZODIAC: Gemini LIFE SPAN 1945 - 2008 DEATH: 11-10-2008 (Age 63)

14 VICTIMS

SERIAL KILLER RAPIST CANNIBAL STRANGLER

Active for **18 years** known to have killed at least **14 victims** between **1972** and **1989**.
previous crimes: ✓ weapon: ✓ gun: ✗ rob: ✗ bound: ✗ strangle: ✓ mutilate: ✓ W M R

Arthur Shawcross (Arthur John Shawcross) an American serial killer known as the Genesee River Killer and the Genesee River Strangler. He was arrested in 1972 for the rape and murder of two children. The charges were pled down to one count of manslaughter and he was released on parole in 1987. Shawcross killed most of his victims from 1988 to 1989 after his parole. He would rape, strangle and beat mostly prostitute victims prior to killing them. Shawcross once claimed to have eaten the vulvas of three victims and the genitals of another. He was also known as The Rochester Strangler and the Monster of the Rivers.

Sentence: life imprisonment without the possibility of parole at Sullivan Correctional Facility in Fallsburg, New York, US. **Death:** cause of death: natural causes, cardiac arrest, heart failure at Albany Medical Center in Albany, New York, US.

Active in: United States DECEASED

Anthony Allen Shore

The Tourniquet Killer

BIRTH: 06-25-1962 YEARS ACTIVE: 1986 - 1995 ARRESTED: 10-24-2003 (Age 41)
GENDER: Male AGES ACTIVE: 23/24 - 32/33 CONVICTED: 10-29-2004 (Age 42)
ZODIAC: Cancer LIFE SPAN: 1962 - 2018 DEATH: 01-18-2018 (Age 55)

4-5 VICTIMS

SERIAL KILLER RAPIST STALKER STRANGLER

Active for **10 years** known to have killed at least **4 victims** between **1986** and **1995**.
previous crimes: ✗ weapon: ✓ gun: ✗ rob: ✗ bound: ✓ strangle: ✓ mutilate: ✗ W M R

Anthony Allen Shore an American serial killer and pedophile rapist known as The Tourniquet Killer. Shore is responsible for the murders of one woman and four young girls. He was convicted of strangling a woman with an unusual ligature in 1992 and confessed to killing three girls including two with the same modus operandi. Shore was also convicted of molesting his two daughters Tiffany and Amber, as a result he was required to provide police with a DNA sample. Detectives pulled Carmen Del Estrada's case from the cold files and tested DNA evidence from underneath Carmen's fingernails. In 2003 the results came back a match to Shore's genetic profile.

Sentence: death penalty at Terrell Unit, Allan B. Polunsky Unit in Livingston, Texas, US. **Death:** cause of death: executed by lethal injection at Texas State Penitentiary at Huntsville, Huntsville Unit in Huntsville, Texas, US.

Active in: United States

DECEASED

Daniel Lee Siebert

Southside Slayer murders

BIRTH: 06-17-1954 YEARS ACTIVE: 1979 - 1986 ARRESTED: 09-04-1986 (Age 32)
GENDER: Male AGES ACTIVE: 24/25 - 31/32 CONVICTED: 03-21-1987 (Age 32)
ZODIAC: Gemini LIFE SPAN: 1954 - 2008 DEATH: 04-22-2008 (Age 53)

10-13 VICTIMS

SERIAL KILLER RAPIST STRANGLER

Active for **8 years** known to have killed at least **10 victims** between **1979** and **1986**.
previous crimes: ✓ weapon: ✓ gun: ✗ rob: ✓ bound: ✗ strangle: ✓ mutilate: ✗ W M

Daniel Lee Siebert an American serial killer and rapist known for commiting at least one of the Southside Slayer murders. Siebert killed ten victims between 1979 and 1986 including two children and a Southside Slayer victim. In 1986, Siebert was apprehended in Hurricane Mills, Tennessee after authorities traced a phone call he made from a phone booth near a restaurant where he was working. Siebert committed at least one of the Southside Slayer murders, and Michael Hughes, Chester Turner, Louis Craine, Lonnie David Franklin and Ivan Hill committed at least one each. In 2008, Daniel Lee Siebert died from complications from cancer at the Holman Correctional Facility in Escambia County, Alabama.

Sentence: death at the Holman Correctional Facility in Escambia County, Alabama, US. **Death:** cause of death: natural causes, pancreatic cancer at the Holman Correctional Facility in Escambia County, Alabama, US.

Active in: South Africa

Norman Afzal Simons

Station Strangler

BIRTH: 01-12-1967 YEARS ACTIVE: 1986 - 1994 ARRESTED:
GENDER: Male AGES ACTIVE: 18/19 - 26/27 CONVICTED:
ZODIAC: Capricorn LIFE SPAN: 1967 - DEATH:

1-22 VICTIMS

SERIAL KILLER RAPIST STRANGLER

Active for **9 years** known to have killed at least **1 victims** between **1986** and **1994**.
previous crimes: ✗ weapon: ✗ gun: ✗ rob: ✗ bound: ✓ strangle: ✓ mutilate: ✗ W M

Norman Afzal Simons a South African serial killer, rapist and primary school teacher known as the Station Strangler. Simons was convicted of only one of twenty-two cases of murder and sodomy of young children near Cape Town, South Africa. Simons victims were all young boys aged between 9 and 13 from the Cape Malays community. He was employed as a teacher at Alpine Primary School in Beacon Valley, Mitchell's Plain. He converted to Islam in 1993, taking on the name Avzal, but converted back to Christianity in 1994. Simons was considered intelligent and spoke seven different languages.

Sentence: life imprisonment at Drakenstein Maximum Correctional Facility in Paarl, Western Cape province of South Africa.

Active in: United Kingdom DECEASED

Angus Sinclair

World's End Murders

BIRTH: **YEARS ACTIVE:** 1961 - 1978 **ARRESTED:**
GENDER: Male **AGES ACTIVE:** - **CONVICTED:** 08-31-1982
ZODIAC: **LIFE SPAN:** - 2019 **DEATH:** 03-11-2019

4-8 VICTIMS

SERIAL KILLER | RAPIST | STRANGLER

Active for **18 years** known to have killed at least **4 victims** between **1961** and **1978**.
previous crimes: ✓ weapon: ✗ gun: ✗ rob: ✗ bound: ✓ strangle: ✓ mutilate: ✗ W M

Angus Sinclair (Angus Robertson Sinclair) a Scottish serial killer known as the World's End Murderer. The World's End Murders refers to the murder of two teenage girls in 1977. Both victims were last seen alive leaving The World's End pub in Edinburgh's Old Town. Sinclair was convicted of the murders of four females and believed to have murdered a total of eight victims. In 1961, Sinclair murdered his eight-year-old neighbor in Glasgow when he was just sixteen-years-old. He was acquitted of the World's End Murders in 2007 under controversial circumstances. He was re-tried and convicted of both murders in 2014. Angus Sinclair was sentenced to life imprisonment with a minimum term of thirty-seven years.

Sentence: life imprisonment at HM Prison Glenochil near Tullibody, Scotland, United Kingdom. **Death:** cause of death: undetermined, a Fatal Accident Inquiry will be held in due course at HM Prison Glenochil near Tullibody, Scotland, United Kingdom.

Active in: South Africa

Moses Sithole

The ABC Killer, The South African Strangler, The Gauteng Killer

BIRTH: 11-17-1964 **YEARS ACTIVE:** 1994 - 1995 **ARRESTED:** 10-18-1995 (Age 30)
GENDER: Male **AGES ACTIVE:** 29/30 - 30/31 **CONVICTED:** 11-03-1995 (Age 30)
ZODIAC: Scorpio **LIFE SPAN:** 1964 - **DEATH:**

38 VICTIMS

SERIAL KILLER | RAPIST | TORTURER | STRANGLER

Active for **2 years** known to have killed at least **38 victims** between **1994** and **1995**.
previous crimes: ✓ weapon: ✗ gun: ✗ rob: ✓ bound: ✗ strangle: ✓ mutilate: ✗ W M

Moses Sithole a South African serial killer and rapist known as The ABC Killer, The South African Strangler and The Gauteng Killer. He is also known as South Africa's Ted Bundy. Sithole preyed on unemployed women, posing as a businessman and luring his victims with the prospects of a job, before leading them to an isolated place, where he raped, tortured, and murdered them. Atteridgeville is the same town serial killer Elias Xitavhudzi was active in. In 1997, Moses Sithole was sentenced to 2410 years imprisonment with a non-parole period of 930 years.

Sentence: life imprisonment, 2410 years at Mangaung Correctional Centre in Bloemfontein, South Africa.

Active in: Russia

DECEASED

Anatoly Slivko

BIRTH: 12-28-1938 YEARS ACTIVE: 1961 - 1985 ARRESTED: 12-28-1985 (Age 47)
GENDER: Male AGES ACTIVE: 22/23 - 46/47 CONVICTED:
ZODIAC: Capricorn LIFE SPAN: 1938 - 1989 DEATH: 09-16-1989 (Age 50)

7 VICTIMS

SERIAL KILLER RAPIST NECROPHILIAC STRANGLER

Active for **25 years** known to have killed at least **7 victims** between **1961** and **1985**.
previous crimes: ✗ weapon: ✗ gun: ✗ rob: ✗ bound: ✓ strangle: ✓ mutilate: ✓ W M

Anatoly Slivko (Anatoly Yelemianovich Slivko) a Russian serial killer, necrophile and rapist. He killed seven young boys in and around Nevinnomyssk, Russia between 1964 and 1985. Slivko was a member of the Young Pioneers (Soviet Boy Scouts), he gained the trust of forty-three young boys over almost three decades, asphyxiated them until they fell unconscious, ritually molested, filmed, photographed and resuscitated them. The seven boys that did not wake up were dismembered and burned. Slivko was interviewed for advice in the investigation of fellow serial killer Andrei Chikatilo's crimes, Chikatilo was unidentified at the time of the interview. In 1989, Anatoly Slivkowas executed by firing squad.

Sentence: death by firing squad at the Novocherkassk prison in Russia. **Death:** cause of death: capital punishment, executed by firing squad at the Novocherkassk prison in Russia.

Active in: Slovakia, Czech Republic

Jozef Slovak

The Bratislava Strangler, The Genius murderer

BIRTH: 04-07-1951 YEARS ACTIVE: 1978 - 1991 ARRESTED: 07-18-1991 (Age 40)
GENDER: Male AGES ACTIVE: 26/27 - 39/40 CONVICTED: 08-20-1993 (Age 42)
ZODIAC: Aries LIFE SPAN: 1951 - DEATH:

5 VICTIMS

SERIAL KILLER RAPIST STRANGLER

Active for **14 years** known to have killed at least **5 victims** between **1978** and **1991**.
previous crimes: ✓ weapon: ✓ gun: ✓ rob: ✓ bound: ✗ strangle: ✓ mutilate: ✗ W M

Jozef Slovak (Jozef Slovák) a Slovak serial killer known as The Bratislava Strangler and The Genius murderer. Slovák murdered at least five women in Slovakia and Czech Republic between 1978 and 1991. He killed his first victim in 1978, Slovák served eight years of his fifteen year sentence and he was released in 1990. He murdered at least four other women before being captured in 1991. In 1993, Jozef Slovák was sentenced to life imprisonment for the four murders and is currently serving his sentence at the Ilavská prison in Ilava, Slovakia.

Sentence: life imprisonment at Ilavská prison in Ilava, Slowakei.

Active in: Australia DECEASED

Arnold Sodeman

Schoolgirl Strangler

BIRTH: 12-12-1899 **YEARS ACTIVE:** 1930 - 1935 **ARRESTED:** 12-02-1935 (Age 35)
GENDER: Male **AGES ACTIVE:** 30/31 - 35/36 **CONVICTED:**
ZODIAC: Sagittarius **LIFE SPAN:** 1899 - 1936 **DEATH:** 06-01-1936 (Age 36)

4 VICTIMS

SERIAL KILLER RAPIST STRANGLER

Active for **6 years** known to have killed at least **4 victims** between **1930** and **1935**.

previous crimes: ✓ weapon: ✗ gun: ✗ rob: ✗ bound: ✓ strangle: ✓ mutilate: ✗ W M

Arnold Sodeman (Arnold Karl Sodeman) an Australian serial killer known as the Schoolgirl Strangler. Sodeman confessed to the murders of four young girls between 1930 and 1935. He preyed on girls between the ages of 8 and 12. He lured at least two of his victims by offering to buy them ice cream and offered another victim a ride on his bicycle. Sodeman would gag, bound and strangle the girls to death. He disposed of the bodies by dumping them at multiple locations in Victoria, Australia. Arnold Sodeman was executed at Pentridge Prison in 1936.

Sentence: death by hanging at HM Prison Pentridge, former maximum-security prison in Victoria, Australia. **Death:** cause of death: capital punishment, executed by hanging at HM Prison Pentridge, former maximum-security prison in Victoria, Australia.

Active in: United States

Morris Solomon

Homicidal Handyman of Oak Park, The Sacramento Slayer

BIRTH: 03-15-1944 **YEARS ACTIVE:** 1986 - 1987 **ARRESTED:** 04-22-1987 (Age 43)
GENDER: Male **AGES ACTIVE:** 41/42 - 42/43 **CONVICTED:** 08-29-1991 (Age 47)
ZODIAC: Pisces **LIFE SPAN:** 1944 - **DEATH:**

6-7 VICTIMS

SERIAL KILLER RAPIST STRANGLER

Active for **2 years** known to have killed at least **6 victims** between **1986** and **1987**.

previous crimes: ✓ weapon: ✓ gun: ✗ rob ✗ bound: ✓ strangle: ✓ mutilate: ✗ W M

Morris Solomon (Morris Solomon Jr.) an American serial killer and rapist known as the Homicidal Handyman of Oak Park. Solomon killed six young women between 1986 and 1987 in Sacramento, California. Solomon would bound, beat and rape his victims burying the body wrapped in bed sheets. He worked as a handyman in Sacramento, California. In 1987, Solomon was arrested after authorities found bodies buried at a residence associated with Solomon. He lived in his abandoned car which was parked on a lot at the residence. In 1992, Solomon was sentenced to death for six of the murders. He was the 342nd person to receive the death sentence in California. Morris Solomon is currently on death row at the San Quentin Prison in San Quentin, California.

Sentence: death at the San Quentin Prison in San Quentin, California, US.

Active in: United States

Erno Soto

Charlie Chop-Off

BIRTH: YEARS ACTIVE: 1972 - 1973 ARRESTED: 05-15-1974
GENDER: Male AGES ACTIVE: - CONVICTED:
ZODIAC: LIFE SPAN: - DEATH:

4 VICTIMS

SERIAL KILLER RAPIST

Active for **2 years** known to have killed at least **4 victims** between **1972** and **1973**.
previous crimes: — weapon: ✓ gun: ✗ rob: ✗ bound: ✗ strangle: ✗ mutilate: ✓ W M

Erno Soto a suspected American serial killer known as Charlie Chop-Off. Soto is suspected of killing three black children and one Puerto Rican child in Manhattan between 1972 and 1973. He was known to stab young boys and cut off their genitals in attempt to transform them into girls. In 1974, Erno Soto was arrested by the police after a failed abduction. He confessed to a 1973 murder but due to his acute mental instability he did not stand trial. Erno Soto was committed to a mental institution for the criminally insane in 1974.

Sentence: preventively detained at an unnamed mental institution in New York City, New York, US.

Active in: United States

Anthony Sowell

The Cleveland Strangler

BIRTH: 08-19-1959 YEARS ACTIVE: 2007 - 2009 ARRESTED: 10-31-2009 (Age 50)
GENDER: Male AGES ACTIVE: 47/48 - 49/50 CONVICTED: 07-22-2011 (Age 51)
ZODIAC: Leo LIFE SPAN: 1959 - DEATH:

11 VICTIMS

SERIAL KILLER RAPIST NECROPHILIAC STRANGLER

Active for **3 years** known to have killed at least **11 victims** between **2007** and **2009**.
previous crimes: ✓ weapon: ✓ gun: ✗ rob: ✗ bound: ✓ strangle: ✓ mutilate: ✓ W M

Anthony Sowell (Anthony Edward Sowell) an American serial killer, kidnapper, rapist and necrophile known as The Cleveland Strangler. He was arrested after the bodies of eleven women were discovered at his residence in 2009. Sowell was convicted of killing eleven women between 2007 and 2009. He was sentenced to death in 2011. In 2018, The City of Cleveland agreed to pay one million dollars to the families of six victims after a botched police investigation into a 2008 rape accusation which allowed Sowell to walk out of jail with no charges. He was suspected in another series of murders in the 1980s, but has not been charged. Sowell resides on death row at Chillicothe Correctional Institution.

Sentence: death at Chillicothe Correctional Institution in Union Township, Ross County, near Chillicothe, Ohio, US.

Active in: United States DECEASED

Timothy Wilson Spencer

The Southside Strangler

BIRTH: 03-17-1962 YEARS ACTIVE: 1984 - 1987 ARRESTED: 01-20-1988 (Age 25)
GENDER: Male AGES ACTIVE: 21/22 - 24/25 CONVICTED: 09-08-1988 (Age 26)
ZODIAC: Pisces LIFE SPAN: 1962 - 1994 DEATH: 04-27-1994 (Age 32)

5 VICTIMS

SERIAL KILLER RAPIST STRANGLER

Active for **4 years** known to have killed at least **5 victims** between **1984** and **1987**.

previous crimes: ✓ weapon: ✗ gun: ✗ rob: ✓ bound: ✓ strangle: ✓ mutilate: ✗ W M

Timothy Wilson Spencer an American serial killer and burglar known as The Southside Strangler, The Southside Slayer and The Southside Rapist. Spencer raped and murdered four women in Virginia from 1987 to 1988, with one murder in 1984. Spencer was the first person in the United States to be convicted of a capital crime through DNA testing. David Vasquez who was wrongfully convicted of Spencer's 1984 victim, became the first to be exonerated following conviction through DNA testing. In 1994, Timothy Wilson Spencer was executed in the electric chair at Greensville Correctional Centre in Jarratt, Virginia.

Sentence: death by electrocution at Greensville Correctional Centre in Jarratt, Virginia, US. **Death:** cause of death: capital punishment, executed by electrocution via electric chair at Greensville Correctional Centre in Jarratt, Virginia, US.

BIRTH: 08-30-1969 YEARS ACTIVE: 1994 - 1995 ARRESTED: 04-19-1995 (Age 25)
GENDER: Male AGES ACTIVE: 24/25 - 25/26 CONVICTED: 04-30-1996 (Age 26)
ZODIAC: Virgo LIFE SPAN: 1969 - DEATH:

3 VICTIMS

SERIAL KILLER RAPIST NECROPHILIAC TORTURER STALKER

Active for **2 years** known to have killed at least **3 victims** between **1994** and **1995**.

previous crimes: ✓ weapon: ✓ gun: ✗ rob: ✓ bound: ✓ strangle: ✗ mutilate: ✓ W M

Jack Spillman (Jack Owen Spillman III) an American serial killer and necrophile known as The Werewolf Butcher. Spillman killed two girls and the mother of one of them in Washington State in 1994 and 1995. His rap sheet includes impending charges on rape in King County and burglary in Spokane County. According to court documents, "Spillman would declare to Miller (his cellmate) that he wanted to be the world's greatest serial killer." Spillman pleaded guilty to first-degree murder in the April 1995 deaths of Rita and Mandy Huffman. Spillman also pleaded guilty to the 1994 slaying of Penny Davis of Tonasket. In 1996, Jack Spillman was sentenced to life in prison without possibility of parole.

Sentence: life imprisonment at the Washington State Penitentiary in Walla Walla, Washington, US.

Active in: United States

Cary Stayner

The Yosemite Killer

BIRTH: 08-13-1961 YEARS ACTIVE: 1999 - 1999 ARRESTED: 07-24-1999 (Age 37)
GENDER: Male AGES ACTIVE: 37/38 - 37/38 CONVICTED: 08-27-2002 (Age 41)
ZODIAC: Leo LIFE SPAN: 1961 - DEATH:

4 VICTIMS

SERIAL KILLER RAPIST STALKER STRANGLER

Active for **1 year** known to have killed at least **4 victims** in **1999**.
previous crimes: ✓ weapon: ✓ gun: ✓ rob: ✗ bound: ✓ strangle: ✓ mutilate: ✓ W M R

Cary Stayner an American serial killer known as The Yosemite Killer. Stayner killed four women in Yosemite, California in 1999. Stayner decapitated the body of his fourth victim. His brother, Steven Stayner was a kidnapping victim of sex offender Kenneth Parnell. Stayner was frequent at Laguna Del Sol, a nudist colony in Sacramento County. He was arrested at Laguna Del Sol in 1999 after witnesses identified his vehicle to authorities. In 2002, Stayner was convicted of four counts of first degree murder. Cary Stayner is currently awaiting execution on death row at San Quentin Penitentiary in San Quentin, California.
Sentence: death at San Quentin Penitentiary in San Quentin, California, US.

Active in: Czech Republic DECEASED

Miroslav Stehlik

Stehno, Thigh

BIRTH: 06-14-1956 YEARS ACTIVE: 1983 - 1983 ARRESTED: 09-01-1983 (Age 27)
GENDER: Male AGES ACTIVE: 26/27 - 26/27 CONVICTED: 10-08-1984 (Age 28)
ZODIAC: Gemini LIFE SPAN: 1956 - 1986 DEATH: 02-25-1986 (Age 29)

2 VICTIMS

SERIAL KILLER RAPIST STRANGLER

Active for **1 year** known to have killed at least **2 victims** in **1983**.
previous crimes: ✓ weapon: ✓ gun: ✗ rob: ✓ bound: ✗ strangle: ✓ mutilate: ✗

Miroslav Stehlik (Miroslav Stehlík) a Czech serial killer known as Stehno (Thigh). In 1983, Stehlik raped fourteen women in Prague during the period of eleven months, with two victims killed. He committed an attempted rape at age fifteen and was sentenced to two years in prison. At eighteen he was sentenced to seven years in prison. He was released in 1982 and placed in institutional sexological treatment. Stehlík committed his first murder while still in treatment, committing his second less than thirteen hours after his release. Stehno (Thigh) was his nickname in prison. In 1984, Stehlik was sentenced to death for two murders, twelve rapes and other crimes. In 1986, Miroslav Stehlik was executed by hanging at the Pankrác prison in Prague.
Sentence: death by hanging at Pankrác Prague Prison in Prague, Czech Republic. **Death:** cause of death: executed by hanging at Pankrác Prague Prison in Prague, Czech Republic.

Active in: Czech Republic

Jiri Straka

The Spartakiad killer

BIRTH: 04-14-1969 **YEARS ACTIVE:** 1985 - 1985 **ARRESTED:** 05-22-1985 (Age 16)
GENDER: Male **AGES ACTIVE:** 15/16 - 15/16 **CONVICTED:**
ZODIAC: Aries **LIFE SPAN:** 1969 - **DEATH:**

3 VICTIMS

SERIAL KILLER RAPIST

Active for **1 year** known to have killed at least **3 victims** in **1985**.
previous crimes: ✓ weapon: ✓ gun: ✓ rob: ✓ bound: ✓ strangle: ✗ mutilate: ✗

Jiri Straka (Jirí Straka) a Czech serial killer known as the Spartakiad killer. In 1985, Straka attacked eleven women in Prague. He was convicted of three murders, two murder attempts, five rapes, three robberies and five thefts. Due to his age, sixteen-years-old, he could not be sentenced to more than ten years in prison. In 1994, Straka's punishment was shortened by a presidential amnesty. In 2004, Jirí Straka was release from prison, he now lives under a different identity.

Sentence: ten years imprisonment at Opava Psychiatric Hospital in Opava, Czech Republic. Jirí Straka was released from custody on December 24, 2004.

Active in: Italy, France DECEASED

Roberto Succo

The Killer of Eyes of Ice

BIRTH: 04-03-1962 **YEARS ACTIVE:** 1981 - 1988 **ARRESTED:** 02-28-1988 (Age 25)
GENDER: Male **AGES ACTIVE:** 18/19 - 25/26 **CONVICTED:**
ZODIAC: Aries **LIFE SPAN:** 1962 - 1988 **DEATH:** 05-23-1988 (Age 26)

7 VICTIMS

SERIAL KILLER RAPIST

Active for **8 years** known to have killed at least **7 victims** between **1981** and **1988**.
previous crimes: ✓ weapon: ✓ gun: ✓ rob: ✓ bound: ✗ strangle: ✗ mutilate: ✗ W M

Roberto Succo an Italian serial killer known as The Killer with the Eyes of Ice, The Monster of Mestre, The Full Moon Assassin and The Cherubino Nero. In 1986, Succo escaped the mental hospital where he was recluded in for murdering his parents five years earlier and began a crime spree in Europe that included burglary, hijacking, kidnapping, rape and murder and earned him the Public Enemy Number One spot in Italy, France and Switzerland. Succo changed his name to Roberto Kurt using fake documents in order to evade police. In 1988, Roberto Succo committed suicide by suffocating himself with a plastic bag in his prison cell after failing to escape a second time.

Sentence: never convicted committed suicide prior to trial at the Treviso prison in Treviso, Veneto, Italy. **Death:** cause of death: suicide, committed suicide by asphyxia, suffocating himself with a plastic bag in his cell at a prison in Vicenza, Italian commune in Veneto, Italy.

Active in: United States

William Suff

Riverside Prostitute Killer, Lake Elsinore Killer

BIRTH: 08-20-1950 | YEARS ACTIVE: 1986 - 1992 | ARRESTED: 01-09-1992 (Age 41)
GENDER: Male | AGES ACTIVE: 35/36 - 41/42 | CONVICTED: 08-17-1995 (Age 44)
ZODIAC: Leo | LIFE SPAN: 1950 - | DEATH:

12-22
VICTIMS

SERIAL KILLER RAPIST TORTURER STRANGLER

Active for **7 years** known to have killed at least **12 victims** between **1986** and **1992**.

previous crimes: ✓ weapon: ✓ gun: ✗ rob: ✓ bound: ✗ strangle: ✓ mutilate: ✓ W M R

William Suff (William Lester Suff) (born Bill Lee Suff) an American serial killer known as the Riverside Prostitute Killer and the Lake Elsinore Killer. Suff was convicted of murdering his first daughter in 1974, he abused and violently shook his infant daughter to death. Once released, he worked as a warehouse clerk for Riverside County and had close involvement with the police department. He would rape, stab, strangle, and sometimes mutilate his victims. William Suff killed twelve or more prostitutes in Riverside County, California between 1989 and 1991. He was convicted of twelve murders in 1995 and sentence to death.

Sentence: death by lethal injection at San Quentin State Prison in San Quentin, California, US.

Active in: Russia

DECEASED

Aleksey Sukletin

The Alligator, The Vassilyevo Cannibal

BIRTH: 03-23-1943 | YEARS ACTIVE: 1979 - 1985 | ARRESTED: 06-04-1985 (Age 42)
GENDER: Male | AGES ACTIVE: 35/36 - 41/42 | CONVICTED: 04-18-1986 (Age 43)
ZODIAC: Aries | LIFE SPAN: 1943 - 1987 | DEATH: 07-29-1987 (Age 44)

7
VICTIMS

SERIAL KILLER RAPIST CANNIBAL TORTURER

Active for **7 years** known to have killed at least **7 victims** between **1979** and **1985**.

previous crimes: ✓ weapon: ✓ gun: ✗ rob: ✓ bound: ✓ strangle: ✗ mutilate: ✓ W

Aleksey Sukletin (Aleksey Vasilevich Sukletin) a Soviet serial killer known as The Alligator and The Vassilyevo Cannibal. Sukletin killed and cannibalized at least seven girls and women in Tatarstan from 1979 to 1985. He had a female accomplice during his crimes, Madina Nurgazizovnaya Shakirova, a native of Vasilyevo. Shakirova was sentenced to fifteen years imprisonment, she was released in 2001. In 1986, the Supreme Court of Tartarstan found Sukletin guilty of seven murders, and he was sentenced to death. In 1987, Aleksey Sukletin was executed by firing squad.

Sentence: death by firing squad at a prison in Kazan, Tatar ASSR, Soviet Union. **Death:** cause of death: executed by firing squad at a prison in Kazan, Tatar ASSR, Soviet Union.

Active in: North Macedonia DECEASED

Vlado Taneski

The Kicevo Monster

BIRTH: YEARS ACTIVE: 2005 - 2008 ARRESTED: 06-22-2008

GENDER: Male AGES ACTIVE: - CONVICTED:

ZODIAC: LIFE SPAN: - 2008 DEATH: 06-23-2008

3-4 VICTIMS

SERIAL KILLER RAPIST STRANGLER

Active for **4 years** known to have killed at least **3 victims** between **2005** and **2008**.

previous crimes: — weapon: ✗ gun: ✗ rob: ✗ bound: ✗ strangle: ✓ mutilate: ✗ W M

Vlado Taneski a Macedonian serial killer and crime journalist known as The Kicevo Monster. He killed at least three victims between 2005 and 2008. Taneski would strangle, bound, torture, and rape his victims before murdering them. Taneski came under suspicion when his articles on the rape and murder of three elderly women included information that had not been disclosed by the police. All the victims were poor, uneducated cleaners and knew Taneski's mother. Taneski killed himself in prison before he could be interrogated for the murder of a fourth woman.

Sentence: never sentenced committed suicide prior to conviction at a prison in the town of Tetovo, Polog, Macedonia. **Death:** cause of death: suicide, committed suicide by drowning himself by dunking his head in a bucket of water at a prison in the town of Tetovo, Polog, Macedonia.

Active in: Spain

Gustavo Romero Tercero

El Asesino de Valdepeñas, The Valdepeñas Killer

BIRTH: YEARS ACTIVE: 1993 - 1998 ARRESTED: 10-09-2003

GENDER: Male AGES ACTIVE: - CONVICTED: 04-22-2005

ZODIAC: LIFE SPAN: - DEATH:

3 VICTIMS

SERIAL KILLER RAPIST

Active for **6 years** known to have killed at least **3 victims** between **1993** and **1998**.

previous crimes: ✓ weapon: ✓ gun: ✗ rob: ✓ bound: ✗ strangle: ✗ mutilate: ✗ W

Gustavo Romero Tercero a Spanish serial killer and rapists known as El Asesino de Valdepeñas and The Valdepeñas Killer. Tercero was an armed robber that killed a couple after the woman recognized him in 1993. He murdered another woman in 1998 after accidentally hitting her with his car, fearing that a possible investigation would link him to the other crimes. A psychiatric evaluation found that Romero had antisocial personality disorder, but could otherwise understand the nature and consequences of his actions. Tercero confessed to the murderes after DNA tied him to one of the victims. In 2005, Gustavo Romero Tercero was sentenced to 103 years in prison.

Sentence: 103 years imprisonment at a prison in Spain.

Active in: United States

John Floyd Thomas

Westside Rapist, The Southland Strangler

BIRTH: 07-26-1936 **YEARS ACTIVE:** 1957 - 2009 **ARRESTED:** 03-31-2009 (Age 72)

GENDER: Male **AGES ACTIVE:** 20/21 - 72/73 **CONVICTED:** 04-01-2011 (Age 74)

ZODIAC: Leo **LIFE SPAN:** 1936 - **DEATH:**

5-25 VICTIMS

SERIAL KILLER RAPIST NECROPHILIAC STRANGLER

Active for **53 years** known to have killed at least **5 victims** between **1957** and **2009**.

previous crimes: ✓ weapon: ✗ gun: ✗ rob: ✓ bound: ✗ strangle: ✓ mutilate: ✗ W M

John Floyd Thomas an American serial killer and rapist known as the Westside Rapist and The Southland Strangler. Thomas has one of the longest criminal careers in the US. The first wave of killings claimed the lives of seventeen women ranging in age from the 50s to the 90s. The murders stopped in 1978 - the same year a witness copied down Mr Thomas's car licence number after he raped a woman in Pasadena and was sent to jail. The second wave began after his release in 1983. Five more elderly white women were raped and strangled in the Claremont area. In 2011, John Floyd Thomas was sentenced to life imprisonment without the possibility of parole.

Sentence: seven consecutive life sentences without the possibility of parole at Richard J. Donovan Correctional Facility in San Diego, California, US.

BIRTH: **YEARS ACTIVE:** 1996 - 1997 **ARRESTED:** 08-14-1997

GENDER: Male **AGES ACTIVE:** - **CONVICTED:** 03-31-1999

ZODIAC: **LIFE SPAN:** - **DEATH:**

16-19 VICTIMS

SERIAL KILLER RAPIST STRANGLER

Active for **2 years** known to have killed at least **16 victims** between **1996** and **1997**.

previous crimes: ✓ weapon: ✗ gun: ✗ rob: ✗ bound: ✓ strangle: ✓ mutilate: ✓ W M

Sipho Agmatir Thwala (Sipho Mandla Agmatir Thwala) a South African rapist and serial killer known as the Phoenix Strangler. Thwala was convicted for ten rapes and the murders of sixteen women. Thwala's nickname came from the area in which he committed his crimes, Phoenix, an Indian township in South Africa. Thwala offered victims employment and was described as charming, he spoke English, Afrikaans and Zulu. Thwala would lure women into sugarcane fields near Phoenix where he would bind, beat and rape them prior to strangling them with their own undergarments. He also set fire to the field and the body the victim in hopes of destroying evidence.

Sentence: life imprisonment a total of 506 years at C Max Penitentiary in Pretoria, South Africa.

Active in: Russia, Ukraine DECEASED

Serhiy Tkach

Sergey, Pologovsky Maniac

BIRTH: 09-12-1952 YEARS ACTIVE: 1984 - 2005 ARRESTED: 08-01-2005 (Age 52)
GENDER: Male AGES ACTIVE: 31/32 - 52/53 CONVICTED: 12-23-2008 (Age 56)
ZODIAC: Virgo LIFE SPAN: 1952 - 2018 DEATH: 11-04-2018 (Age 66)

37-100 VICTIMS

SERIAL KILLER RAPIST NECROPHILIAC STRANGLER

Active for **22 years** known to have killed at least **37 victims** between **1984** and **2005**.
previous crimes: ✗ weapon: ✗ gun: ✗ rob: ✓ bound: ✗ strangle: ✓ mutilate: ✗ W M

Serhiy Tkach (Serhiy Fedorovich Tkach) a Soviet-Russian serial killer known as the Pologovsky Maniac. Tkach was a former Ukrainian police criminal investigator turned serial killer. He suffocated girls aged between 8 and 18 years of age. He performed sexual acts on their bodies after they were dead. He claimed to have killed one hundred victims. Tkach confessed to numerous crimes but refused to apologize for any of them, he demanded the death penalty. Tkach was sentenced to life imprisonment for the murder of thirty-seven women and girls over more than two decades. The death penalty in Ukraine was abolished in 2000. Serhiy Tkach died from a heart attack in 2018 while still in prison.

Sentence: life imprisonment at Prison No. 8 of Zhytomyr in the Ukraine. **Death:** cause of death: natural causes, heart attack at Prison No. 8 of Zhytomyr in the Ukraine.

Active in: United Kingdom

Peter Tobin

Bible John murders

BIRTH: 08-27-1948 YEARS ACTIVE: 1991 - 2006 ARRESTED: 10-03-2006 (Age 58)
GENDER: Male AGES ACTIVE: 42/43 - 57/58 CONVICTED: 05-04-2007 (Age 58)
ZODIAC: Virgo LIFE SPAN: 1948 - DEATH:

3-13 VICTIMS

SERIAL KILLER RAPIST

Active for **16 years** known to have killed at least **3 victims** between **1991** and **2006**.
previous crimes: ✓ weapon: ✓ gun: ✗ rob: ✓ bound: ✓ strangle: ✗ mutilate: ✗ W M

Peter Tobin a Scottish rapist and serial killer known to have killed at least three young women between 1991 and 2006. Also a suspect in the Bible John murders, committed in Glasgow during the late 1960s. His three proven victims have the same hair color as the Bible John's sacrifices, and they were all strangled the same way, except for Angelika Kluk. In 2012, Tobin was hospitalized after suffering a suspected heart attack. In 2015, Peter Tobin was left severely injured and permanently disfigured by a fellow inmate when he was attacked with a razor blade. In 2016, Tobin was hospitalized after he suffered a suspected stroke. In 2019, Peter Tobin is reported to be suffering from cancer and too frail to leave his cell most days.

Sentence: life imprisonment at the HM Prison Edinburgh in Stenhouse, Edinburgh, Scotland.

Active in: Slovenia

DECEASED

Metod Trobec

The Monster of Gorejne Vasi

BIRTH: 07-06-1948 | YEARS ACTIVE: 1976 - 1978 | ARRESTED:
GENDER: Male | AGES ACTIVE: 27/28 - 29/30 | CONVICTED:
ZODIAC: Cancer | LIFE SPAN: 1948 - 2006 | DEATH: 05-30-2006 (Age 57)

5 VICTIMS

SERIAL KILLER | RAPIST | STRANGLER

Active for **3 years** known to have killed at least **5 victims** between **1976** and **1978**.
previous crimes: ✓ weapon: ✗ gun: ✗ rob: ✓ bound: ✗ strangle: ✓ mutilate: ✓ W M

Metod Trobec a Slovene serial killer and rapist known as The Monster of Gorejne Vasi. He murdered five women between 1976 and 1978 in Slovenia. In 1974, Trobec was sentenced to thirteen months in a prison in Slovenia. Trobec would rape, murder and cremate his victims. He was known to strangle at least one of his victims and multiple victims had their corpses cremated in a wood oven. Trobec was sentenced to death which was later commuted to twenty years in prison. While in prison, Trobec attempted to murder two other inmates adding fifteen years to his sentence. He spent twenty-seven years in prison. In 2006, Metod Trobec committed suicide in his cell at Dob pri Mirni Prison in Slovenia.

Sentence: death commuted to twenty years in prison at the Dob pri Mirni Prison in Slovenska Vas, Slovenia. **Death:** cause of death: suicide, committed suicide by hanging himself in his cell at the Dob pri Mirni Prison in Slovenska Vas, Slovenia.

Active in: United States

Chester Turner

Southside Slayer murders

BIRTH: 11-05-1966 | YEARS ACTIVE: 1987 - 1998 | ARRESTED: 10-01-2002 (Age 35)
GENDER: Male | AGES ACTIVE: 20/21 - 31/32 | CONVICTED: 06-10-2007 (Age 40)
ZODIAC: Scorpio | LIFE SPAN: 1966 - | DEATH:

15 VICTIMS

SERIAL KILLER | RAPIST | STRANGLER

Active for **12 years** known to have killed at least **15 victims** between **1987** and **1998**.
previous crimes: ✓ weapon: ✗ gun: ✗ rob: ✗ bound: ✗ strangle: ✓ mutilate: ✗ W M

Chester Turner (Chester Dewayne Turner) an American serial killer known as the Southside Slayer. Turner was convicted of killing fifteen victims in Los Angeles, California in the 1980s and 1990s. Chester Turner committed at least one of the Southside Slayer murders, and Michael Hughes, Daniel Lee Siebert, Louis Craine, Lonnie David Franklin and Ivan Hill committed at least one each. Chester Turner was sentenced to death and is serving on death row at San Quentin State Prison with an admission date of October 1, 2002.

Sentence: death, execution by lethal injection at San Quentin State Prison in San Quentin, California, US.

Active in: Austria, United States, Czech Republic — DECEASED

Jack Unterweger

Jack the Writer, Häfenliterat

BIRTH: 08-16-1950 YEARS ACTIVE: 1974 - 1992 ARRESTED: 02-27-1992 (Age 41)
GENDER: Male AGES ACTIVE: 23/24 - 41/42 CONVICTED: 06-29-1994 (Age 43)
ZODIAC: Leo LIFE SPAN: 1950 - 1994 DEATH: 06-29-1994 (Age 43)

10-12 VICTIMS

SERIAL KILLER RAPIST STRANGLER

Active for **19 years** known to have killed at least **10 victims** between **1974** and **1992**.
previous crimes: ✓ weapon: ✗ gun: ✗ rob: ✗ bound: ✗ strangle: ✓ mutilate: ✗ W M R

Jack Unterweger (Johann Unterweger) an Austrian serial killer known as Jack the Writer, Häfenliterat, Knastpoet, Vienna Woods Killer and The Vienna Strangler. Unterweger served fourteen years in Austrian prison for a murder in 1974. Unterweger raped, strangled and killed at least nine prostitutes after his release. He was a small star in Austrian media in the early 1990s and was arrested in the United States, where he may have killed another three prostitutes. Jack Unterweger committed suicide by hanging himself in 1994 after being sentenced to life in prison.

Sentence: life imprisonment with possibility of parole at Graz-Karlau Prison in Gries, Graz, Styria, Austrian. **Death:** cause of death: suicide, committed suicide by hanging himself in his jail cell at Graz-Karlau Prison in Gries, Graz, Styria, Austrian.

Active in: United States — DECEASED

Andrew Urdiales

BIRTH: 06-04-1964 YEARS ACTIVE: 1986 - 1996 ARRESTED: 04-23-1997 (Age 32)
GENDER: Male AGES ACTIVE: 21/22 - 31/32 CONVICTED: 05-23-2002 (Age 37)
ZODIAC: Gemini LIFE SPAN: 1964 - 2018 DEATH: 11-02-2018 (Age 54)

8 VICTIMS

SERIAL KILLER RAPIST

Active for **11 years** known to have killed at least **8 victims** between **1986** and **1996**.
previous crimes: ✗ weapon: ✓ gun: ✓ rob: ✗ bound: ✓ strangle: ✗ mutilate: ✗ W M

Andrew Urdiales an American serial killer convicted for the murders of eight women between 1986 and 1995 in Illinois, Indiana and California. Urdiales abducted, raped and shot his victims, before dumping the bodies. Some of his murders were committed while he was enlisted in the Marines. He was arrested in connection with a series of murders in 1997. While police ran ballistic tests on his gun, Urdiales confessed to all eight murders. He was convicted of three murders in 2002 and five murders in 2018. In 2018, Urdiales committed suicide by hanging himself in his cell at San Quentin State Prison in San Quentin, California.

Sentence: death, commuted to life imprisonment at San Quentin State Prison, San Quentin, California, US. **Death:** cause of death: suicide, hanging in prison cell at San Quentin State Prison, San Quentin, California, US.

Active in: Russia

DECEASED

Anatoly Utkin

Ulyanovsky maniac

BIRTH: 01-01-1943 YEARS ACTIVE: 1968 - 1973 ARRESTED: 02-09-1973 (Age 30)
GENDER: Male AGES ACTIVE: 25/25 - 30/30 CONVICTED: 12-13-1974 (Age 31)
ZODIAC: Capricorn LIFE SPAN: 1943 - 1975 DEATH: 09-12-1975 (Age 32)

9 VICTIMS

SERIAL KILLER RAPIST

Active for **6 years** known to have killed at least **9 victims** between **1968** and **1973**.
previous crimes: ✓ weapon: ✓ gun: ✓ rob: ✓ bound: ✗ strangle: ✗ mutilate: ✓ W

Anatoly Utkin (Anatoly Viktorovich Utkin) a Soviet serial killer and rapist known as the Ulyanovsky maniac. Utkin operated in the Ulyanovsk and Penza regions in the late 1960s and early 1970s. He killed eight girls and one man from 1968 to 1973. He was known to rape at least one of his victims. He had other charges including theft and robbery. He was found guilty on all counts and sentenced to death by firing squad. He made petitions for a pardon but all requests were rejected. Anatoly Utkin was executed by firing squad in 1975.

Sentence: death by firing squad at a prison in Russia. **Death:** cause of death: executed by firing squad at a prison in Russia.

Active in: France

DECEASED

Joseph Vacher

The French Ripper, The South-East Ripper

BIRTH: 11-16-1869 YEARS ACTIVE: 1894 - 1897 ARRESTED: 08-04-1897 (Age 27)
GENDER: Male AGES ACTIVE: 24/25 - 27/28 CONVICTED: 10-28-1898 (Age 28)
ZODIAC: Scorpio LIFE SPAN: 1869 - 1898 DEATH: 12-31-1898 (Age 29)

11-27 VICTIMS

SERIAL KILLER RAPIST NECROPHILIAC

Active for **4 years** known to have killed at least **11 victims** between **1894** and **1897**.
previous crimes: ✓ weapon: ✓ gun: ✓ rob: ✗ bound: ✗ strangle: ✗ mutilate: ✓ W M

Joseph Vacher a French serial killer known as The French Ripper and L'eventreur du Sud-Est (The South-East Ripper). He murdered eleven to twenty-seven victims between 1894 and 1897. Vacher raped, stabbed, sodomized and disembowelled women, teenage boys and girls who worked alone in the countryside as farm laborers. Vacher claimed he was insane but was pronounced sane and fit to stand trial. He was arrested in 1987 and sentenced to death in 1898. In 1898, Joseph Vacher was executed via guillotine at a prison in Bourg-en-Bresse, Ain, France.

Sentence: death by beheading via guillotine at a prison in Bourg-en-Bresse, Ain, France. **Death:** cause of death: capital punishment, executed by beheading via guillotine at a prison in Bourg-en-Bresse, Ain, France.

Active in: United States

Darren Deon Vann

Donald Vann

BIRTH: 03-21-1971 YEARS ACTIVE: 2013 - 2014 ARRESTED: 10-18-2014 (Age 43)
GENDER: Male AGES ACTIVE: 41/42 - 42/43 CONVICTED: 05-04-2018 (Age 47)
ZODIAC: Aries LIFE SPAN: 1971 - DEATH:

7-18 VICTIMS

SERIAL KILLER RAPIST STRANGLER

Active for **2 years** known to have killed at least **7 victims** between **2013** and **2014**.

previous crimes: ✓ weapon: ✗ gun: ✗ rob: ✓ bound: ✗ strangle: ✓ mutilate: ✗ W M

Darren Deon Vann an American serial killer and rapist also known as Donald Vann. Vann confessed to the murders of at least seven women in Gary, Indiana between 1995 and 2010. Vann would rape and strangle victims prior to leaving their bodies in abandoned structures in Gary, Indiana. He was captured after police traced the missing cell phone of one of his victims, which Vann astir had n his possession. In 2018, Darren Deon Vann was convicted on seven counts of murder and was sentenced to seven concurrent life sentences. Thomas Hargrove, founder of the Murder Accountability Project, together with a Gary, Indiana deputy coroner, attempted to persuade police that there were eighteen similar murders. Authorities denied any connection in the cases.

Sentence: life imprisonment, seven concurrent terms at Wabash Valley Correctional Facility in Sullivan County, Indiana, US.

Active in: Spain DECEASED

Jose Antonio Rodriguez Vega

El Mataviejas, The Old Lady Killer

BIRTH: 12-03-1957 YEARS ACTIVE: 1987 - 1988 ARRESTED: 05-19-1988 (Age 30)
GENDER: Male AGES ACTIVE: 29/30 - 30/31 CONVICTED: 12-05-1991 (Age 34)
ZODIAC: Sagittarius LIFE SPAN: 1957 - 2002 DEATH: 10-24-2002 (Age 44)

16 VICTIMS

SERIAL KILLER RAPIST

Active for **2 years** known to have killed at least **16 victims** between **1987** and **1988**.

previous crimes: — weapon: ✗ gun: ✗ rob: ✗ bound: ✗ strangle: ✗ mutilate: ✗ W M

Jose Antonio Rodriguez Vega a Spanish serial killer and rapist who was known as El Mataviejas (The Old Lady Killer). Rodriguez Vega raped and killed at least sixteen elderly women, ranging in age from 61 to 93 years old, in and around Santander, Cantabriam, between 1987 and 1988. He was known to beat, rape and suffocate elderly victims at the home of the victim. In 1992, Rodriguez Vega was sentenced to 440 years in prison. In 2000, Jose Antonio Rodriguez Vega died after being attacked and stabbed 113 times by two fellow inmates, El Carrot and Daniel RO, at a prison in Topas, Spain. Rodriguez Vega had already met at least one of his two murderers in the prison of Dueñas.

Sentence: 440 years in prison at a prison in Topas, Spain. **Death:** cause of death: homicide, stabbed by two fellow inmates at a prison in Topas, municipality of Spain.

Active in: Romania DECEASED

Romulus Veres

The Hammer Man, The Man with the Hammer

BIRTH: 01-23-1929 YEARS ACTIVE: 1970 - 1970 ARRESTED: 02-14-1974 (Age 45)
GENDER: Male AGES ACTIVE: 40/41 - 40/41 CONVICTED: 02-02-1976 (Age 47)
ZODIAC: Aquarius LIFE SPAN: 1929 - 1993 DEATH: 12-13-1993 (Age 64)

5 VICTIMS

SERIAL KILLER RAPIST STALKER

Active for **1 year** known to have killed at least **5 victims** in **1970**.
previous crimes: ✗ weapon: ✓ gun: ✗ rob: ✓ bound: ✗ strangle: ✗ mutilate: ✓ W

Romulus Veres a Romanian serial killer known as The Hammer Man or The Man with the Hammer. He would kill his victims with a hammer or by stabbing them with a knife. One victim was pregnant and found in a pool of blood, the neighbors thought she had given birth. Discovering that the woman had been hit in the head, she was rushed to the hospital and later survived. Veres set fire to the bodies of two of his later victims and was known to have raped at least one victim. Veres blamed the Devil for his actions, he suffered from schizophrenia which was used as the grounds of insanity. In 1976, Romulus Veres was institutionalized in the Stei Psychiatric Hospital in Romania where he died from liver disease in 1993.

Sentence: preventively detained at the Stei Psychiatric Hospital in Romania. **Death:** cause of death: natural causes, liver disease at the Stei Psychiatric Hospital in Romania.

Active in: Spain, Italy, France DECEASED

Manuel Delgado Villegas

El Arropiero, El Estrangulador del Puerto

BIRTH: 01-25-1943 YEARS ACTIVE: 1964 - 1971 ARRESTED: 01-18-1971 (Age 27)
GENDER: Male AGES ACTIVE: 20/21 - 27/28 CONVICTED:
ZODIAC: Aquarius LIFE SPAN: 1943 - 1998 DEATH: 02-02-1998 (Age 55)

7-48 VICTIMS

SERIAL KILLER RAPIST NECROPHILIAC STRANGLER

Active for **8 years** known to have killed at least **7 victims** between **1964** and **1971**.
previous crimes: ✓ weapon: ✓ gun: ✗ rob: ✓ bound: ✗ strangle: ✓ mutilate: ✗ W M

Manuel Delgado Villegas a Spanish serial killer and wandering criminal known as El Arropiero (The Arrope Trader) and El Estrangulador del Puerto (The Strangler of Puerto). Villegas confessed to the murders of forty-eight people of different gender, age and sexual orientation in three separate countries, police only investigated him for twenty-two murders in Spain. Villegas would beat, suffocate, strangle, rob and/or rape his victims. Some of his victims were killed with hand to hand combat techniques that he learned while in the Spanish Foreign Legion. He was diagnosed with a severe mental disorder and XYY syndrome. Villegas interned in a mental institution until his death in 1998.

Sentence: preventively detained at Carabanchel Penitentiary Psychiatric Hospital in Madrid, Spain.
Death: cause of death: natural causes, lung disease, chronic obstructive pulmonary disease at Hospital Can Ruti, a psychiatric hospital located in Badalona, Catalonia, Spain.

Active in: United States

Henry Louis Wallace

The Taco Bell Strangler

BIRTH: 11-04-1965 YEARS ACTIVE: 1990 - 1994 ARRESTED: 03-13-1994 (Age 28)
GENDER: Male AGES ACTIVE: 24/25 - 28/29 CONVICTED: 01-07-1997 (Age 31)
ZODIAC: Scorpio LIFE SPAN: 1965 - DEATH:

9-10 VICTIMS

SERIAL KILLER RAPIST STALKER STRANGLER

Active for **5 years** known to have killed at least **9 victims** between **1990** and **1994**.

previous crimes: ✓ weapon: ✓ gun: ✗ rob: ✓ bound: ✗ strangle: ✓ mutilate: ✗ W M

Henry Louis Wallace an American serial killer and rapist known as the Taco Bell Strangler. Wallace confessed to the murders of ten women in Charlotte, North Carolina. He would rape, strangle, or stab his victims prior to murdering them. Wallace was a supervisor at Taco Bell, some of his victims were his employees at Taco Bell in Charlotte, North Carolina. In 1997, Wallace was convicted on nine counts of murder and was sentenced to nine death sentences. Henry Louis Wallace is awaiting execution at Central Prison in Raleigh, North Carolina.

Sentence: death at Central Prison in Raleigh, North Carolina, US.

BIRTH: 03-06-1959 YEARS ACTIVE: 1984 - 1986 ARRESTED: 02-14-1999 (Age 39)
GENDER: Male AGES ACTIVE: 24/25 - 26/27 CONVICTED: 12-30-1999 (Age 40)
ZODIAC: Pisces LIFE SPAN: 1959 - DEATH:

5 VICTIMS

SERIAL KILLER RAPIST TORTURER STRANGLER

Active for **3 years** known to have killed at least **5 victims** between **1984** and **1986**.

previous crimes: ✓ weapon: ✓ gun: ✗ rob: ✗ bound: ✓ strangle: ✓ mutilate: ✗ W M R

Faryion Wardrip an American serial killer and rapist known as The Wichita Falls Body Snatcher. Wardrip assaulted and murdered a total of five women around Wichita Falls, Texas between 1984 and 1986. He was convicted and sentenced to thirty-five years in prison for only one of the murders, he was released on parole in 1997. Wardrip was arrested and convicted in connection with the other murders in 1999. He was sentenced to death plus three life terms. Faryion Wardrip remains on death row at Allan B. Polunsky Unit in Livingston, Texas.

Sentence: death by lethal injection plus three life terms at Allan B. Polunsky Unit in Livingston, Texas, US.

Active in: United States

Lesley Warren

The Babyface Killer

BIRTH: 10-15-1967 YEARS ACTIVE: 1987 - 1990 ARRESTED: 07-21-1990 (Age 22)
GENDER: Male AGES ACTIVE: 19/20 - 22/23 CONVICTED: 09-15-1993 (Age 25)
ZODIAC: Libra LIFE SPAN: 1967 - DEATH:

4-8 VICTIMS

SERIAL KILLER RAPIST TORTURER STRANGLER

Active for **4 years** known to have killed at least **4 victims** between **1987** and **1990**.
previous crimes: ✓ weapon: ✓ gun: ✓ rob: ✗ bound: ✓ strangle: ✓ mutilate: ✗ M R

Lesley Warren (Lesley Eugene Warren) an American serial killer and rapist known as The Babyface Killer. Warren was the oldest of two siblings he also had a half-sister and half-brother. He had been physically and psychologically abused since birth by his father. Warren received a sentence of death for killing Velma Gray, and the Asheville murders of Jayme Hurley and Katherine Johnson. Investigators believe that he is responsible for at least eight to ten other murders, all women. Lesley Warren is now on Death Row at Central Prison, located in Raleigh, North Carolina.

Sentence: death by lethal injection at Central Prison in Raleigh, North Carolina, US.

Active in: United Kingdom

Rosemary West

The Gloucester House of Horrors

BIRTH: 11-29-1953 YEARS ACTIVE: 1971 - 1987 ARRESTED: 02-25-1994 (Age 40)
GENDER: Female AGES ACTIVE: 17/18 - 33/34 CONVICTED: 11-22-1995 (Age 41)
ZODIAC: Sagittarius LIFE SPAN: 1953 - DEATH:

10 VICTIMS

SERIAL KILLER RAPIST TORTURER STRANGLER

Active for **17 years** known to have killed at least **10 victims** between **1971** and **1987**.
previous crimes: ✓ weapon: ✗ gun: ✗ rob: ✗ bound: ✓ strangle: ✓ mutilate: ✓ W M

Rosemary West (born Rosemary Pauline Letts) a British serial killer who along with her husband Fred West are known as The Gloucester House of Horrors. In 1995, Fred and Rosemary were convicted of ten murders, nine young women between 1973 and 1987, and her own son in 1971. The majority of these murders were committed at the couple's home, 25 Cromwell Street in Gloucester, England. On November 22nd 1995, Rosemary West was found guilty and sentenced to life imprisonment at HMP Low Newton, Brasside, Durham, England. She was the second woman to receive a life sentence in Britain, the first was serial killer Myra Hindley in 1990.

Sentence: life imprisonment at HMP Low Newton in Brasside, Durham, England.

Active in: United Kingdom DECEASED

Fred West

The Gloucester House of Horrors

BIRTH: 09-29-1941	YEARS ACTIVE: 1967 - 1987	ARRESTED: 02-24-1994 (Age 52)	12-13
GENDER: Male	AGES ACTIVE: 25/26 - 45/46	CONVICTED:	VICTIMS
ZODIAC: Libra	LIFE SPAN: 1941 - 1995	DEATH: 01-01-1995 (Age 53)	

SERIAL KILLER | RAPIST | TORTURER | STRANGLER

Active for **21 years** known to have killed at least **12 victims** between **1967** and **1987**.
previous crimes: ✓ weapon: ✗ gun: ✗ rob: ✗ bound: ✓ strangle: ✓ mutilate: ✓ W M

Fred West (Frederick Walter Stephen West) a British serial killer who along with his wife Rosemary West are known as The Gloucester House of Horrors. In 1995, Fred was suspected of twelve to thirteen murders, nine young women between 1973 and 1987, and his own son in 1971. Fred West committed suicide by asphyxiating himself while on remand at HM Prison Birmingham on January 1st 1995. West's suicide note: "In loving memory. Fred West. Rose West. Rest in peace where no shadow falls. In perfect peace he waits for Rose, his wife."

Sentence: never sentence committed suicide prior to conviction at HM Prison Birmingham in Winson Green, Birmingham, West Midlands, England. **Death:** cause of death: suicide, asphyxiated himself by hanging in prison cell with a blanket and tags from a prison laundry bag at HM Prison Birmingham in Winson Green, Birmingham, West Midlands, England.

BIRTH: 11-11-1966	YEARS ACTIVE: 1990 - 1997	ARRESTED: 01-31-1997 (Age 30)	10
GENDER: Male	AGES ACTIVE: 23/24 - 30/31	CONVICTED: 02-23-1998 (Age 31)	VICTIMS
ZODIAC: Scorpio	LIFE SPAN: 1966 -	DEATH:	

SERIAL KILLER | RAPIST | CANNIBAL | NECROPHILIAC | TORTURER

Active for **8 years** known to have killed at least **10 victims** between **1990** and **1997**.
previous crimes: ✓ weapon: ✗ gun: ✗ rob: ✗ bound: ✗ strangle: ✓ mutilate: ✗ W M

Stewart Wilken an African serial killer, cannibal and necrophile known as Boetie Boer (Brother Farmer). Wilken's raped, sodomised and murdered ten victims between 1990 and 1997 in Port Elizabeth, on the east coast of South Africa. Wilken's committed acts of cannibalism and necrophilia during his crimes. Wilken's was reported to have cut off and ate a nipple of one of his victims. One of his victims was his own daughter who disappeared in 1995, her body was found in 1996 wrapped in a tarpaulin behind the Holiday Inn Garden Court in South Africa. Stewart Wilken was sentenced to seven terms of life imprisonment on February 23st 1998.

Sentence: life imprisonment, seven terms at St Albans Correctional Facility, Uitenhage Farms in Port Elizabeth, South Africa.

Active in: Canada

DECEASED

Peter Woodcock

David Michael Krueger

BIRTH: 03-05-1939 YEARS ACTIVE: 1956 - 1991 ARRESTED: 01-21-1957 (Age 17)
GENDER: Male AGES ACTIVE: 16/17 - 51/52 CONVICTED: 04-11-1957 (Age 18)
ZODIAC: Pisces LIFE SPAN: 1939 - 2010 DEATH: 03-05-2010 (Age 71)

4
VICTIMS

SERIAL KILLER RAPIST NECROPHILIAC STRANGLER

Active for **36 years** known to have killed at least **4 victims** between **1956** and **1991**.
previous crimes: — weapon: ✓ gun: ✗ rob: ✗ bound: ✗ strangle: ✓ mutilate: ✓ W M

Peter Woodcock a Canadian serial killer and child rapist known as David Michael Krueger. Woodcock was a sexual sadist who killed three young children in Toronto in the 1950s. He was sentenced to a psychiatric facility, where he murdered a fellow inmate while on unsupervised release in 1991. Once captured Woodcock stated "My fear was that Mother would find out. Mother was my biggest fear. I didn't know if the police would let her at me." On March 5th 2010, his 71st birthday, Krueger died of natural causes while in custody at Penetanguishene Mental Health Centre in Canada.

Sentence: preventively detained, not guilty by reason of insanity at Penetanguishene Mental Health Centre in Penetanguishene, Ontario, Canada. **Death:** cause of death: natural causes, on his 71st birthday, Krueger died of natural causes. at Penetanguishene Mental Health Centre in Penetanguishene, Ontario, Canada.

Active in: United States

Randall Brent Woodfield

The I-5 Killer,The I-5 Bandit

BIRTH: 12-26-1950 YEARS ACTIVE: 1979 - 1981 ARRESTED: 03-07-1981 (Age 30)
GENDER: Male AGES ACTIVE: 28/29 - 30/31 CONVICTED: 06-26-1981 (Age 30)
ZODIAC: Capricorn LIFE SPAN: 1950 - DEATH:

18-44
VICTIMS

SERIAL KILLER RAPIST

Active for **3 years** known to have killed at least **18 victims** between **1979** and **1981**.
previous crimes: ✓ weapon: ✓ gun: ✓ rob: ✓ bound: ✓ strangle: ✗ mutilate: ✗ W M

Randall Brent Woodfield an American serial killer, rapist, kidnapper, and robber who was dubbed The I-5 Killer or The I-5 Bandit by the media due to the crimes he committed along the Interstate 5 corridor running through Washington, Oregon, and California. Woodfield was sentenced to life in prison on June 26, 1981. Woodfeild, 6 foot 1 inch tall man weighing 170 pounds, drafted by the Green Bay Packers in the 1974 NFL Draft as a wide receiver, 428th pick, but did not make the final roster. Woodfield was later convicted of three murders and is now suspected of killing up to 44 people. Later crimes and DNA evidences later raised Woodfields confirmed victims to 18. Depicted by Anne Rule in her book titled "The I-5 Killer" as Award-winning student Randall Woodfield was every college girl's dream - and nightmare..

Sentence: life imprisonment plus 165 years at Oregon State Penitentiary (OSP) Salem, Oregon, United States.

Active in: China

DECEASED

Yang Xinhai

Monster Killer, Yang Zhiya, Yang Liu

BIRTH: 07-29-1968 YEARS ACTIVE: 1999 - 2003 ARRESTED: 11-03-2003 (Age 35)

GENDER: Male AGES ACTIVE: 30/31 - 34/35 CONVICTED: 02-01-2004 (Age 35)

ZODIAC: Leo LIFE SPAN: 1968 - 2004 DEATH: 02-14-2004 (Age 35)

67 VICTIMS

SERIAL KILLER RAPIST

Active for **5 years** known to have killed at least **67 victims** between **1999** and **2003**.

previous crimes: ✓ weapon: ✓ gun: ✗ rob: ✓ bound: ✗ strangle: ✗ mutilate: ✓ W M

Yang Xinhai a Chinese serial killer and rapist known as the Monster Killer, Yang Zhiya and Yang Liu. Yang committed sixty-seven murders and twenty-three rapes between 1999 and 2003. His spree spanned four provinces in four years. He was known to enter victims' homes at night and kill with axes, cleavers, hammers, and shovels. He was known to rape at least one of his victims. In 2003, Yang was arrested during a routine police inspection of entertainment venues in Cangzhou, Hebei. He confessed to the sixty-seven murders and twenty-three rapes, authorities also matched his DNA with that found at several crime scenes. In 2004, Yang Xinhua was executed by firing squad in Luohe, Henan, China.

Sentence: death by firing squad at a prison in Luohe central province of Henan, China. **Death:** cause of death: capital punishment, executed by gunshot to the head on Valentines Day at a prison in Luohe central province of Henan, China.

Active in: India

DECEASED

Akku Yadav

Bharat Kalicharan

BIRTH: YEARS ACTIVE: 2004 - 2004 ARRESTED:

GENDER: Male AGES ACTIVE: - CONVICTED:

ZODIAC: LIFE SPAN: - 2004 DEATH: 08-13-2004

3 VICTIMS

SERIAL KILLER RAPIST

Active for **1 year** known to have killed at least **3 victims** in **2004**.

previous crimes: ✓ weapon: ✓ gun: ✗ rob: ✓ bound: ✗ strangle: ✗ mutilate: ✓ W

Akku Yadav (born Bharat Kalicharan) a rapist and serial killer also known as Bharat Kalicharan. Yadav murdered at least three victims, dumping their bodies on railroad tracks near Nagpur, India. He had numerous been reported of committing rape, the police never arrested him for the crimes. A mob of his neighbors burnt down his house, Yadav turned himself over to the police for protection. A bail hearing was set on August 13th 2004, during the hearing Yadav called one of his previous rape victims a prostitute and threaten to rape her again. Akku Yadav was lynched by a mob of around two-hundred women at the Nagpur district court. The police arrested a handful of women that were in the mob, they were all later released for lack of evidence.

Sentence: lynched by a mob prior to arrest at the Nagpur district court room in Nagpur, India. **Death:** cause of death: homicide, lynching, lynched by a mob of around two-hundred women at the Nagpur district court room in Nagpur, India.

Active in: Turkey

Yavuz Yapicioglu

The Screwdriver Killer

BIRTH: YEARS ACTIVE: 1994 - 2002 ARRESTED: 12-24-2002
GENDER: Male AGES ACTIVE: - CONVICTED: 12-25-2002
ZODIAC: LIFE SPAN: - DEATH:

18-40
VICTIMS

SERIAL KILLER RAPIST

Active for **9 years** known to have killed at least **18 victims** between **1994** and **2002**.
previous crimes: ✓ weapon: ✓ gun: ✗ rob: ✓ bound: ✗ strangle: ✗ mutilate: ✗ W M

Yavuz Yapicioglu a Turkish serial killer and arsonist known as The Screwdriver Killer. Yapicioglu killed victims in various cities of Turkey between 1994 and 2002. He has eighteen proven victims and is accused of more than forty murders by eyewitnesse testimony, some of the eyewitnesses were relatives of Yapicioglu. Yapicioglu had previously been a patient at several psychiatric hospitals in Turkey. He was given a medical examination and was found fully criminally liable for the offenses he committed. Yavuz Yapicioglu has been preventively detained at the Tekirdag Prison since 2013.

Sentence: preventively detained at Tekirdag Prison in Tekirdag, Turkey.

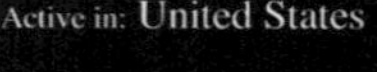

Active in: United States

Robert Lee Yates

Spokane Serial Killer

BIRTH: 05-27-1952 YEARS ACTIVE: 1975 - 1998 ARRESTED: 04-18-2000 (Age 47)
GENDER: Male AGES ACTIVE: 22/23 - 45/46 CONVICTED: 10-26-2000 (Age 48)
ZODIAC: Gemini LIFE SPAN: 1952 - DEATH:

18-23
VICTIMS

SERIAL KILLER RAPIST

Active for **24 years** known to have killed at least **18 victims** between **1975** and **1998**.
previous crimes: ✓ weapon: ✓ gun: ✓ rob: ✓ bound: ✗ strangle: ✗ mutilate: ✗ W M R

Robert Lee Yates an American serial killer known as the Spokane Serial Killer. Yates was known to have murdered at least thirteen women, all of whom were prostitutes in the Skid Row area of East Sprague Avenue in Spokane, Washington between 1996 and 1998. He confessed to three additional murders from 1975 to 1988 and was convicted of two more murders in Pierce County. Robert Lee Yates was sentenced to death by lethal injection in 2002 which was commuted to life without parole in 2018. Robert Lee Yates is currently serving life in prison at the Washington State Penitentiary.

Sentence: death commuted to life without parole at Washington State Penitentiary at Walla Walla, Washington, US.

Active in: China

DECEASED

Huang Yong

BIRTH: 11-18-1974 | YEARS ACTIVE: 2001 - 2003 | ARRESTED: 11-12-2003 (Age 28)

GENDER: Male | AGES ACTIVE: 26/27 - 28/29 | CONVICTED: 12-09-2003 (Age 29)

ZODIAC: Scorpio | LIFE SPAN: 1974 - 2003 | DEATH: 12-26-2003 (Age 29)

17-25 VICTIMS

SERIAL KILLER | RAPIST | TORTURER | STRANGLER

Active for **3 years** known to have killed at least **17 victims** between **2001** and **2003**.

previous crimes: ✗ weapon: ✗ gun: ✗ rob: ✗ bound: ✓ strangle: ✓ mutilate: ✗ W M

Huang Yong a Chinese serial killer and homosexual rapist. Huang lured victims to his apartment, where he would drug, strangle, rape, murder and bury seventeen teenage boys. He is suspected of twenty-five murders between 2001 and 2003. In 2003 a victim escaped Huang's apartment, after four days of torture and alerted police. Huang was quoted saying "I've always wanted to be an assassin since I was a kid, but I never had the chance." He was convicted of seventeen murders and sentenced to death in 2003. Huang Yong was executed by firing squad on December 26th 2003.

Sentence: death by firing squad at a prison in Beijing, Henan, China. **Death:** cause of death: executed by firing squad at a prison in Beijing, Henan, China.

Active in: South Korea

Yoo Young-chul

Raincoat Killer

BIRTH: 04-18-1970 | YEARS ACTIVE: 2003 - 2004 | ARRESTED: 07-15-2004 (Age 34)

GENDER: Male | AGES ACTIVE: 32/33 - 33/34 | CONVICTED: 12-13-2005 (Age 35)

ZODIAC: Aries | LIFE SPAN: 1970 - | DEATH:

21-26 VICTIMS

SERIAL KILLER | RAPIST | CANNIBAL

Active for **2 years** known to have killed at least **21 victims** between **2003** and **2004**.

previous crimes: ✓ weapon: ✓ gun: ✗ rob: ✓ bound: ✗ strangle: ✗ mutilate: ✓ W M

Yoo Young-chul a South Korean serial killer and self-confessed cannibal known as the Raincoat Killer. Yoo used a hammer to murder mostly older victims, until his focus shifted to the decapitation and mutilation of escorts after being dumped by a girlfriend who worked in that profession. He burned three and mutilated at least eleven of his victims. Yoo admitted he had eaten the livers of some of his victims. He was arrested in 2004 and confessed to murdering a total of twenty-one victims. Yoo Young-chul was sentenced to death in 2005 and is currently awaiting execution.

Sentence: death at Seoul Detention Center, Uiwang, Gyeonggi Province, South Korea.

Serial Killer Rapists by Confirmed Victims

#	Confirmed	Possible	Name	Page
1	147	300	Luis Garavito	58
2	110	300	Pedro Lopez	89
3	80	200	Gilles de Rais	111
4	78	81	Mikhail Popkov	109
5	72	150	Daniel Camargo	30
6	67	67	Yang Xinhai	147
7	60	93	Samuel Little	87
8	52	56	Andrei Chikatilo	33
9	49	90	Gary Ridgway	115
10	45	45	Wang Qiang	111
11	38	38	Moses Sithole	127
12	37	100	Serhiy Tkach	137
13	36	55	Gennady Mikhasevich	96
14	33	33	Ali Asghar Borujerdi	27
15	33	34	John Wayne Gacy	57
16	32	32	Ramadan Abdel Rehim Mansour	92
17	30	36	Ted Bundy	29
18	28	29	Dean Corll	38
19	27	35	Maoupa Cedric Maake	90
20	25	25	Juan Vallejo Corona	38
21	24	24	Bela Kiss	79
22	24	27	Fritz Haarmann	65
23	23	23	Ronald Dominique	43
24	22	29	Earle Leonard Nelson	102
25	21	43	Patrick Wayne Kearney	77
26	21	26	Yoo Young-chul	149
27	21	50	Manuel Octavio Bermudez	21
28	20	35	Paul John Knowles	80
29	20	20	Abdullah Shah	124
30	20	20	Bulelani Mabhayi	90

Serial Killer Rapists by Possible Victims

#	Confirmed	Possible	Name	Page
1	147	300	Luis Garavito	58
2	110	300	Pedro Lopez	89
3	80	200	Gilles de Rais	111
4	8	185	Keith Hunter Jesperson	73
5	72	150	Daniel Camargo	30
6	8	100	Rodney Alcala	17
7	37	100	Serhiy Tkach	137
8	9	100	Nikolai Dzhumagaliev	47
9	60	93	Samuel Little	87
10	49	90	Gary Ridgway	115
11	78	81	Mikhail Popkov	109
12	3	70	Donald Leroy Evans	51
13	3	70	Tommy Lynn Sells	124
14	67	67	Yang Xinhai	147
15	16	67	Randy Steven Kraft	82
16	52	56	Andrei Chikatilo	33
17	36	55	Gennady Mikhasevich	96
18	14	54	Larry DeWayne Hall	67
19	21	50	Manuel Octavio Bermudez	21
20	3	50	Robert Ben Rhoades	114
21	11	49	Juana Barraza	20
22	6	49	Robert Pickton	107
23	7	48	Manuel Delgado Villegas	142
24	12	46	Jake Bird	24
25	45	45	Wang Qiang	111
26	18	44	Randall Brent Woodfield	146
27	21	43	Patrick Wayne Kearney	77
28	18	40	Yavuz Yapicioglu	148
29	11	40	Sergey Golovkin	63
30	7	38	Roger Kibbe	78

Serial Killer Rapists by Years Active

#	Years	Confirmed	Name	Page
1	52	5	John Floyd Thomas	136
2	35	60	Samuel Little	87
3	35	4	Peter Woodcock	146
4	33	110	Pedro Lopez	89
5	30	5	Willem van Eijk	49
6	29	5	David Edward Maust	95
7	27	33	Ali Asghar Borujerdi	27
8	25	3	Altemio Sanchez	121
9	25	9	Richard Biegenwald	23
10	24	7	Anatoly Slivko	128
11	24	5	Harvey Carignan	31
12	23	18	Robert Lee Yates	148
13	23	1	Bobby Jack Fowler	54
14	22	7	Terry Blair	26
15	22	8	Gilbert Paul Jordan	75
16	22	10	Lonnie David Franklin	55
17	22	5	Anthony Kirkland	79
18	21	14	Joachim Georg Kroll	83
19	21	7	Walter E. Ellis	49
20	21	37	Serhiy Tkach	137
21	20	2	Paul Rowles	119
22	20	5	William Patrick Fyfe	56
23	20	12	Fred West	145
24	19	5	Edward Edwards	48
25	19	3	Tommy Lynn Sells	124
26	18	10	Jack Unterweger	139
27	18	8	Yoshio Kodaira	80
28	18	78	Mikhail Popkov	109
29	18	49	Gary Ridgway	115
30	18	7	Sataro Fukiage	56

Some serial killers on this list may be unidentified or using an alias as their main name, alphabetical order is a very loose term. Also consider that in many parts of Asia, as well as some parts of Europe and Africa, the family name is placed before a person's given name. In these cases, for simplicity, we have used the last section of the name.

Zodiac Sign	Killers
Libra	26
Capricorn	26
Sagittarius	25
Gemini	21
Aries	20
Pisces	20
Leo	19
Aquarius	16
Scorpio	16
Cancer	15
Virgo	15
Taurus	10

Aquarius - 16 killers

	Page
Robert Berdella	21
Mohammed Bijeh	23
Anatoly Biryukov	24
Jerome Jerry Brudos	29
Daniel Camargo	30
Gordon Cummins	40
Luis Garavito	58
Erwin Hagedorn	66
Robert Christian Hansen	68
Yoshio Kodaira	80
Cody Legebokoff	86
Roy Lewis Norris	104
Gary Ridgway	115
Friedrich Schumann	123
Romulus Veres	142
Manuel Delgado Villegas	142

Aries - 20 killers

	Page
Robert Black	25
Lucious Boyd	28
John Christie	34
Andre Crawford	39
John Martin Crawford	40
Martin Dumollard	45
Michel Fourniret	53
Bernard Giles	61
Keith Hunter Jesperson	73
Paul John Knowles	80
Lam Kor-wan	82
Joachim Georg Kroll	83
David Edward Maust	95
Gennady Mikhasevich	96
Jozef Slovak	128
Jiri Straka	133
Roberto Succo	133
Aleksey Sukletin	134
Darren Deon Vann	141
Yoo Young-chul	149

Cancer - 15 killers

Name	Page
Westley Allan Dodd	43
Kenneth Erskine	50
Donald Leroy Evans	51
Leonard Fraser	55
Gerald Gallego	57
Sean Vincent Gillis	61
Kwauhuru Govan	64
Rodney Halbower	66
Charles Ray Hatcher	70
Carl Panzram	106
Glen Edward Rogers	118
Charles Schmid	122
Tommy Lynn Sells	124
Anthony Allen Shore	125
Metod Trobec	138

Capricorn - 26 killers

Name	Page
Marcelo Costa de Andrade	17
Juana Barraza	20
Wayne Boden	26
Ian Brady	28
Thor Nis Christiansen	34
Dean Corll	38
Juan Vallejo Corona	38
Ronald Dominique	43
Billy Glaze	63
William Henry Hance	67
Vincent Johnson	74
Buddy Earl Justus	75
Israel Keyes	78
Joseph Naso	101
Kiyoshi Okubo	105
Clifford Olson	105
Robledo Puch	110
Wang Qiang	111
John Edward Robinson	116
Jose Rodriguez	117
Sergei Ryakhovsky	120
Altemio Sanchez	121
Norman Afzal Simons	126
Anatoly Slivko	128
Anatoly Utkin	140
Randall Brent Woodfield	146

Gemini - 21 killers

Leo - 19 killers

Sagittarius - 25 killers

	Page
John Eric Armstrong	18
Johnny Avalos	19
Cesar Barone	20
Jake Bird	24
Ted Bundy	29
John Duffy	44
Scott Erskine	50
Wayne Adam Ford	53
Harvey Glatman	62
Sergey Golovkin	63
Larry DeWayne Hall	67
Jacobus Dirk Hertogs	71
Gilbert Paul Jordan	75
Joseph Kallinger	76
Edmund Kemper	77
Timothy Krajcir	83
Eddie Leonski	87
Richard Laurence Marquette	93
Damaso Rodriguez Martin	94
Dennis Nilsen	103
Francisco de Assis Pereira	107
Harvey Miguel Robinson	116
Arnold Sodeman	129
Jose Antonio Rodriguez Vega	141
Rosemary West	144

Scorpio - 16 killers

	Page
Gao Chengyong	33
Alton Coleman	35
Joseph James DeAngelo	42
Marc Dutroux	46
Nikolai Dzhumagaliev	47
Fritz Haarmann	65
Genzo Kurita	84
Derrick Todd Lee	86
Robert Pickton	107
Robert Ben Rhoades	114
Moses Sithole	127
Chester Turner	138
Joseph Vacher	140
Henry Louis Wallace	143
Stewart Wilken	145
Huang Yong	149

Taurus - 10 killers

	Page
Harvey Carignan	31
David Carpenter	31
Daniel Conahan	36
Milton Johnson	74
Lee Roy Martin	93
Cory Deonn Morris	98
Vladimir Mukhankin	99
Earle Leonard Nelson	102
Paul Rowles	119
Issei Sagawa	121

Virgo - 15 killers

www.ingramcontent.com/pod-product-compliance
Lightning Source LLC
Chambersburg PA
CBHW060853280326
41934CB00007B/1035

* 9 7 8 1 7 3 3 6 3 0 6 1 0 *